THE ADULTS-ONLY STORY
OF A GREAT CHILD STAR

What was it like to reign as America's favorite child star? To be a slave to the studio's bizarre whims?

To hear your own uncle threaten to shoot your dog when you couldn't cry on camera? Then to actually hear the shots?

To suffer the torments of first love with Judy Garland, and receive an advanced erotic education from Joan Crawford at 17?

To ride a roller-coaster of triumph and tragedy from Hollywood to Broadway to TV, going through money like water and taking women like aspirin? To have the luck to survive it all and the sheer guts to tell it all . . .

. . . and finally get even.

D0958776

PLEASE DON'T SHOOT MY DOG

THE AUTOBIOGRAPHY OF

Jackie Cooper

with Dick Kleiner

BERKLEY BOOKS, NEW YORK

This Berkley book contains the complete
text of the original hardcover edition.
It has been completely reset in a typeface
designed for easy reading, and was printed
from new film.

PLEASE DON'T SHOOT MY DOG

A Berkley Book / published by arrangement with
William Morrow and Company, Inc.

PRINTING HISTORY
William Morrow and Company edition published 1981
Berkley edition / March 1982
Second printing / July 1982

All rights reserved.
Copyright © 1981 by Jackie Cooper.
This book may not be reproduced in whole or in part,
by mimeograph or any other means, without permission.
For information address: William Morrow and Company, Inc.,
105 Madison Avenue, New York, New York 10016.

ISBN: 0-425-05306-7

A BERKLEY BOOK ® TM 757,375
Berkley Books are published by Berkley Publishing Corporation,
200 Madison Avenue, New York, New York 10016.
The name ''BERKLEY'' and the stylized ''B'' with design
are trademarks belonging to Berkley Publishing Corporation.
PRINTED IN THE UNITED STATES OF AMERICA

DEDICATION

It is said there is a little boy in all men. Boys play and fight and teach each other to become big boys. Big boys go through school and learn to become men. Through the teachings of their mothers and fathers, feeling men learn to love and respect women. This is a normal process, having usually come to pass through an everyday kind of growing up—going to school, competing in games, earning grades, getting pimples, dating, and going to work.

But there is a small legion of some who've been denied that process, and they are forever trying to grow up—in spite of those who will not let them. They are forever trying to learn— in spite of those who do not teach them. They are forever trying to love—in spite of those who do not love them.

This is the story of more than five decades in the life of one of that legion—dedicated to Barbara, who for twenty-seven years has lovingly given me so much I'd been denied in the years before, taught me so much I'd never learned in the years before, and loved me through one crisis after another.

Few of us in the above-mentioned legion have survived our lot. I'm grateful to Barbara not only for my survival but for showing me the joy of truly loving—which is, after all, life itself.

A Note of Appreciation and Explanation

The authors wish to thank all of those who took time to talk to us in connection with this book. The contributions of all of them are basic to the integrity of the work, and we are deeply grateful. Since the names of these people appear in the book, there is no need to list them here.

There is one conspicuous omission, however. And that is Norman Taurog, who played such a vital role in this story. Every effort was made to seek Mr. Taurog's cooperation, but we were rebuffed totally. We talked to him on the telephone and asked for an appointment. No. We suggested we could ask him our questions on the phone. No. We wrote him a letter with questions, but there was never a reply.

It is unfortunate that he elected to choose the path of non-cooperation. What he might have said might have helped unravel a few mysteries. And certainly, his point of view would have been helpful.

Maybe next time.

J.C. AND D.K.

PART ONE

The Boy

1.

It was 1951. A year earlier I had been in England, where I had indulged myself and bought a Jaguar XK-120. It wasn't just for showing off; it was for racing. I raced that car a lot. That summer of '51 I drove it across country to Los Angeles to see my little boy, then I took it up to Pebble Beach, raced it there, and I was on my way back to New York.

Driving cross-country in a good car was relaxing for me. I preferred driving at night, especially in the summer, across the plains states, where the heat can be brutal in the daytime. It gave me a chance to think about myself, my problems, my future, my past, whatever.

I had plenty to think about. My first marriage had broken up; my second was shaky. I had a small son I loved very much but saw too little. My career in Hollywood had fallen apart, but fortunately New York had accepted me, and I enjoyed working on the stage. It was a new world for me, a film kid, on Broadway. New work, new people, new skills.

The blue-black world of Kansas at night sailed past me, unnoticed. Every fifteen minutes or so there came a cluster of neon lights, signaling a town. A gas station, a diner, a general store. I would slow down until the neon glow was behind me, then take off again.

Ahead of me, in New York, there was a new play waiting and a romance that was causing me, in turn, joy and grief. The road was arrow-straight. At night, on terrain as flat and unvarying as that, you can see a car in either direction from miles away. So there was nothing to slow me down. I was sailing along, doing eighty or so. It was hot, still, humid. I'm sure it was up around ninety degrees. Off to my left, I could see flashes of heat lightning, and a few drops of rain struck my face. They felt good.

As I drove steadily east, I noted a slender finger of light behind me. Just one beam. It couldn't be the police. As it gained on me, I realized it wasn't on the road, but off to my right, and it was too high and too powerful for a car. Then I heard a whistle and realized it was a train. It kept creeping up on me, and I couldn't help smiling. A race! I floored the accelerator, and the Jag leaped forward. Very quickly it was doing 100, but I was just about holding the train even.

The top of the Jag couldn't take it. There was what seemed like an explosion, a ripping and tearing, and the canvas shredded into a mass of fluttering strips. I slowed down and watched the train roar past me. The rain began in earnest, and I was getting soaked. I drove that way for another half hour, drenched to the skin, hot, clammy, miserable. I knew that eventually I would hit Kansas City, and an increase in traffic told me that I had reached the city's western outskirts.

It was very early in the morning. My chances of finding a garage of any kind were slim, and the odds against finding any place that had the equipment, material, and skill to replace a Jaguar top were astronomical. So I figured I'd find a motel, get a little sleep, and hope I could get the car fixed later in the day.

But fate—or perhaps something a little stronger—guided me down a street where I saw a garage. By the faint light of the dawn, just beginning to break, I could make out a sign: CONVERTIBLE TOPS REPAIRED. There was nobody about, but I got out and knocked on the door. A man came out, and I pointed to my poor wounded vehicle. He looked at it, professionally. He was also looking at me, but I was used to that.

He was a pleasant man. He looked at my car and said he could make a new top in about two hours. He started working on it. I tried to help, handing him whatever tool he indicated. All the while he worked, he kept stealing glances at me every minute or so. I could tell—you get to recognize every reaction—that he was screwing up his courage, getting ready to say something to me about who I was. Finally, it came.

"Hey, you're Jackie Cooper, aren't you?"

I smiled and said yes.

He worked a while longer, stretching and fitting the canvas. I could tell he had something else on his mind. An autograph? A picture for his kid? A script? Well, I would know soon enough.

It took him five minutes or so before he could get around to it. Then he didn't say anything, just took me by the arm, led me off to one side, and pointed to a dimly lit window over his garage.

"See that window there?" he said, pointing up.

I said yes, I saw it.

"I live there with another fellow," the mechanic said.

I waited. There was something more.

He looked me right in the eye for the first time.

"That other fellow I live with," he said, "is your father."

My father.

A hundred thoughts flashed through my mind in the next few seconds, as I stood there and stared at that window.

Who was my father? Was it John Cooper? Was John Cooper still living? Why had he left me? Where had he been all those years I needed him? Why had he deserted my mother? And other mysteries, private mysteries I had spent a childhood wondering about.

The mechanic didn't press the issue. He just stood there and let me digest the information.

"His name is John Cooper?" I asked. I had to establish the fact that we were talking about the same person.

"That's right."

John Cooper. He wasn't even a shadow in my life because you can see a shadow. He wasn't even a whisper because you can hear a whisper. I never knew him. I had seen him, but not since I was two, and I recalled nothing of the man. Nothing at all. Only what I had heard from my mother, which was polite, and from my grandmother, which wasn't.

"Your father was a good man," my mother had said very often.

"Your father was a lousy kike bastard," my grandmother had said just as often. And louder.

I don't know if I said it aloud, but a thousand times—a million times—I had said to myself, "Why did he leave?" People like my mother and my aunts had told me what a great guy he was, so talented, so much fun. Okay, but if he was so great, why did he leave?

They told me, during my childhood, that he had died. I could believe that. That made sense. Even great guys die, and then they have an excuse for abandoning their sons. So for years, as a child, I believed my dad, a great guy named Johnny Cooper, had died. Then, at thirteen, I found out that was a lie. Johnny Cooper was still living.

The shop owner was talking. He was saying Johnny Cooper had been sick. He was still in pretty poor health. He played piano in a nearby bar, the mechanic said. He said if it was okay with me, he'd go upstairs and tell Johnny I was there. He said Johnny was so proud of me, that he had pictures of me all over his room, that he would be so happy to see me.

"How about it, Jackie? Let me tell him you're here, okay?"

He seemed to assume that I would say yes. He turned to go into the building.

"No," I said. I turned my back on the window. "No, please don't. I don't need to be confused."

The look in his eye accused me of an emotional crime. But he didn't try to change my mind. He said that Johnny Cooper had told him all about his life, about our relationship, such as it was. He had even told him how I had them stop sending the $100 to him every week. He had told him that he walked out— left to get a pack of cigarettes when I was two—and had never come back. He knew everything, maybe more than I knew.

He went back to working on the top of my car. I looked up at the window. I shook my head. I meant what I had said when I told him I didn't want to be confused. The years, the war, maybe even maturity had helped me bury the question of my father in the back of my head. Earlier it had bothered me. When I grew up, in a house without an adult male figure, I had been unhappy because I didn't have a father. After my father had walked away from us, there was only me and my mother, Mabel, and her mother, my grandmother. And my two aunts, Florence and Julie. And my uncle, Big Jack, although I never called him Uncle because he was only ten years older. He was hardly a father figure.

In most of my early movies—*The Champ*, as the prime example—the father-son relationship had been a key factor. All day at the studio I would talk about "Daddy" or "Pa" or whatever I was supposed to call him. I would cry if this make-believe father was hurt or drunk or beaten up. I would jump in his arms when he was well or sober or victorious. All day long I was the son and there was a strong father. Then I would go home, and there was no father.

It hurt me. I envied the kids I played on the screen, and I envied my friends who had fathers. Yes, it sure as hell bothered me.

But gradually I put it in perspective. If I didn't have a father, okay, I didn't have a father. I had other things. So I pushed the question into a far corner of my mind, and there it stayed, never completely forgotten, yet no longer troublesome. I didn't want it to come back out again and trouble me now.

Yes, I think that I wanted to see him, but I could never forgive him for deserting my mother and me. It was an anger I think I had carried with me since I was old enough to realize what had happened. How could he have left like that?

Maybe if he had written or called or come and tried to explain, we could have made our peace. He had done none of those things. I believed him dead, for so long, because my mother and grandmother and all the rest had told me he was dead.

"Good riddance the bastard is dead," my sweet little old grandmother had said so often. My mother would nod her agreement, with a weary look on her thin, beautiful face.

I was eleven when my mother had remarried. That was after they had Johnny Cooper declared legally dead. That wasn't news to me. I was certain he was dead. If he had been alive, why, then, of course, he would have come to see me, to talk to me, to take me fishing, to take me to the ball game, to do all those great father things. He hadn't come, so obviously he was totally dead.

A year or so after that my mother had heard from my father.

"Your father's turned up alive, Jack," she said. "I want you to hear it from me."

She told me what she knew. She said he had written to her. He had been in a bad accident. He told her he was badly hurt and, in fact, crippled. He wanted money. That was all. I don't know if he even asked about me. He must have known I was a success and there was money to be had.

I don't remember what, if anything, I said to my mother at that time. So my father was alive—so what? He was just a name to me and a very few pictures in the old family photograph album. I had never known him, so I didn't love him. How could I love him? He was only a concept to me, he had served a function in creating me, but he was not a person. I suppose I had a natural curiosity about him, but that curiosity was more than outweighed by my hatred of him for deserting us. And now I hated him even more—if he had been dead, okay, but to be alive and never come around, that was just incomprehensible. He hadn't even had the decency to stay dead.

Sometime in 1948, when I decided to get out of Hollywood

and settle permanently in New York, I told my business manager I was quitting California and wouldn't need his services any longer, and would he please send me all my records and files? That was when I found out the true story or some of it.

Every week, from 1935 to 1948, some twelve years plus, a check for $100 had gone to John Cooper. Even when they had been telling me he was dead, they knew better. I had paid more than $60,000 to this man—it was all money I had earned because nobody else in the family made that kind of money. And there were also some canceled checks to a Kansas hospital, indicating that over and above the weekly stipend, my mother (i.e., I) had also paid many hundreds of dollars for an operation and hospital care for John Cooper.

Okay, what was the money for? It couldn't have been because my mother still loved the man, not after he had deserted her and her child. It couldn't have been because she felt guilty—she had been the wronged party. It couldn't have been part of any settlement because there had been no settlement.

So I began to wonder if it had been hush money. The more I thought about it, the more plausible that explanation became. John Cooper was being paid off so he wouldn't talk, wouldn't spoil things for the son he had walked out on.

All through my youth the fan magazines wrote about my mother and father as though theirs had been one of the great love stories of the century. They didn't want John Cooper to smear that pretty picture.

I must admit that my mother was just as guilty of that deception as the rest of the world. I have an old manuscript of a book she started, around 1932, with a writer named Ruth Biery. I don't believe it was ever even finished or submitted to a publisher. Miss Biery must have been a fan magazine writer my mother liked. My mother, in fact, was very popular with the Hollywood press corps; she was always pleasant to them, always ready with an interview, always cooperative.

Anyhow, *The Story of Jackie Cooper* has a chapter about "Jackie's Daddy."

"He [John Cooper] had started life in a serious way. He had wanted to be a priest; studied for it."

That, of course, is simply untrue. John Cooper, according to everybody who knew him, was Jewish. Maybe not a good Jew or a work-at-it Jew, but he sure didn't study for the priesthood. But that was typical of the kind of stuff they passed out when I was a kid. In the thirties they didn't want anybody in films to be Jewish *or* have a Jewish father, certainly not "America's Boy," as I was known then. It was bad enough that I was half Italian; there was no way of concealing the fact that my mother's family was Italian. So maybe he got $100 a week to keep from spilling the beans.

The book goes on to talk about how Mabel Leonard (my mother) met John Cooper. They were both musicians, and at the time Cooper ran a little store in Los Angeles selling piano music and other musical odds and ends. Mabel Leonard came to work for him.

"It was only natural that these two should fall in love as soon as they began to work in the same tiny room," the book continues. "They were drawn together by their love of music as a magnet draws a piece of steel to it."

I guess that was true. My mother never talked much about that time. Everybody says Johnny Cooper was a lot of fun and a good musician. He must have had some talent; he wrote a couple of songs that became standards—"Do You Ever Think of Me?" and "Under the Bamboo Tree"—but he never made much money from them. I don't know if he sold his interest or what, but he sure didn't become rich. Today, with ASCAP watching out for songwriters, a couple of all-time standards like those could have helped him all his life.

My mother and her collaborator go on to tell of my birth, of how the Victrola came along and hastened the demise of the little music store selling sheet music, of the financial troubles the young couple had, of how Johnny Cooper went out to work and played on silent movie sets (they liked to have music to inspire the actors) in the daytime and played in nickelodeons at night. As for Mabel and the baby—"she hated loneliness, but there was nothing else to do. She would have to make the best of it." It's hard for me to sort out the truth from the fan magazine gush in this material. God knows now if the young couple were struggling nobly against odds, as the book implies, or whether it was a nasty, squabbling, unpleasant scene. For all I know, Johnny Cooper could have been a boozer and a womanizer, although, to his credit, everything I've heard (which wasn't much) painted him as a decent guy.

"The days were dismal enough," the book continues. "She had never before been alone for a moment. But the nights were worse. Then it was dark; she was afraid of every tiny, squeaky sound."

One might expect to read any moment it had started snowing

in Los Angeles and my mother was out in the cold, selling matches. Things did get worse, although the snow never fell. Instead, the roof caved in, figuratively. Debts piled up so badly that my mother, who never regained her health completely after my birth (and that, unfortunately, is all too true), had to go back to work to help out. I wasn't in such great health, either, at the time.

"Jackie was not strong. You have seen a frail fishing vessel tossed like a kite on the ferocious waves of the ocean during a terrific windstorm? Jackie was like that frail, tiny ship during the first years of his life. Tossed hither and thither. Never certain of a sure landing."

The hither wasn't so bad, but the thither damned near killed me. But that comes later.

As for Johnny Cooper, the book explains what was happening to him this way:

"John Cooper was not happy. He was living with his wife's mother and sisters. He was lonesome for Mabel and the little home he had thought they would have together. He knew his wife had to work to help out, but that knowledge only made him feel bitter."

Sounds reasonable. But you don't just walk out, bitter or not, if you have a little boy that you theoretically sired and that you theoretically love.

"One night he left his mother-in-law's home as he always did—at six o'clock in the evening. He never came back. He did not take even an extra handkerchief with him; his clothes hung in the closet; his shirts lay in the drawer; his brush and comb lay on the dressing table. He left no note; sent no word about leaving."

Then this one sentence was added: "To this day no one knows what happened to John Cooper."

I don't know if that sentence was something they really believed or not.

Anyhow, exit one father. But even though I was totally surrounded by women—my grandmother, my mother, my aunts Florence and Julie—there were some males around. My aunts began to attract beaux and eventually got married. Uncle Roddy Kenmore married Aunt Florence. Uncle Norman Taurog married Aunt Julie. That would be Norman Taurog, the director, the man who directed me in my first feature picture and played such an important part in my life for many years after that.

And there were others. My mother had several boyfriends. Most memorable was good old Bill Smith, a traveling salesman she met during a vaudeville tour back east. He came west and eventually went to work for 20th Century-Fox, where he became a man of some importance. Earlier he was married to Ethel Merman for a few fast months. Later he was my best man at my first wedding. He often helped me in the father department.

There was a rat named Howard Something who used to beat me up when my mother and the others weren't around. And then, eventually, there was my stepfather, Charles J. "Chuck" Bigelow. When he was courting my mother, he was everything a boy dreamed about having as a stepfather. At first, I was happy about the marriage, figuring now, at last, I'd have a father. But he pretty soon showed himself to be not quite kosher.

And there was my uncle Jack, the kid brother in my mother's family, who was only ten years older than I was and more of a big brother than a father figure.

There were all around, from time to time, uncles and friends and the stepfather.

Still, the figure of Johnny Cooper haunted me always. I might have denied it then, I might have said that I never gave him a thought, but I'm pretty damn sure that whenever I played a part of a boy with a father, or whenever I read a book about a boy with a father, or whenever I saw a friend of mine with his father, I'd be thinking about him, Johnny Cooper.

And that brings me back to that Kansas garage and the last chance I ever had to run after my father, to spin him around, to ask him those questions that had preyed on my mind forever:

Why did you leave?

Why didn't you write?

Where were you all those years that I needed you?

But the answers might be worse than not getting a chance to ask the questions. For what I feared, I think, all along was that either (a) Johnny Cooper was not really my father, but only some convenient scapegoat, a good guy willing to make my mother's pregnancy legal; or, at the very least, (b) Johnny Cooper and my mother had never been married.

Today I think I could deal with the truth. But when I was younger, such knowledge would have thrown me for a loop. I was still too young, too vulnerable, too inexperienced.

I didn't want to know. I didn't want to be confused.

■ ■ ■

BILL SMITH: Mabel was a helluva swell girl. Johnny Cooper was a piano player, you know. Now I can't prove this, but I don't think he and Mabel were ever married. As a matter of fact, I'm positive of it, but who the hell cares? Johnny went out at two in the morning to get a sandwich or something—they lived over on Yucca then—and that was the end of him.

They didn't hear from him again until Mabel was dying. I had gone with her for years and years and years, and she had a terrible death; she was about sixty pounds when she died. One day I walked in the room, and she was dying, and she was crying, she could hardly talk. And I pegged it right away.

She had a letter in her hand, and I says, "From Johnny?"

And she says, "Yeah."

He was in a veterans' hospital somewhere in Missouri or some goddamn place, I don't know, I've forgotten now. This was the first time she had heard from him in years.

So Mabel says, "What'll I do, Bill?"

I says, "Tear it up."

Whether the letter asked for some dough or what, at this point I've forgotten. I think he did ask for some few bucks or something, if my memory—it's so long ago. At any rate, that was that for Johnny.

■ ■ ■

FLORENCE KENMORE: Mabel and Johnny did get married. I was there. Clarence Jackson, who was a friend of ours—he used to take Julie out—he stood up for Johnny, and I stood up for Mabel. There was a judge. Of course, this was after Jackie was born, I guess about a year after.

Let me tell you this. My father was very, very calm, a very calm man. He just made one horrible mistake. When Mabel was pregnant, he put her out of the house. He was a very quiet man, Dad was, but I guess we were all afraid of him, although he never set a hand on me. I guess he scared the dickens out of Mabel, Jackie's mother—she was a little frightened of him. He never touched her, he never whipped her, he never put a hand on her, but to him what she did was horrible and a shame on the family.

My brother Jack and I would go to see her. Johnny had put her in an apartment. This lady, she was a family friend or something, she sort of just looked after her. Jack walked in with me, and he was a little kid, and he said, "Oh, Mabel's gained so much weight," but I'd bring her little things to eat, and so forth, and she was terribly neglected. It was very sad. Jack and I would bring her things to eat, because I don't think she ate properly. Johnny was in the shop, working, and maybe he stayed clear of Mabel. Maybe they didn't get married because he hadn't gotten his divorce yet, I'm not sure about that. He could have brought Mabel dinner every night, but he didn't. She used to tell Jack and me that all she had to eat was a loaf of bread. She said that's why she was so fat, from eating only bread.

■ ■ ■

The mechanic kept working on my car top, and he didn't say anything more about Johnny Cooper. I think he was mad at me; after all, Johnny was his buddy, and he felt I was being a lousy son. But he didn't know; nobody knew.

He finished. I paid him. I drove out of there. I didn't look back.

2.

My childhood, from the time I was eight or so, was public property. Like Jackie Coogan before me, my comings and goings were reported in innumerable magazines and newspapers all over the world.

Yet I remember very little. There are people, I suspect, who know more about my childhood than I do. Despite some rumors to the contrary, I was just a little boy. Normal, I'd like to think, and average and ordinary—except for the fact that by the time I was eight I was a movie star.

I remember almost nothing about my earliest years. I have lately tried very hard to piece them together, but there are still gaps and unanswered questions.

Why, for example, was I sent away when I was around two? Norman, my uncle, tried for a while to be a father to me after my mother died, and he told me about that experience. But I have come to realize that he lied to me about a lot of things, so perhaps he lied about that, too. He told me that after Johnny Cooper left, my mother had the problem of supporting me. She and I went to live with my grandmother, but my grandmother demanded money for our keep. (Norman never liked my grandmother, so when he cast her as the villain of his piece, he could have been exaggerating her villainy.) So my mother went back on the road and boarded me with a friend of hers, a woman named Irene Watts. Mrs. Watts's son, D. P. Watts, sent me a few of my mother's letters to "my darling Rene," dated 1925 (I was three then), which he unearthed, along with some pictures of the two of us.

In one, from New York, my mother writes:

> Rec'd your dear sweet letter and was so glad to get it.
> Well, I know I've caused a heap of worry & trouble out
> there & I'm terribly sorry, but was always trying to do what
> I thought the right thing. Now I think I've done more than
> my share & as far as I'm concerned, that guy [presumably
> she is here referring to Johnny Cooper] can go to Hell

forever. But never again. I get the dirty end of it. When he divorced Wilma he had to give her alimony & she was all wrong & now he won't even support the baby. Well, I have an appointment here [the letter was written on the stationery of the Hotel Claridge in New York] with an attorney tomorrow A.M. I'll be willing to go without alimony to get rid of the fool. Yes, I would love to see mother take the baby. Then I would be happy. But I don't think that she really wants to & unless she can give him all the love she would one of her own, I'm sure he would be better off where he is. At times, I'd give anything to be home but what good would I be, earning a measly little salary and never get out of debt. . . . Well, I hope to make something out of myself & make a little money, too. It does seem a shame that that darling who is so good should be the one to suffer. I wrote and told my mother just how I felt & to do as she wished about taking him. . . . Well, I pray to God some girl grabs him [Johnny, I think] and hangs on to him so he won't ever bother me again. Honestly, if I saw him in the gutter I wouldn't speak to him.

In another letter, my mother wrote to her friend:

Haven't heard from mother since Edith's letter. She seemed very peeved at me in it. I felt terribly and she said I broke she and Jack's heart when I took the baby from him. Naturally, I felt bad about that but I figured they had lots of time to decide whether or not they wanted him and then I know how they all hate Johnny and I do, too, but at the same time, I can't figure why the baby should suffer. I just feel that I had him and he is me and that's the way they should figure and just forget that Johnny ever existed. I have. He never enters my mind and when he does, it is just like thinking about some animal.

That's the beautiful love story that the fan magazines wrote about later on, when I became America's Boy.

There were more letters in the same vein in that same period. My mother wrote frequently about money, about how she wished she could send more. Apparently Rene wrote often (none of her letters were preserved), and mother wrote back to thank her for her reports on me and my progress.

I have no memory of that time. I don't know how long it lasted. I don't know if it began when my mother and grandmother had a fight over my grandmother's keeping me and ended when they reached an understanding, but I would assume so.

I get the feeling from the letters and the pictures with them that the Watts home was a pleasant one and I was happy there. That period had to end by 1926 because that was when I began working in pictures. I lived with the Wattses a year or so, I suppose.

The book my mother started says that Rene—she is called Irene in the book—and her husband wanted to adopt me, that they kept me for two years and spoiled me and loved me and tried to convince Mabel that it would be better for everyone if they adopted me. Mabel resisted the idea, of course. And then the singer she was working with—Edith Clifford—was just about to go to Europe, and that was the big decision Mabel faced. Edith wanted her to go to Europe with her. That would mean another year away from me. By the time she returned I probably wouldn't have known her. So she came back, told Irene she wanted me back again, and that was when my life with our family began in earnest.

My first memory dates from around that time. I was with my grandmother in the living room, and we were hiding behind the couch, and the doorbell kept ringing and ringing. My grandmother had her hand over my mouth so I couldn't make a sound. Eventually whoever was ringing the bell stopped, and I could hear his footsteps walking down the path and away. She got up and walked slowly and stealthily to the window, turning around once and wagging a finger at me and saying, "You keep goddamn quiet, you hear?"

A few minutes later the mailman came up the path. He was okay; we didn't have to hide from him. She opened the door, and I was next to her, and she said, "Say hello to the man, Jackie," and to emphasize her point, she pinched me on the backside. That was her way of pointing out to me that she meant what she said. It made me mad, but I couldn't fight her; not yet. The mailman was being nice, trying to talk to me. I tried to answer him politely, while keeping a wary eye on my grandmother; she pinched, and when she wanted to vary her attack, she would kick.

Many years later, when I was seeing a psychiatrist in New York, he tried to get me to remember something, anything before that memory, but I couldn't dredge one up. That was my first, that scene in the living room, first hiding from someone (bill collector? personal enemy?) and then talking to the mailman while my grandmother pinched me.

She was, I suppose, the strongest person I met in my childhood. My mother was sunshine and light; my grandmother was thunderstorms. You remember thunderstorms more clearly.

Her real name was Mary Babbino Polito Leonard. Mary Babbino was the name she was born with, Polito was the man she married, and Leonard was the name they later changed it to.

She had many names. She herself preferred Marie or Mary. When I was growing up, her daughters and son and the rest of the family (including me) called her Nonnie to her face. Later, years later, my stepfather, Chuck Bigelow, christened her Queenie. Queenie fitted her so well I still think of her as that. My uncle Jack, when he got to be a teenager and started experimenting with the language, called her Moose Tits, although never to her face, naturally.

As a little boy I thought she was immense. She probably stood about five feet two inches—none of the women in the family grew more than that—and must have weighed 150 or so. She was pretty hefty. I always remember her with a cigarette in her mouth. She coughed a lot, probably because of her smoking, and my mother was always on her to cut it down or out. Nonnie would yell back—she was a yeller—and curse. I had my introduction to basic American cursing right at home, listening to my grandmother.

I guess she liked me. Later Bill Smith said that she ignored me, that Big Jack was her pet—understandable, because he was her youngest child and only son—and that I was only tolerated. Of course, when I became a movie name, that changed things considerably around the house.

My maternal great-grandparents, the Babbinos, were part of the early San Francisco Italian crowd that included the Gianninis. The Gianninis started the Bank of America. The Babbinos didn't. Instead, they had a little grocery store, and after my grandmother married John Polito, they still had it, and everybody (including my grandfather) lived in back of the store.

Then my great-grandfather had some physical problem or other, and he was told to get out in the country, that the city air (this was long before we'd heard of smog, but city air was always a villain to doctors) was harmful. So they bought a huge ranch—1,400 acres, according to family legend—near Santa Rosa. It didn't cost much, which was good, because they didn't have much.

When Marie Babbino Polito was seventeen, she began having children. My aunt Florence was the first; then Mabel, my mother, came along a year and a half later; then, another year and a half after that, enter my aunt Julie. It was another ten years before Jack was born.

For some reason, inexplicable to me now, my great-grandparents took Florence, and so my aunt Flo spent her first fourteen years up on the ranch in Santa Rosa. But my mother and Julie stayed with their parents in San Francisco. My grandfather changed his name to Leonard and studied for the bar and became a lawyer. He was not too successful, I'm told, and dabbled in real estate, too, to earn more money.

Ultimately he decided to try his luck in Los Angeles, and so they all moved down south. By that time Florence was back in the nest.

None of the girls stayed in school very long. In those days, of course, it wasn't considered important for girls to have much of an education. One by one, they dropped out. My mother, who had the musical ability in the crowd, became a piano player and played at music stores, demonstrating sheet music. And that is how, theoretically, she met Johnny Cooper.

I know nothing about him or his family background. He had been married before. Some of the stories about him, when he died, said he was of German ancestry. One said his real name was Cooperman. I heard, somewhere along the way, that Cooper was his mother's name and that his real name, from his father, was one of those multisyllabic Russian or Polish names.

Maybe because of the confusion in my head, as a small child, about who my mother was—my real mother was away often; then there was my grandmother and my aunts and the lady who took care of me when I was boarded out—I developed a special name for my real mother. Perhaps she instigated it, I don't recall. But I do know that until I was ten or twelve, I called her Mother Dearest.

If that rings a bell, it could actually be one of two bells. The first bell is that when I was a kid, all the fan magazine ladies seized on that. They all thought it was so cute for this kid to call his mother Mother Dearest, and so they wrote about it often.

The second bell is that book by Christina Crawford about her mother, Joan, which she called *Mommie Dearest*. According to that story, Joan made her four adopted kids call her Mommie Dearest.

I think she got the idea from me. Joan Crawford came over to our house when I was first signed by MGM—lots of movie people did; it was fashionable at the time to bask in a child star's reflected glory—and she was clearly impressed by the name I had for my mother. So I think it very possible that when she began adopting children of her own, she remembered how little Jackie Cooper had called his mother Mother Dearest.

3.

I don't really have one fond memory of my grandmother. It's a sad thing to have to say, but it's true. Yelling, pinching, slapping, hitting, pulling me from one place to the other by the ear—that's what I remember.

My mother would try to get her to stop, defending me as best she could, but she was a gentle soul, she was away a lot, she was sick a lot. She didn't pull much weight around there, at least not until I became famous.

I think I was around four or five when my grandparents got divorced. Obviously they weren't very good Catholics for that to happen. My grandfather was the one to instigate the split; he walked out and later married a young woman and had a few more children. My grandmother, never a cheerful soul, turned from bitter to acid overnight.

For some reason, she took me with her (maybe there was no one to leave me with) when she went to the lawyer's office to discuss the divorce with her soon-to-be-ex. I think Big Jack was with us, too. My grandparents had been married twenty-four years. She really laced into him that day. Never before or since have I heard one human being talk so badly about another. Words I never have used were flung around that room. Nonnie grew red in the face, and the anger spewed forth like an eruption. My poor grandfather just sat there, and I seem to remember his cheeks turning pink.

So the household shrank. John Philip Leonard was gone, and John Cooper, Sr., was gone, and my mother was on the road most of the time with Edith Clifford, she of the bleached blond hair, beauty mark, and risqué songs. Then Florence married Rodger Kenmore, and I gained a nice uncle who took his wife and left. Julie married Norman Taurog, and she left, too. That meant only my grandmother, my uncle Big Jack, and I were left at home in those years.

My mother was never in good health, as long as I knew her. I don't know if it was all downhill after I was born, but it was never good. Besides saving up money to send home for my support, she was saving up money to buy herself a hysterectomy. I think Verdi and his librettists could have put together a masterpiece of a tragic opera about my mother, out there playing the piano while trying to support her son, and all the while her health was slipping away.

But she kept up a brave front. She was, whenever I saw her, cheerful and bright and optimistic. There was music around her, as there is with some people. Maybe it should have been a dirge, but it wasn't—it was jazz.

4.

I grew. I had been a scrawny, sickly infant. My months or years or however long it was with the Watts family changed me into a healthy, husky kid. And I began to get compliments. I don't remember any of them, of course, but later the family would tell me that people stopped me in the street and told my grandmother or whoever I was with how cute I was.

There is a story that may be apocryphal. My mother repeats it in the book she wrote, or started to write, with Ruth Biery.

She quotes my grandmother as saying, when I was about four, "Mabel, everyone thinks Jackie is an unusual child. He is not only cunning but bright. Listen to the way he talks—like a child of seven. Get him to sing his songs and speak his rhymes for you. He can imitate anyone. He is like his father. I think he has much talent. I think we should put him in pictures!"

That was great stuff for the fan magazines, but I seriously doubt the truth of that story. In the first place, as I remember my grandmother's attitude toward me before I became famous, she never thought very much of me. To her, I was a nuisance, certainly not "cunning and bright." And that bit about my being like my father—no way. She had no use whatsoever for my father, so certainly she would not have used him as a flattering comparison.

The story, as I got it, as I seem to recall it, and as I am pretty sure it happened, is more or less like this:

Money was never plentiful, certainly after John Leonard took off. He supposedly never sent a nickel back to help support his wife, children, and grandchild. Florence was gone, and Julie never worked, as I remember it. And Nonnie, naturally, didn't work. So the only support for all of us was whatever Mabel, my mother, could mail home.

We lived near some of the studios. And for most of the ladies in that poor neighborhood, it became common practice to walk to the studio gate in the morning and see if any of the directors needed extras. This was, of course, years before the

Screen Extras Guild was formed, so the business of hiring was all very casual.

The director, or one of his assistants, would walk out of the gate where the neighborhood people were standing and point to the ones he wanted. "You, you, you, and you." That was the hiring practice in those days in Hollywood. If you were picked, you got $2 and a box lunch.

My grandmother would go down to the gate with all the other people in the neighborhood. She didn't have anything else to do, and besides, she could use the $2, and the box lunch would mean one less meal to prepare. She was picked often because she had a little towheaded kid with her—me.

The directors looking for extras would get two for the price of one. They would get a motherly-looking lady—she was only in her early forties then—with a little kid in tow. They didn't pay me, and I had to share her box lunch.

That's how I began a movie career, as the kid with his grandmother, working as an extra in dozens of films. Once I began going to school, that stopped. During school vacations and summers I was hauled down to the studio gates again.

I think I put up a fuss a lot of times. I had not had a very serene childhood, with the result that I had a temper, and I'm told some of my tantrums were major disturbances. But my grandmother was equal to that, laying about with her rough hands in strong fashion. I seem to have this vague but disturbing recollection of many tears on many mornings in those dear dead days (happily) beyond recall.

My mother came back home to stay when I was five or so, in 1928. She got a job as a secretary during the day, and at night she played piano for rehearsals. She was working for a trio of musical film songwriters at Fox—Con Conrad, Archie Gottler, and Sid Mitchell, who were writing the songs for something they were going to call *Fox Movietone Follies of '29*. There was a sequence in the picture in which a song called "That's You, Baby" would be done in a montage—first by a couple of kids, then by some teenagers, and finally by the stars of the film, Sue Carol and Nick Stewart.

Somebody got the bright idea that I should audition for that number as one of the kids who would sing it first. Maybe it was my mother, maybe my grandmother, I don't know.

My mother knew the song, of course, so she taught it to me at home. I was a quick study always, so I got it down fast.

And so my mother put my name on the list. But she didn't think it would be a good idea if the film's producer, or whoever was doing the auditioning, knew I was her son. So my grandmother was drafted to bring me in and make believe she was my mother, and I was carefully coached to ignore my mother. When I got there, they told me, I was NOT—repeat NOT—to run over and hug and kiss my mother, as I would ordinarily have done, but to make believe I had never seen her before in my life. I guess they made it into a game—I could understand games.

I have a vague memory of a barnlike room, a lot of kids, my mother at the piano, my grandmother gripping me extra-tight by the wrist (no ear this time). And I went in and did the song.

Of course, I had a head start because I knew the song so well—the others had just heard it that day—and maybe that helped. I was hired.

Many, many years later, I directed fifteen of the first thirty episodes of M*A*S*H, which were filmed on the Fox lot. That was the first time I had been on that part of the lot since I was a child, since those first few films I did. And, compounding the curious, the producer of M*A*S*H at the time, Gene Reynolds, made his office in a cottage—the same cottage where those three songwriters, Conrad, Gottler, and Mitchell had worked. And Reynolds's secretary sat in the same exact spot (and, with what I know of movie studios, conceivably at the same exact desk) where my mother sat when I first went to that studio.

It was hardly instant stardom, but I did go from the small bit in that film to another small bit in another one, and the chain reaction that is responsible for much of Hollywood's star system had begun. Once you get rolling in Hollywood, it is very hard to stop yourself, short of deliberately screwing up or causing problems. You may not become a star, of course, but you will probably work continually. They like to hire people they know, who are known quantities.

Anyhow, I soon found myself in another film called *Sunny Side Up*, with Charles Farrell and Janet Gaynor, directed by David Butler, then at the height of his career. I was supposed to be an amateur contestant in a talent contest at a fair, reciting "Under the Spreading Chestnut Tree" while urgently having to go to the bathroom. (I never saw that bit of film, strangely, until 1964, when I was in England on business and was a guest on a British talk show. They had that clip and showed it on the show.)

David Butler liked the work I did in the film. He became my first champion. It was Butler, I understand, who approached Leo McCarey and said that he had a good kid if he needed one. McCarey had worked for Hal Roach, and he apparently told Roach that David Butler had a good young kid if he needed one. Roach was always looking for good kids because he produced the *Our Gang* comedies, which much later became TV's *Little Rascals*.

I auditioned for Roach, and he hired me. I was there in 1929 and 1930, and I was in maybe a dozen *Our Gang* shorts. While I was there, they made the transition from silent to sound, so some of the ones I did were silents and some were talkies, as we called them.

I was making $50 a week. We were poor no more, thanks to me.

5.

I was working; my mother was working; we had a better house, one near the beach, plenty to eat. And my mother, who always did have a big heart, had taken a girl friend under her wing—Dixie Lee. Dixie lived with us. I liked her. More important, my mother liked her. My mother needed friends. Dixie was a few years younger than my mother, but that didn't matter.

Dixie's man, then, was Bing Crosby. He was around our house a lot, of course, because he and Dixie were in love. So Bing had dinner with us a few nights a week for about a year.

Mother and Dixie had met at the Fox studio because my mother was still playing rehearsal piano and Dixie was a chorus girl in a musical. Later I remember my mother's telling me that Dixie had seemed so young (she was) and so naïve (maybe that, too), and she feared for her morality, so she brought her home. She told her that she could stay with us as long as she wanted.

Bing was then singing with Paul Whiteman's band. I remember my grandmother said he was "part of a degenerate trio." That was the Rhythm Boys, and Bing was one-third of the "degenerate" trio. He and Dixie had met somewhere, he liked her and vice versa, and they began seeing each other pretty steadily. But my mother, who became Dixie's unofficial big sister, laid down the rules, that Bing had to have her home at a certain hour, that their behavior in our house had to be circumspect, all that. In those days people behaved. Mostly.

So Bing was around the house frequently. I particularly remember the Sunday morning ritual. I'd get up early, and as soon as some grown-up told me it was okay, I'd be out of the house and down to the beach. When I went outside those Sunday mornings, there would be Bing Crosby, asleep on the front porch swing, in his tuxedo and shoes with a flower in his buttonhole. I would get him a pillow and a blanket. He never paid me much attention—he wasn't the kind of man to play with kids or to kid around with them—but he wasn't mean either.

Well, they got married. Dixie and Mabel stayed close. As Bing did better and better, they moved up and up in the world. Then they bought the old Tom Mix house, north of Sunset Boulevard in Beverly Hills, where all the big movie star estates, like Pickfair, were located. Mother would take me there once in a while when she went to visit Dixie. I remember a few pre-Christmases there because my mother was a great gift wrapper. She wrapped and wrapped for days before Christmas for the Crosbys. I would often be there, watching, helping, handing her ribbon and scissors. (How did we manage before Scotch tape?)

The two ladies stayed close. For years they visited back and forth, talking on the phone, exchanging secrets and girl talk. But they finally dropped it because, I came to understand, my mother and Dixie realized they were lying to each other. They were lying about what was happening to Dixie and Bing and their marriage.

I didn't see too much of Dixie or Bing after a while. My mother went there for dinner by herself or sometimes with a date and then, after she remarried, with my stepfather. I seldom went. I liked Dixie very much because she never talked down to me. So many adults did talk down to me. But she was one of the good ones. Bing I could take or leave, he stayed out of my way, and so, of course, I stayed out of his.

Then there came an illuminating experience. In 1931 we were both—Bing and I—invited to appear at a benefit of some sort at the El Capitan Theater, which later became the Hollywood Palace. My mother and Dixie decided we would all go together, so we rented a car, hired a chauffeur, and rode to the affair, with Dixie and Bing, Mother, me, and my grandmother all in the back seat. I was going to sing "I Found a Million Dollar Baby—in a Five and Ten Cent Store." It was one of Bing's hit records of the moment, and my mother thought it would be cute to have me do one of his hit records. And so, as we drove to the benefit, my mother mentioned that I was doing his song.

He blew up. He said that he was going to do it, that she should have known that he was going to do it, and that he had already rehearsed it with the band. He said that I would have to do some other number because I had only my mother as accompanist and wouldn't have to change a whole band. He said it all very angrily, and my mother was deeply hurt by his attitude. She tried to explain that we weren't following each other on the program and that the whole idea was that my singing the song was meant as something of a tribute to him. The atmosphere in the back of the car was very tense.

Crosby, when we got to the theater, loudly told the orchestra he was changing his song, and that made my mother feel rotten, but it was the only song she and I had rehearsed. I sang my heart out. When we went home, the Crosbys were not with us.

That cooled any friendship that had existed between my mother and Bing, but the Dixie-Mabel friendship was too strong to be broken. The two women were still buddies, and when Gary Crosby was born, there was as much excitement in our house as there was in the Crosbys'. And as the other Crosby boys came along, it was almost as though my mother had given birth, too, such was her joy. We visited them often, my mother taking me with her—but always when Bing was out, always in the daytime. When Bing was home, the only subject he and my mother had in common was Dixie's health. My mother tried to tell him to see his children a little more and to see his golfing cronies a little less because she knew that his ultracasual attitude toward his sons was breaking Dixie's heart.

I grew up, and Bing had his tremendously popular radio show, *The Kraft Music Hall*, and so it was inevitable that I was booked as a guest on his show several times in the late thirties. I was honestly impressed by him as a performer, as a star, and the fact that he was—or, at least, had been—a close family friend impressed me even more. I thought, when I went on his show, that we would be palsy-walsy, more than just the usual host-guest relationship, that he'd reminisce with me about those hundreds of meals he cadged at our house, about the days when I'd tucked him in on the porch swing and brought him a pillow. But it didn't work out that way. He paid me very little attention. Rather than be friendly, if anything, he went out of his way to put me and my mother down.

My mother was still at Dixie's often and growing increasingly concerned about her. Dixie had begun to drink too much—for whatever reason—and Bing wasn't there very often. His boys obviously needed their father more than he allowed himself to be present. Dixie and Mabel talked often. But their talk wasn't the giggling, happy chatter of earlier days. Now it was heavy, serious, and often punctuated with tears.

The Crosbys' new house burned down one night, totally.

My mother said maybe it was an omen. Maybe when Bing rebuilt the house, he would also rebuild his life. They rented a house. I didn't like to go there. Dixie was drinking more all the time, and the booze turned her mean. Mean to everyone, including my mother, but my mother took it because she realized her friend was very troubled and because, too, they were old friends and her definition of friendship included taking the bad along with the good. Now Bing sent his sons off to school, had his wife guarded in that rented house, and went his merry way. I wasn't asked to do any more guest shots on his radio show.

When my mother was dying, Bing (along with many others who I feel came out of guilt) showed up at our home. When I got to her room that evening after work, he was sitting next to her, and my mother said he had been there for hours. They hadn't talked in about a year, and of course, that was the last time they saw each other. He didn't come to her funeral, but I didn't blame him for that. I shouldn't have gone either. I did think, however, that he could have written a note, but he didn't.

Once, sometime later, I thought I'd like to see Dixie. Somebody—I can't remember who—told me I couldn't. Maybe she wasn't up to having visitors. Then she died, in 1952. I didn't write him a note either.

With the war and then my years in New York, I didn't see Bing Crosby again until 1970. At the time I had an office at the NBC television studio in Burbank. Bing was rehearsing a special there, so I dropped down to see what he looked like. I got there when they were all taking a break. He was in his dressing room. I knocked and went in. He was talking to an agent I had known for a long time, a man named Johnny Dugan. Bing was cordial, not exactly throwing his arms around me, but polite, although I could tell he wasn't about to ask Dugan to leave so we could be alone together. He asked me proper questions about my career, my family, my health, but he never once mentioned my mother.

So I did. I had thought of something I thought he might enjoy hearing. At the time I had a partner, Bob Finkel, who was producing Bing's special, and our company was about to make a series with Pearl Bailey which would emanate from the Hollywood Palace. It was for ABC, and that network was going to give us office space in the Hollywood Palace, too. So I told Bing that when I moved in there, it would be just about forty years to the day from that time we were doing that benefit there and had that silly tiff about who was going to sing "I Found a Million Dollar Baby—in a Five and Ten Cent Store." As I told the story, Bing was occupied with opening some mail. When I finished the story, he said, "How about that?" and he never looked up from the mail he was reading.

I never saw him again.

6.

The movie that gave me my first big push was *Skippy*. It was made in 1930. I was eight.

Until then my memories of working in films are sparse and, naturally, childlike. The dog in the *Our Gang* shorts impressed me more than the other kids did. I loved that dog, and one of the great events of my childhood career occurred the weekend Pete Stringer, the man who owned the dog, let me go home with him. To stay a whole weekend with Pete and his dogs was my idea of glory and paradise combined. As for the rest of it, to me working was good because when I worked, I didn't have to go to school. And I was no scholar at that point in my life.

The longer I stayed on the set, the less time I had to spend in school—a simple equation that even I could understand, poor mathematician though I was. There were no laws then about taking it easy on kids—those came later—so we worked from eight in the morning until six at night like everybody else. But I never minded the work. It was make-believe, a children's game, and the smarter grown-up actors even now admit that acting is game playing. It's fun, and it lets a man or woman mature while still permitting him to play childish games.

So I'd go in and out of grammar school. I was supposedly attending the Grant School, not far from the Gower-Sunset intersection, and when I wasn't working, I'd walk to school. But when I was working, I didn't have to go.

So I preferred to work. I was too young to realize what I was missing. To me, at the time, "work" meant a jumble of things which I reacted to positively—the absence of school; the chance to play that make-believe game; the opportunity to talk to grown-ups on a grown-up level; the dog. I didn't know that back there in the schoolyard, normal kids were having normal and much healthier fun.

Later, people tried to rationalize to me that I had gained more than I lost by being a child star. They talked to me about the money I had made. They cited the exciting things I had done, the people I had met, the career training I had had, all that and much more.

But no amount of rationalization, no excuses, can make up for what a kid loses—what I lost—when a normal childhood is abandoned for an early movie career.

I've thought about this a lot, naturally, and I've talked about it to a few of my fellow former child stars, the ones—such as Roddy McDowall—who are thoughtful enough to have considered all the pros and cons deeply.

Roddy tells a horror story about meeting a little girl actress who came to an audition with her mother. The little girl, a shy, pretty thing, was hanging back, and her mother was pushing her forward. And the producer or director or whoever was doing the interviewing asked the little four-year-old girl why she wanted to be an actress. The child hesitated, so the mother plunged in and said, "It's been her lifelong dream."

But everybody knows horror stories about stage mothers. I'm talking now about the non-horror story that, in a sense, is even more horrible. I'm talking about the child who grows up empty and doesn't realize it until it's too late.

I'm talking about me.

I gained a lot, as those rationalizers are quick to point out— money, experiences, career—but think of what I lost. I had no friends. That deprived me of the early competition which I have discovered is so valuable in the growing-up process. I did not receive a good education. Tutors on the set can be manipulated by a street-smart kid and a succession of directors who just want to get the work done and the hell with the kid's education. For many adult years, because of that, I had trouble reading because I simply wasn't properly trained.

I grew up with pressure and responsibility. Most children don't experience them until they are teenagers, if then. I had it from the time I was seven or eight. The pressure to get the scene right, to learn the words, to act this way or that way, to smile or cry or look scared for the cameraman, to do a nice interview. The responsibility to work correctly for the director who tells you that if you don't do a good job, he may get fired and he has three little babies at home to feed.

Why should an eight-year-old kid have to have that kind of pressure?

It isn't a normal life, and we've all seen what it has done to some of my friends, like Garland and Bartholomew and Rooney.

■ ■ ■

JOHN FORSYTHE: When I first met Jackie [rehearsing for the national company tour of *Mister Roberts* in 1949], he was very secure about his acting talents—marvelously secure—but very insecure about his own personal life and what he was and where he was going. For example, I had been a ballplayer in school and in college, and when a lot of the guys in our company—Lonny Chapman and Jack Klugman and Cliff Robertson and Frank Campanella—wanted to start a softball team, of course, I was very involved. We went out, and we played in a league—this was in Chicago—and we did exceptionally well. Jackie used to come out, and one day I asked him. I said, "Come on, let's throw a ball around." He said no, he didn't think so. I said, "Don't you like it?" And he said it wasn't that; it was just that he had never played ball. It was a very revealing moment.

He had never had the time to go out and play with his peers. Subsequently anything he's taken up, he's taken up with tremendous enthusiasm. He's tried to interest me in some of these things, but they are always things—like skeet shooting—that you do by yourself. Never a team sport, not even tennis or golf in which you play with someone else. Always by yourself. He got to be a very good skeet shooter. Auto racing. Flying a plane. By himself.

■ ■ ■

I never rebelled or even thought about rebelling. I wouldn't have, not then. Anyhow, I was happy. Besides, I was told, over and over, that I was a performer, that was my job, that was what I had to do. A kid doesn't question it when adults tell him that.

Later, when my mother had a run-in with Louis B. Mayer and I was blackballed and I knew I wouldn't be able to work for a year, I was torn. I was going to go to Beverly Hills High

School, and I was looking forward to that very much, to be in with the other kids, one of the crowd, that sort of thing. Yet there was a side of me that felt terrible guilt about not working because it had been drummed into me for so long that I was an actor and that was my lot. If I didn't work, then I would be a nobody, and they had told me that I was a somebody.

That was later. In 1930 came *Skippy*. There was a cattle call at Paramount, and I was taken there, with a few hundred other kids. I got the part. I have only a slight memory of that day. When Paramount wanted to sign me, they discovered that I was already signed to Hal Roach for *Our Gang*, and they had to borrow me from Roach through procedures which were common in those days.

I was signed when Victor Schertzinger was supposed to be the director. For some reason, he was replaced by Norman Taurog. By then Taurog was my uncle, having married my aunt Julie about three years before, and our whole family was happy about that.

Taurog was a good director—I discovered later, when I began having a basis for comparison, that he was one of the best—but from the first he frightened and confused me. I hadn't really known him well before *Skippy*. Although he had been married to my aunt for some time, they had been living in New York. My pre-*Skippy* memories of him are scant.

But as soon as the *Skippy* project was put together, he became a vivid figure in my life. His position in our family was curious. As far and away the most successful member—before *Skippy*, he had directed many shorts and one or two minor features—he automatically became the big cheese in the Leonard family. When he was invited for dinner, he was served first and given the choicest morsels. He was listened to, kowtowed to, and seemingly respected. But that was only to his face. Behind his back my grandmother used to call him "that fat Jew bastard."

They would tell me that I must do his bidding, obey him totally on the set, because he was the director and also because he was my uncle. At the same time my grandmother would tear him down while I listened to every word. I was thoroughly confused. I was privy to the family's thoughts that he was something less than human on the one hand, and on the other, I was given instructions to listen to him and to do exactly what he told me to do because he was so smart.

Maybe in that dichotomy were sown the seeds of my eventual dislike of the man. I never did out and out hate him; much later, I felt sorry for him. But also I never did love him or like him very much. I did have, for a time, a great deal of respect for him as a director. He won the Academy Award for his direction of *Skippy*, and looking back, I think he deserved it.

At the beginning, when we were working together on the scenes for *Skippy*, we were frequently at his house. I began to notice that he was constantly putting down his wife, my aunt Julie, and I didn't like that. She was my least favorite aunt, but still, she was flesh and blood, and he wasn't.

When we started working, I did what I was told. My grandmother was with me on the set. If I got it right, I was a good boy. If I didn't, she'd slap me. She didn't pinch me anymore because now I was old enough to tell my mother when I got home. But somehow getting slapped wasn't so bad, so I'd just forget that.

Skippy was the picture that established me for my ability to cry. I had three crying scenes in the picture. They weren't easy.

We were shooting on location in San Bernardino, and the first crying scene came at the end of a long, hard day. Taurog told everybody on the set to be quiet, to let me concentrate on my work. My grandmother said, "Be a good boy and cry." They waited. I tried. No tears.

Taurog had a temper. He was a short man, and he peered over his glasses, and that—all the kids on the picture had come to recognize—was a bad sign. This day he peered, and he screamed, and he hollered. He shouted that it had been a mistake for him to have hired me (I knew I had been hired first, but I wasn't about to dispute him), and he called me a "lousy ham actor" (the first time I had heard that phrase), and he told his assistant to start getting the standby kid ready to replace me.

I suppose all of that tirade was designed to make me unhappy, so I would burst into good, usable tears. Instead, it made me angry, rather than unhappy. Angry kids don't cry. I guess, knowing my reputation, I hit things and slammed things and maybe even broke things, but not one tear was shed.

It was an impasse. As I waited, I saw a new figure on the set, another kid dressed exactly as I was dressed, in the Skippy costume. Evidently they had gotten the spare costume—they always have two of everything on a set, in case the original is rendered unusable for any reason—and quickly put it on one of the other kids. It was Robert Coogan, Jackie's kid brother, a couple of years younger than I was. The idea that they would give my part to any other boy was enough to make me very sad very quickly.

I came apart at the tear ducts. I really cried for Uncle Norman. They rushed me into the scene, and I did it, and then they gave me an ice cream cone, and Uncle Norman said I was a fine actor, and my grandmother said I was a good boy.

From then on, for a while, everything was fine. Norman kept telling me how important it was to my mother that I work hard because my mother was still having to work and she—as we all knew, always—wasn't in the best of health. I was still under contract to Hal Roach for *Our Gang*, so I was being paid only $50 a week for *Skippy*, while Roach had loaned me to Paramount for about $25,000. I didn't know much, if anything, about those money aspects, but I did know I had to work much, MUCH harder, so she wouldn't have to work and maybe she would feel better.

I worked hard, as hard as I could. But I knew there were two more big scenes coming up when I would have to cry. By then I understood how they had tricked me the first time, and I was sure that they were going to try to trick me again. So I determined that when the time came, I would cry by myself.

Of course, when the time came, I couldn't. Dry-eyed, I faced their wrath. I knew I was being very, very bad by not crying—hurting my mother's health, disappointing my grandmother, making my uncle Norman unhappy—but I simply could not bring forth a tear.

A short time before *Skippy* began, a friend of my mother had given me a little dog. I have always loved dogs, and this one—name long since forgotten—was a favorite. I remember him as quiet, well behaved, obedient. I kept him tied to my chair on the set, and he mostly slept all day.

But that dog was suddenly a *cause célèbre*. Norman vented his wrath on him. He said the dog was a nuisance, disturbing everybody on the set, making him nervous.

He said he was going to take the dog away. I asked him where he was going to take my dog. He said to the dog pound. He said if I finished work in time—i.e., if I cried for him—

I could maybe get to the pound before they put my dog away. If I didn't, well, that was too bad.

I smelled a rat. This was the trick they were trying to use to get me to cry. I didn't dare risk a smile, but inwardly I congratulated myself for being too smart for them. This one wasn't going to work. I stood there and watched as my grandmother took the dog, untied him, carried him out. She said she was going to put him in the car and drive to the pound.

I heard my little dog yelp. I knew she had pinched him to make him do that. Again, anger, not tears. Another tantrum. I was so mad I threw anything I could get my hands on.

Norman said okay, that was the end. If I didn't stop that immediately, he said, he'd have the policeman—there was always a security guard on the set—shoot my dog. I said he didn't have the guts. Norman nodded to the security guard. I saw him draw his gun out of the holster and watched him as he went in the same direction my grandmother had gone with my dog.

The set was deathly still. I couldn't see them. Then I heard a single shot. It echoed a moment. Then total silence.

I could visualize my dog, bloody from that one awful shot. I began sobbing, so hysterically that it was almost too much for the scene. Norman had to quiet me down by saying that perhaps my dog had survived the shot, that if I hurried and calmed down a little and did the scene the way he wanted, we would go see if my dog was still alive. So I did the scene as best I could.

Later, of course, I found my dog totally unharmed, and Norman and Nonnie and the security guard grinned at each other, proud of the little trick they had pulled.

That night I couldn't eat, and I couldn't stop crying, and I couldn't sleep. They had to call a doctor, who came and gave me a little something to calm me down. I kept throwing up and crying, and I was a mess. The shot the doctor gave me let me go to sleep. In the morning my grandmother said that I had worried everybody. I felt very bad about that.

I knew I had one more crying scene to do. I was very worried about it because I now knew, from past experience, that I probably would not be able to cry on my own, and I knew that they would once again do something terrible to me so I would cry. What would it be this time? I tried to think of all the bad things they might try. As the dreaded day drew closer, I became more and more frightened.

On that day, however, my mother came to the set with me instead of my grandmother. I suppose she had heard about the first two times, and she certainly had seen what their conduct had done to me. I imagine she took a day off from work so she could come with me on that day.

When it came time to do the scene, my mother did something nobody else had thought of doing before. She explained the scene to me. She told me what had happened to Skippy and why he was crying. We went over all the lines together, and we took the scene apart and discussed it completely. It was a scene in which I was supposed to be praying, and crying, for a little friend, and she dissected the scene and my emotions. She never talked *down* to me. As we talked about Skippy and his friend and all that, I began to cry because now I knew and I sympathized and I cried honest tears. Still crying, I went out and took my place, and it was all done in one take. And most people who remember *Skippy* at all remember that scene the clearest. Taurog received all the credit for it, of course.

The rest of that day, after that scene was shot, I half expected Uncle Norman to say that I had done well, to tell me how happy he was I had done that scene without any problems. He never mentioned it again. My mother kept telling me what a good little boy I was, but since my uncle, the director, didn't say so, somehow I didn't really believe it.

7.

I believe that for both Norman and me, *Skippy* was a turning point. For the next decade our lives would be intertwined, although we made only one more film together. But as he was also my uncle, there was more than a director-star relationship; we were family. He was also the closest thing to a father I ever had.

In fact, for some time I entertained the fear that perhaps he might have been my actual father. It was simple to create a scenario that would explain things—before marrying my aunt, he had one night of passion with my mother, she got pregnant, and Norman, panicky, arranged for Johnny Cooper to marry Mabel to give her child a name and to take the heat off himself.

Little things had made me think about that with some seriousness. Even after Norman and my aunt were divorced, he still maintained an interest in me that seemed far more paternal than avuncular. And we fought, often, and surely our fights smacked more of a father-son than uncle-nephew relationship. He often, I felt, demanded a great deal from me—and I had seen enough fathers to know that they frequently tempered their love with too strong demands.

During this period I would frequently stare at his picture and then at my own face in the mirror, searching for similarities. Sometimes I would imagine that I saw some—a bit about the ear or the eyes or the chin—and at other times, depending on my mood, I would find none at all.

That scenario would, at least, answer the most nagging question in my mind, a question that arose when my mother died. She was, during her final illness, still legally married to my stepfather, Chuck Bigelow. And I was still legally underage, so I was very worried that Bigelow, a man I despised, would adopt me or at least try to.

My mother had always said that if I had any problems, I should talk to Uncle Norman. So I did. He told me to see Jack O'Melveny. The firm of O'Melveny, Tuller and Meyers ("In

Los Angeles," my grandmother always said, "you have to have a Jew in a law firm somewhere") was our family lawyers. O'Melveny was nice and polite, and he smiled nicely and politely and told me to do what Mr. Taurog told me to do. He said that I didn't have to worry about Bigelow, that he couldn't adopt me, that I could rest easy on that score.

Soon after that meeting Uncle Norman called me and asked me to come over. I did. He said he would be my legal guardian if and when anything happened to my mother, so that Bigelow was completely out of the picture.

Then he said there were only two things I had to do. First, I should never mention a word about this conversation to Bigelow. He didn't think I would ever find myself in a position with Bigelow where it might come up, but just in case it did, he wanted to forewarn me not to say a word about his future guardianship of me.

"The second thing, Jackie," Taurog said, "is that I want you to pick up that telephone and call your uncle Jack and say thanks."

"Thanks? For what?"

"Never mind for what. Just do it."

He picked up the receiver and handed it to me.

"Dial the number," he said. "And say to Big Jack, 'Norman said to tell you that even though I don't know what it's for, thanks.'"

I didn't know what it was all about. I was nineteen and frightened by that strange request. But he looked very serious, and he waggled the telephone receiver in front of me. I took it, dialed the home number, and spoke to my young uncle.

"Hello, Jack?"

"Yes?"

"Jackie. Norman said to tell you that even though I don't know what it's for, thanks."

"Oh, I see." Jack's voice seemed very serious. And I had the feeling that he almost had been waiting for my call. "Okay, Jackie. You don't ever have to mention it to me again."

He hung up. I hung up. I looked at Norman. He smiled, and as I left, he told me not to mention the call to anyone and never to ask Big Jack about it. I didn't. I saw Big Jack off and on for the rest of his life—he died in 1955 in his early forties—and we never talked about that phone call.

What had my uncle, Jack Leonard, done for me that required that mysterious telephone call? Why at that time, with my mother on her deathbed and my uncle Norman being given guardianship of me when she died?

■ ■ ■

FLORENCE KENMORE: Do you think it [having to thank Jack Leonard] could have been because of the birth certificate? The birth certificate was picked up, I don't know who picked it up. There had to be a birth certificate. I don't know if they got one that said "John Cooper." The first one did not, I guess. It might not have had any name on it, for the father. At least that was my understanding. Later on they got another one.

■ ■ ■

Perhaps that puzzling telephone call was designed to thank Jack Leonard for not blowing the whistle on Norman's infidelity, which might have resulted in my conception. That, at least, was the troubling thought that pursued me for many years. Maybe Uncle Jack knew the truth, and I was simply innocently thanking him for keeping his trap shut.

Then, on further reflection, I would realize that if that scenario were true, it would cast my mother in a bad light. And I knew she was a very good and proper woman. No prude, but hardly the promiscuous sort. The family—even dear old Nonnie—had a very high standard of morality.

■ ■ ■

FLORENCE KENMORE: Oh, Johnny was Jackie's father, there is no doubt about that. Why, the first time I went to a senior prom, I had to take a chaperone along with me. Our mother was that way with us. Not that we were wild in any way, it's just that Mother was that way. Mabel certainly wasn't wild at all. This thing with Johnny just happened. She didn't run around with guys. Johnny was the only man she slept with.

■ ■ ■

I suppose there are secrets in most families. Over the years what the secrets were is forgotten; what is remembered is only that somebody knows something about somebody else.

I remember that phone call. But now there is nobody else left who does or who might be able to explain it to me. Big Jack is long gone. My uncle Norman—no longer my uncle, but I still think of him like that—is a recluse; he's lost his sight and sits, brooding, in his big house. Even before he shut himself away, we had lost contact. So nobody knows why I had to call my uncle Jack and thank him.

To me it is a mystery of almost as much significance as that of life and death. I know now that I will never learn the answer. And I truly don't care anymore.

I think having had only a wisp of a father has helped me, in turn, be a better father to my own children, Jack, Russell, Julie, and Cris. I've been trying to supply them with everything I missed.

8.

In 1955 I was filming *The People's Choice*, my first TV series, and one day, on the set, somebody handed me a bunch of telegrams. They were all from people back east, friends who had heard that John Cooper, the father of Jackie Cooper, had died. Somehow they had gotten the news earlier in the East than we had in California. One of our advertising agency men asked me if I wanted him to check it out. I said yes. He said later that he had called his office in New York, and they had checked, and it was true. John Cooper had died of cancer of the throat.

> WICHITA, Kan., Nov. 19 (AP)—John G. Cooper, father of former child movie star Jackie Cooper, died here yesterday.
>
> Mr. Cooper was active in show business until 1941 and wrote several songs.

No tears. No regrets. I don't think I thought much about it, one way or the other. I guess about all he ever gave me was my blond hair and hazel eyes, maybe some musical sense.

Taurog gave me more. His influence was stronger, although it took me many years to realize that much of it was malevolent. At the beginning, though, when we made *Skippy* together, he was certainly an influence for good. You could make a case that he went about it the wrong way—his trickery to make me cry—but the aim was to make the picture a success, and that, in turn, would make me a success.

Taurog was a small man, physically, and like so many small men, he made up for his short stature with a tall ego. When *Skippy* turned out to be a smash, he was at once impossible to live with. Julie stuck it out for ten more years.

Right away they had to live like Hollywood royalty. They bought a big, big house in Beverly Hills, and to me, as a boy, it seemed like a castle. They bought the lot next door for a swimming pool and tennis court. We would go there once a week for dinner. Since they lived in a castle, they lived like nobility. Butler. Several maids. Cook. Chauffeur.

■ ■ ■

BILL SMITH: Norman was doing big and was married to Julie, who was at this point a beautiful dame—she had worked in pictures. Norman was a big fat guy. Can I be frank about this now? I was very, very close to them. I was at their house every day. It was pathetic. He ruined Julie's life. It was one of those things which happens plenty of places, who the hell knows? They built a house. Mabel furnished it and did it in beautiful taste. The fag champion tennis player who was a real nice guy—I knew him quite well—Bill Tilden, he built the tennis court. They had an Olympic pool, the most beautiful place you've ever seen. The only things they moved in that house when they moved in there were a set of glasses and their clothes. Everything else in that house was brand-new, believe it or not. One set of glasses they used in the bar—I don't know what the hell they brought them for. At any rate, they had nine in help. They really lived, see. She had her own suite, and so did he. After they separated, I moved in with him—he was alone up there.

■ ■ ■

I found it hard to be affectionate toward Uncle Norman. He smelled of cigar smoke—both his clothes and his breath—and I found it unpleasant to embrace him. But I was required to do so frequently. I was also very confused about his religion. I knew he was Jewish—certainly my grandmother reminded me often enough—but he himself never said anything about religion or his faith.

He was, I came to realize as I grew older, strictly a closet Jew. He never contributed to any Jewish causes, even during the increasingly critical years before World War II, when Hitler's raging, maniacal anti-Semitism made Jews everywhere work together in a common cause. I had the feeling, which I still feel was correct, that Norman's religion was something he tried to live down. Anything that smacked of Jewishness he avoided. He told stories in a Jewish dialect and told them very well, and he would always punctuate them with cliché descriptions—the ugly little Jew, the guy with the little Jew beard, the fat little Jew tie salesman—and my grandmother led all the laughter.

■ ■ ■

FLORENCE KENMORE: I don't think religion was very important in our family. I guess Johnny Cooper was Jewish, but I don't really know. It wouldn't have made any difference. My mother used to have holy pictures and would take them down when it was her turn to have the whist party, which is sinful, of course. I don't think my mother was prejudiced. I don't see how she could have been because so many of her friends were Jewish.

■ ■ ■

It didn't take me long, even as a youngster, to learn to distinguish between the good directors and the men who were just faking it. That latter group—and there were more of them—I could easily hoodwink. The good ones I couldn't. Kids are smart that way; they can quickly smell out the grownups they can bamboozle.

When *Skippy* made us both famous, and when Norman and Julie built their grand mansion, suddenly our family was thrust into the forefront of Hollywood society, such as it was. The Taurogs began entertaining lavishly. We were frequent guests there. I don't know if we were invited because of the family tie or because I had become a celebrity, too, and my presence would help make their party a grand occasion.

I remember meeting people such as Russ Columbo, Carole Lombard, Sue Carol, Lew Ayres, Maurice Chevalier, George Gershwin, and Jerome Kern at the Taurogs.

When Julie became pregnant, I thought and wondered about sex for, I suppose, the first time. Julie's pregnancy was the first one I was consciously aware of. Somehow—I imagine from my mother, who was always frank in answering my questions—I had learned the facts about conception. I tried in my mind to picture my aunt and my uncle in that arrangement. He was short and getting fatter all the time; she was short and slender. Try as I might, I could not construct an image of those two people in the position I had been told was necessary to make a baby. The given facts did not permit those particular bodies to dispose themselves in such a manner for the deed to be done. And yet Aunt Julie was undeniably with child.

Norman was proud as a peacock and positive that he would have a son. And I reached the conclusion that I wanted him to have a son. I reasoned that if he had a boy, then somehow the load on my shoulders would be lightened. So we were both rooting for a son. Norman went so far as to have the room designated to be the nursery painted a bright, boyish blue. I suppose that when Patricia Taurog was born, he swallowed his disappointment, but I am sure he felt somehow let-down.

Norman is now estranged from us all—from Julie, from Patricia and her family, from me. Norman and Julie were divorced when Patricia was eleven. She was their only child. At the time of the divorce Norman bragged to me how he had worked on her and coached her and prompted her so that she would, when she was fourteen and went to court, tell the judge that she preferred to live with him. And that is exactly what happened. Later Patricia told me she realized she had made a mistake. She told me Norman had been miserable to her, and his actions as a father consisted almost entirely of shipping her off to various schools.

He always had a tendency toward tyranny. He had been a tyrant toward me on numerous occasions. After my mother died, and he tried to take up the slack and become parental, he would tell me what to do. I often thought what he told me was wrong, but there was the echo in my head of the words I thought my mother would say—"Do what Uncle Norman tells you"—and so, for years, I did what Uncle Norman told me.

I had had no training to stand on my own feet, really. Things had always been done for me as a star. Money was a subject as alien to me as Swahili grammar. Similarly, other practical subjects were foreign to me. I had never had to cope with anything because the studio did everything, and what it didn't do, my mother and grandmother did. My mother was gone, and for some time, my grandmother and I had not been talking. That left Uncle Norman. I had always done what I was told. I continued to.

So perhaps the tyranny was as much my abject acceptance

as it was his dictatorial behavior. Still, he did it in such a way that I felt mentally abused. I obeyed—up until I went into the Navy during World War II.

Not long after the war I went to New York and stayed for years. When I came back, I began starring in television series. I hadn't seen Norman for some time. Then, early in 1960—I remember it was soon after my daughter Julie was born, and that was in December 1959—Sheldon Schrager came to my office. At the time he was an assistant director; now he is vice-president in charge of production for Columbia Pictures. He had been married to Patricia, Norman's daughter, for some years, and, even though Patricia and her father didn't get along anymore, Schrager, a strong family man, had pity for his father-in-law.

"Jackie," Schrager said, "I know that Norman is a crabby old son of a bitch, but he wants to see you. After all, you two are family, and this is silly."

So the three of us had lunch. I hadn't seen him for nearly fourteen years, I guess, not since he married his second wife, Sue. Then we arranged for dinner at Chasen's—Norman and Sue, Barbara, my wife since 1954, and I. It was edgy all the way. Sue had something she wanted to get off her chest, she said—why had Barbara and I named our daughter after Norman's first wife, Julie? We explained that we hadn't. It was a name that Barbara had always liked and that I liked, too. It was one sticky subject. Everything we moved on to was equally sticky. We got on politics, and that was much worse. Sue is a dedicated Republican to the right of John Wayne, and Barbara and I are staunch Democrats. The election would be coming up later that year. Barbara and I were hoping Senator John Kennedy of Massachusetts would be the nominee, and Sue was a big backer of Vice President Richard Nixon. I sincerely believe politics is one reason why Sue Taurog and I could not be friends to this day.

But for the sake of old family ties, and maybe still because I felt my mother would want it, I did see Norman after that. Once Norman and his two adopted children, Prissy and John, came to our house. John was fifteen or so and goggle-eyed over my 300SL and had to have a ride in it. So I drove over to his house one day, picked him up, gave him a ride in my car. That was fine.

Later, when I was running Screen Gems, I hired Sheldon

Schrager as an associate producer on our first two-hour movie. And Schrager said I had to see Norman. We had lunch. He was fast losing his sight. Earlier he had lost the sight in one eye from diabetes. Now the other one was going.

Schrager and I worked together a few more times, and each time he said I had to get together with Norman. Schrager is big for the family concept. I'm not, except for my own—my wife and children. But a few times we had lunch or dinner or just visited with Norman. He was retired, practically blind; he went out only to do some lecturing at USC.

I haven't seen him now in maybe ten years. I see Sheldon Schrager once in a great while. He has since divorced Pat and remarried. Sheldon keeps saying that Norman and I should get together.

I don't think we will.

9.

I was a normal boy, although there was a rumor spread around that I was a midget. I suppose I should have considered that a compliment—it meant that I was acting so skillfully they couldn't believe I was only a boy—but I didn't. Walter Winchell gave the rumor its biggest boost when he not only wrote that I was a midget but insisted he had met me a dozen years before, when I was already established in the Singer Midgets act.

The December 1931 issue of *Motion Picture* carried an article by someone named Dorothy Calhoun, entitled "Is Jackie Cooper a Midget?" It was a very serious discussion of the pros and cons of that question. Under a picture of me, when I was four, is this caption: "This picture of Jackie Cooper was taken in 1927. Does he look like a four-year-old here?"

For a time it was a subject of some national concern. It happened to all of us—Shirley Temple, particularly—when we were first famous. It is hard for the public to accept the fact that little children can have big talent.

I was a normal boy. But I was also famous and hence valuable. So I couldn't do things which might hurt me. No bicycle riding—I might fall off and break something or skin my nose or knee. No football playing with the other kids—again, too risky. No crossing the street without a grown-up to assist me—I could get run over. So at home I would walk around the block endlessly, without crossing a street, watching the other kids play but banned from participating.

I was nine when they began calling me America's Boy, the boy every American family knew and loved. Typically American—blond, hazel-eyed, clear-skinned, brave, fearless, loved by mother and father, popular with dozens of buddies.

You know by now how tainted that picture was. America's Boy was the illegitimate son of a Jewish father and an Italian mother, living with a mixed-up family, no close friends at all. If the WASPish Midwest and South had known the truth, they

49

would have dropped me as their idol before they swallowed their next broiled catfish.

They began putting me in film after film—most of them variations on the same theme. It was the theme that had captured the public's fancy in *The Champ*, the first picture I made with Wallace Beery. It was the theme of the boy and his father, motherless, together facing the blows and curses of an unfeeling world.

I made others between *Skippy* and *The Champ*, but few memories remain. I do remember, in *Donovan's Kid*, having a scene with the villainous Boris Karloff. He played a character called Cokey Joe, and he was trying to make me sniff some white powder. Then Richard Dix burst in to save me; he beat Karloff up and carried me away to safety. I kept asking everybody what the white powder was and why Mr. Karloff was trying to get me to sniff it. They told me it was a drug. It wasn't until recently that I have seen any film in which cocaine was shown so clearly.

When a Fella Needs a Friend had me and Chic Sale, a gentle, kindly man. He knew how to talk to kids. He didn't pat me on the head. I used to hate head patters, and I have realized that all children dislike being patted on the head. I think it is because that gesture reminds children of the great disparity in height between themselves and the head patter, and thus, they don't like it. Never pat a kid on the head.

There was a picture, called *Divorce in the Family*, which sticks in my mind only because it was my first distant location. We were out on the Mojave Desert, in the town of Mojave itself. The actual location was thirty miles from there into the desert, and I found I could easily avoid the teacher by taking off and hiding among the rocks. She was, I suspect, afraid of following me because of the threat of snakes.

Then came *The Champ*.

Wallace Beery is long gone now, so I guess it can be said without fear of hurting anybody's feelings, but I really disliked him. It began the very first day on *The Champ*. There was to me then no warmth to the man. He always made me feel uncomfortable.

I had begun to look forward to the men in these pictures. Maybe it was the feeling that he—whoever he was—would be a father to me for the duration. And it worked out so I had some very nice, fatherly actors to work with. Richard Dix had been great—he'd spar with me, walk around with his arm draped casually across my shoulder. All very macho, very boy-and-dad. I'd worked with Chic Sale and Lewis Stone, and they had both been great.

My mother had begun to take me to some films before my pictures, so I'd know who these men were. I had, for example, been taken to see *Cimarron* before I worked with Richard Dix, so I knew who he was. When the news reached our house that my next costar would be Beery, there was great elation. My grandmother was particularly pleased. She was a big fan of Beery's. So was my uncle Big Jack. They kept telling me how great it was going to be.

So I looked forward to the first day's shooting on *The Champ*. On the Metro lot we were doing a scene supposedly set in a Tijuana hotel room, where I had to put Beery to bed because he was drunk. That took the morning, and then in the afternoon we moved on to another scene with the old-time character actor Edward Brophy and Beery and me.

King Vidor was the director. As the day wore on, I felt uncomfortable. I could sense tension on the set, and that is always uncomfortable. As a child, too, whenever there is something that is not right, you immediately conclude that somehow it must be your fault. So I started to wonder what I had done, particularly when I saw them all glance my way once in a while.

Beery was obviously angry. Vidor and Brophy and Vidor's assistant, Red Golden, were trying to make him do something, but—he was a big star—trying to josh him into doing it, rather than telling him to do it.

I gradually got the drift of it. They were accusing him of trying to upstage me. (For the uninitiated, upstaging is the fine art of one actor doing things in the background of a scene to make the audience look at him, rather than at the person who is theoretically the star of that particular scene.)

They couldn't come right out and say, "Wally, don't upstage the kid." But in effect, that was what they were doing, without saying those words. He had apparently been going through his repertoire of mugging and broad gestures while I was supposedly in the foreground, doing or saying something vital to the action of the piece.

Beery knew what he was doing, and he knew what Vidor, Brophy, and Golden were telling him. He couldn't get angry at them, so he got angry at me. And I had never had one of the father figures in my movies angry at me.

Over the years I have seen *The Champ* many times, and damned if Beery didn't upstage me very often.

He rebuffed all my affectionate advances. As a young boy I was demonstrative—that trait had been encouraged by most grown-ups I had met—and I liked to hug and kiss people. Beery brushed me off. He would also tell me to do things in the picture one way when the director, Vidor, had already told me to do them an entirely different way. I was used to doing what I was told by my elders, but it was confusing when two elders gave me contradictory instructions.

Beery was childless when we made *The Champ*. Later he did adopt a little girl, and in the other pictures we made together, he would have her visit the set occasionally. My mother, probably to cheer me up when he would thrust me away, would tell me he wasn't even affectionate toward his own child.

One of Beery's traits that was famous in Hollywood was his tendency toward miserliness. My mother and I witnessed one excellent example of that quality when, for some reason, we had lunch with him one day in the MGM commissary. As we left, my mother noticed that he had not left a tip. She offered to lend him some change if he didn't have any. He held up one of those big hands of his and said that he didn't ever leave a tip. My mother couldn't believe that. He said he was very serious. He explained that tipping was designed to be a reward for special service. Since he was Wallace Beery, he said, he automatically got special service, and therefore, a tip would be a waste of money.

The Champ was a monster of a success, and so Louis B. Mayer immediately demanded that his story department find another story of the same sort for the two of us to do. *O'Shaughnessy's Boy* was the one they came up with. It was basically the same story as *The Champ*, only this one had a circus background and Beery was a one-armed lion tamer instead of a boxer.

Richard Boleslawski, an import from the Polish theater, was the director. Now, with Taurog and Vidor behind me, I was aware of a good director. Boley was one of those. And he was the first to treat me, in any way, like an actor. He would tell me what to do, but respectfully. Some of the others I had had would ask me how I wanted to do a scene. A kid needs to be told. Boley was strong. He and Beery often clashed because of that strength. And frequently they would have to call the producer down to the set to arbitrate the dispute. I would be pleased (and so would the crew, who unanimously disliked Beery) when Boleslawski won more than he lost.

I would come home and tell everybody about Beery. And my grandmother, who had started out admiring him so much, gradually came to refer to him, almost without exception, as "that fat Polish prick." But my mother, as always, tried to be understanding. I would pour out my grievances to her—many she had seen firsthand—and she would try to find some rationale for his behavior. She was that way. It made me tolerate him, which perhaps was her game. I never did actually hate him, although I never liked him.

We made *The Bowery* together; it was Darryl Zanuck's first with his new company, Twentieth Century Pictures. Beery and I had another actor with us in this one—George Raft. And I fell in love with him. As cold and distant as Beery was, that was how warm and friendly Raft was. My grandmother, who read fan magazines, told me that she had heard he wore a girdle and said I should find out if it was true. So I snooped—I had gotten good at snooping around sets—and I found out that it was indeed true. But it wasn't what I had expected. To me, living in an almost totally female society, a girdle was a pink thing with fasteners hanging down. One day my snooping paid off, and I got a peek of George Raft changing, and he was wearing something, all right, but it wasn't pink. It was just a tight elastic garment around his middle, attached to his shorts.

I had overheard my mother say that she had heard he had gangster connections. In the thirties, gangsters were all the rage. Raft had played a lot of gangsters, so the rumors began. I have no idea if there was any truth to them, but the thought of Al Capone frightened me, as it did any child of my era. He was the bogeyman of the thirties. Raft was very kind and patient with me, and I tagged after him all day, and I often wondered, when he made a telephone call, if he was talking to Scarface Al or any of those colorful characters. But even though we became friends, I never had the guts or the bad manners to ask him. I had been taught never to ask personal or embarrassing questions.

Beery continued his upstaging tricks, not only with me but also with Raft. George was not about to take that and, being an old pro, countered tit with tat. So the two old pros waged an upstaging battle that forced the director, Raoul Walsh, to call for retake after retake. Consequently, the film began falling behind schedule. Dozens of takes would be ruined because of the jockeying for position between Beery and Raft or because while one was speaking, the other would be scratching his head or rubbing his chin or one of the other time-tested tactics for stealing a scene. Walsh would blow up, and Zanuck would come down to the set. Darryl was something of a ham, too, so Beery and Raft and Zanuck would go at it, arguing about who did what to whom, when and how, and how to make it come out even.

There was the first faint glimmer of friendship from Beery toward me then. I think it was motivated by jealousy. He could see how Raft had captivated me, and faced with the prospect of losing me (he never had had me, of course), he tried to do something about it. What he did was typical. He started to tell me bad things about his rival. He whispered that he had heard from a reliable source that Raft had actually killed a few people. He said that, of course, I knew that Mr. Raft was associated with Chicago gangsters, didn't I? Well, the story he had heard was that in Chicago, to prove his mettle, George had been given a gun and told to rub out two gangsters and he had done it.

Naturally, the first thing I did was run to George Raft and tell him what I had heard. Raft laughed but glowered at Beery.

The other picture I did with Beery was the biggest of them all, from the standpoint of budget and ambition—*Treasure Island*. Lots of my contemporaries, or people who grew up in the era when they could have seen that as children, feel it was one of the high spots of their childhood. It was, of course, based on the Robert Louis Stevenson adventure novel, and so it was a solid story, a real old-fashioned adventure.

For me, at twelve going on thirteen, it was the hardest work of my life, and some of the most unpleasant. There were some bright spots, mostly from my association with the director, Victor Fleming. To begin with, I was miscast. I didn't know it then—I had not read the book (reading was, as I have said, something I had not yet learned to do with enjoyment)—and the character I played was a boy (Jim Hawkins) who was a bright, sensitive English boy of fourteen or fifteen, the man of the family with his father gone. They should have gotten an older boy, preferably English, one with more maturity. I didn't realize I was wrong then (and the public eventually accepted me), but Fleming knew it. And he tried to get me to act older.

I would read the lines as I had always read lines. Fleming would tell me not to whine, to try to act more mature. It was the first time anyone had made me think about what I was doing, really to consider my character and how to make him come alive.

Louis B. Mayer, when we began making the picture, was having one of his periodic bouts of worry. *The Bowery* had been made but not yet released, and he wasn't sure how that would do. If it did poorly, maybe *Treasure Island* was a poor risk. Our producer, Hunt Stromberg, Sr., wanted to shoot it in the South Seas, but Mayer quickly squashed that idea, and we went to Catalina. Then Mayer broke Fleming's heart by turning down color for the film. Fleming had thought— rightly—that to do a splashy adventure film without color would be almost sinful. Stromberg and Fleming had wanted to find a real oceangoing frigate for the ship scenes that figure so prominently in the story. That, too, was an expense Mayer vetoed. Instead, he borrowed a 110-foot yacht from his friend Joe Schenck, and had a superstructure built on top to convert it from a modern schooner to an old frigate of that period, the 1700's. The yacht-turned-pirate ship was moored off Catalina. Because of the additions, the poor vessel had become top-heavy. It rolled badly in any sea, and when we worked aboard her, it was difficult to keep our footing.

We stayed at a hotel on Catalina but were out at sea for twelve hours a day, six days a week. One bright spot was that I learned dancing. There was a little orchestra in the hotel, and every night the unit manager's wife—Mrs. Ulrick Bush— would teach me dancing. She was very nice to me.

Beery wasn't, as usual. For one thing, he had his own speedboat. The rest of us were ferried out to the converted yacht via a water taxi, a trip which, if I remember correctly, took almost an hour. On the way home I'd almost always sleep, my head on my mother's shoulder. But Beery had demanded, and gotten, a separate speedboat to zip him in and out. I would look longingly at the long, lean, and very fast speedboat every day. He never once offered me—or anyone else—a lift.

To me, at twelve, a high spot of the film would be when

I got to fire a gun. Jim Hawkins pitches in to help the good guys beat the pirates, led by Long John Silver (Beery) and his pegleg. When Jim does, he grabs a couple of the old pistols and shoots his way out of a trap.

The special effects men, in charge of guns and such on a film set, were experimenting with the guns. They just used flash powder, of course, but they wanted to make sure they worked and had the right effect when they were fired. I prevailed on them to let me try once, using the excuse that I was going to have to fire them sooner or later and should really have a chance to experiment now. So they loaded one for me, told me what to do, and I fired. The flash powder landed right on Wallace Beery's foot. That was the foot on the leg he had to have strapped up behind him for the pegleg effect. It was an uncomfortable rig, so between scenes he was unstrapped. His bare foot was stretched out on the deck, and my gun was pointed right at his foot.

He yelled bloody murder. I have since been attacked by flash powder myself, and I can testify that it is no more painful than being run into by a lit cigar. But Beery's screeches and gyrations aroused the whole company. Naturally I was scared to death. I was frozen in that one spot, the telltale gun with its telltale trail of smoke clutched in my telltale hand.

Then the crew burst into laughter and applause. They had no use for Beery—no crew ever did—and they were giving me a standing ovation for having shot him in the foot. Strangely that applause did not please me. The stricken look on his face, the humiliation of having his injury become the cause of joy got to me. I went to a private spot down below and cried about it. I was stunned at the fact that grown men would take pleasure in another's pain and discomfort. I realized that his own actions had created the climate under which those actions could thrive, but still, it troubled me.

We were on *Treasure Island* for almost three months, which was a tremendously long shooting schedule in those days. Even so, we were all called back later. Louis B. Mayer wanted retakes. Retakes were a big thing at Metro then. It was a studio dedicated to perfection, and it often recalled a company to add a scene or reshoot a scene. It made the films more expensive, but they turned out well, and Mayer was a man who demanded things be done his way.

When he saw *Treasure Island*, he was miserable. Obviously

he had never read the book or the movie script. The film did not have a happy ending. Furthermore, there was no scene in it of Jackie Cooper crying. That was what I was famous for, tears, and Mayer felt the public would be disappointed if I didn't cry at least once. But mostly it was the happy ending he demanded. It was pointed out to him that the film followed the book, but that cut no ice with L.B. He had a new ending written—Jim Hawkins frees Long John Silver just before the end of the film, but first, he cries because his piratical friend will be gone forever.

We were all unhappy at the summons to return to work. Fleming nearly had a stroke; to him, the idea of mucking about with a Stevenson ending was damned near sacrilegious. But if Fleming was mad, Beery was raging. It was the crying scene that infuriated him. He knew that the public would like it and that in the scene he would merely be support. So he did everything in his power to ruin the scene. He knew that it was never easy for me to cry. Now, when I was almost thirteen, it was getting harder. So Beery would stall. He would blow lines. He would turn to Fleming, in the middle of a scene, and apologize for doing something wrong, even though he hadn't done anything wrong. And so the retakes, which had been scheduled for a day—it was only a two-and-a-half-page scene—stretched out to almost a week.

Beery would go to his dressing room and stay there. When he came out, he would almost immediately take a break to go to the men's room. I remember once a poor assistant director being sent to fetch him out of the can—he had been there, easily, for a half hour—and Beery roaring at the little man from inside, "Just because I'm paid ten thousand a week doesn't mean that I have to shit faster than anybody else." (I think he even exaggerated that—the rumors were he was getting $5,000 a week.)

When that retake was finally completed, that was the end of the Beery-Cooper films. I doubt if I saw him five times after that. I remember the day after his brother, Noah, had died, in 1946, soon after I had gotten out of the Navy. I was having lunch at Romanoff's, and there was that buzz when somebody important comes in, so I looked up, and there was Wallace Beery. He was with a young lady—he had long since separated from his second wife—and as he walked to his table, everybody, from waiters to patrons, was offering condolences on his brother's death. But Wally was never one to share the limelight, and now he growled because his dead brother was upstaging him. So he just plunged ahead, waving aside all the kind, sympathetic remarks—"Yeah, yeah, just skip it, will ya?"—and sat down.

It made me uncomfortable all over again. But I never did have a comfortable moment with the man who costarred with me in those famous films. He never even bought me an ice cream cone.

Somehow, over the years the Beery mystique has endured. I think that the question people have asked me most often has been "What kind of guy was Beery?" It would be too complicated to explain to them what my real attitude toward him was and, anyhow, they ask that question expecting me to say how great he was, and I wouldn't want to burst their beautiful bubble. So I've always said, "He was a swell guy, a real swell guy."

But I really don't think he was a swell guy at all. When I first started with him, I wanted him to be. He was a big disappointment. I've had a bunch of disappointments like that. But at the time I was just making my name as an actor, in *Skippy*, Beery was still a hero to me.

10.

YUMA, Ariz., April 29 (AP)—Mrs. Mabel Cooper, mother of Jackie Cooper, juvenile film star, and Charles J. Bigelow, of Chicago, were married here early this evening by Judge Earl A. Freeman. The wedding party left immediately for Palm Springs.

That was in 1933, and I was a member of that wedding party. The matron of honor was Louis B. Mayer's executive secretary and right-hand lady, Ida Koverman. It was a happy trip. I was happy for my mother. And she was happy for me because she felt that the marriage would give me a father.

We had met him through the man he shared an apartment with, Red Golden, King Vidor's first assistant. Red had met my mother when we made *The Champ*, and he had dated her a few times. I expect I was jealous, as any boy would be when his mother begins going out. I didn't like Red much, and I think my mother knew that, so she really never was serious about him. I think she was serious about Bill Smith, but he wasn't the marrying kind, and I don't believe she ever had any illusions about him. To me, he had almost become family, he was just a man who was around, who gave me presents, who was fun.

Then Bigelow got into the picture. At first, we got along very well. There were things about him I liked. He was a horseman, of sorts, and I liked horses and people who liked horses. When I was a boy, anything to do with horses was my meat—from merry-go-rounds to pony rides to western movies to cowboy clothes. And when Mr. Bigelow—that was what I called him at first—casually mentioned that he played polo, well, he was all right with me.

I liked his car, too. He had a two-seater Chrysler, fire engine red, with two spare tires in back. It was pretty neat. He took me for rides in his car, and then he took me out horseback riding with him, and he and I got along very well. He was a very enterprising fellow.

Because I was recognizable then, the three of us couldn't go away just anywhere. They were always looking for out-of-the-way places. They began to go to Twentynine Palms, a desert resort which is more secluded and, hence, more private than Palm Springs. I was eleven or so, and I knew the facts of life, but the idea of my mother and Mr. Bigelow's sleeping together never dawned on me. We were just all three of us away for the weekend. We had a two-room bungalow, and when I woke up in the morning, my mother was always in the other bed in my room.

I fell off a horse, one of those weekends in Twentynine Palms. Bigelow and I were out riding—I imagine I was calling him Chuck by this time—and he was smart enough to make me get right back on again. I was crying—not seriously hurt, but I ached and my feelings were deeply insulted—but I knew that he was doing the right thing when he insisted that I get back on the horse again. I liked him for that.

My mother said she thought she was going to marry him. We talked about it. My big concern was where everybody would sleep in the house. She told me that married people sleep together. I was a little bothered—the jealousy thing, mostly—but I liked Chuck, and I guess I really wanted a father. It always seemed so nice to have one in the movies I did.

The marriage resulted in a grand upheaval of the family. I think my mother thought we should make it look as though Chuck were supporting us on his salary—he was an executive of some sort with Consolidated Film, an independent film lab—and his earnings wouldn't be enough for our Beverly Hills house. So she rented that out, brought Queenie and Big Jack to a place at the beach, and the Bigelow-Cooper family moved into a small rented house in a less expensive part of the city.

I was no longer the only man in my mother's life, and it rankled. He got home late, and she had dinner with him. I ate earlier. She sat with me, but she didn't eat with me. But still, I liked him, liked having a man around the house.

The honeymoon between him and me didn't last very long. For a while things were okay. And to those who cared, it looked as if America's Boy were now complete. In fact, that image persisted for years, long after it had actually shattered at home. Here is a quote from an article in the fan magazine *Screenland* in 1939:

Perhaps the nicest thing Mabel Cooper ever did for Jackie was to select Charles Bigelow for his stepfather. As a matter of record, it was Jackie who was calling him "Dad" before Mr. Bigelow had popped the question! Never has there been a closer association or a finer understanding between a father and son. In Charles Bigelow, Jackie has a real friend, a confidant, with tolerance and a broad-minded approach to all the problems of youth, life and living.

About that "closer association" and "finer understanding": It started with angry words and ended with a punch in the face. I really can't pinpoint what started the change, but it happened about the time I had my appendix out. In those days appendectomies required a two-week hospital stay. When I came home, Chuck and I began sniping at each other. My mother, caught in the middle, sometimes took my side, sometimes took his side. I can see now that she was trying desperately to keep the peace, but at the time I resented it, of course, when she went against me. I had my bratty side. I was now almost thirteen.

Pretty soon the façade of living on Chuck's salary vanished. We moved back to Beverly Hills. To be fair about it, I had something to do with that return. The little house we lived in when they were first married was one I didn't like, primarily because there were no kids my age around. So I coaxed my mother into going back to Beverly Hills. I think Chuck coaxed her some, too.

He was beginning to live pretty high on the hog. He liked to entertain, to throw big parties. He liked to dress flashily, to drive long, loud cars, to give gaudy gifts.

But I was, obviously, the main source of the family income. He got a job at Monogram Studios, but it didn't pay well. And then, at fourteen, I stopped working, too, for about a year. So there wasn't much of anything coming in. That didn't seem to slow down Chuck Bigelow's high life.

Our house in Beverly Hills was one of a comparative few in that era that had a swimming pool. Today swimming pools are as common there as refrigerators, but then they were still somewhat rare. And so our home was mecca for my newfound teenaged friends. When I stopped working, I began going to Beverly Hills High, and suddenly I had that priceless commodity I had never had before—friends. Most of them were not show business kids, not a lot of rich kids; they were mostly ordinary middle-class kids. A swimming pool was a big deal. They loved to come over to my house.

In those days, too, a kid could get a driver's license on his fourteenth birthday, and I was down there bright and early when I turned fourteen. I already had a car. I had done a guest-starring role on a popular radio show of that period, *Al Pearce and His Gang*, and that program was sponsored by Ford, which had offered me a car in lieu of a paycheck. I had jumped at the deal over my mother's protest, and so I had a car before I had a license.

I felt like a normal kid for a year, with a car and friends, and they liked me—I think almost as much because I was a good guy as because of the pool, although that certainly helped boost my popularity.

My year of inactivity ended when I did a cheapie at Chuck's studio, Monogram, called *Boy of the Streets*. I was something then, driving myself to and from work, a pocketful of cash ($10 was the maximum), plenty of friends—and, increasingly, girls on the scene. That summer, 1937, I was doing *White Banners* at Warner Brothers, with Claude Rains and Fay Bainter and Bonita Granville. Mother and Chuck and I stayed, for the summer, at the beach with my grandmother. Mother bought the house next door so we would have some privacy—beach houses weren't very expensive then.

That was when I began to hear Mother and Chuck arguing. I tried to listen. Kids will do that. I overheard my mother saying how their relationship had changed, how he hadn't slept with her for over a year, and she demanded to know why. I was old enough to understand.

Because of that and because of a general deterioration of our relationship, Chuck and I hardly spoke anymore. After the summer and when we moved back to Beverly Hills, it grew worse. So did the entire climate in the family. Virtually every night at dinner there was an argument. At fifteen, I tried to stay out more and more, with my new circle of friends, my pals from Beverly Hills High, plus others I had met, like Sidney Miller and Junior Coghlan and Buddy Pepper.

They—Chuck and my mother—always had a few belts at the bar before dinner. Dinner itself was full of tension and contention. I loved it when they went out, so I was by myself, and I'd plug in my radio and listen to music while the maid served me dinner. No arguments!

One night the usual arguments, the usual tension. I had had it, and I slammed whatever I was holding on the table, and I said, "Can't we ever eat without an argument?"

Bigelow stood up.

"Don't you ever talk like that again to your mother and me," he said as he came over and pulled me out of my chair.

I didn't know until that moment that I don't like to be touched in anything approximating anger. Thinking back on it, I should have known. I had had many hours of boxing and wrestling lessons—ex-fighter Johnny Indrisano had taught me at home, and Max Baer's trainer had taught me at MGM, and I had always been an effective counterpuncher. When anybody tagged me, I fought back like a tiger.

When Bigelow touched me, I became very mad. By then I was a pretty husky kid—I was five feet nine inches and weighed about 160, and I was pretty strong—and I brushed his hand off and stared him straight in the eye.

I don't remember my exact words—they were few—but the import was that if he didn't take his hands off me, I would break his neck. He was a couple of inches taller than I was but he backed away and gestured to me to take it easy, he meant me no harm.

His backing down cost him the last vestige of respect I had for him. A teenage kid really knows that he shouldn't talk to his elder the way I had talked. He is looking for a stern word or a stern look or maybe even a stern slap in the face. When the elder just backs down and slinks away, that's the end of all respect.

Something or someone—perhaps Bill Smith, who never did like Bigelow—made me begin to wonder about his honesty. I began watching him very closely after that incident at the dinner table. Since I knew, after that, I could never again like him, I no longer had to feign respect for him. It followed that I could keep a disrespectful eye on him.

There was a lot to watch. Whenever the three of us went out to dinner, he always paid by check. There were no credit cards then, of course, so it was either cash or check. Bigelow would write out a check for considerably more than the bill had come to and pocket the change. He wangled a fancy car—a Cadillac "60 Special"—out of my mother. I figured if he could do it, I could, too, and I wangled a Lincoln Zephyr out of her.

Bigelow had made a kind of office out of a little upstairs sitting room. When I walked by and looked in on him, he would always close the books he was working on and shove them into a drawer. I saw that he had installed a safe in a closet off that sitting room, and I frequently found him putting things in the safe at night. Once I found a pair of girl's panties in the glove compartment of his car. I found myself keeping track of everything he did, financial and otherwise.

I made a picture called *That Certain Age* with Deanna Durbin—I was the first to kiss her, or was it Robert Stack?—and there was a pretty little girl in the cast. Her name was Peggy Stewart, but it was her older sister, Pat, who interested me. Pat Stewart and I began going out seriously. Eventually Pat married Wayne Morris, but that was a long time ahead. When we were in our teens, we were very much in love.

Pat and I often had parties at the house now, as my old friends began to pair off, boy-girl, and so did our new friends. Forrest Tucker, Ann Rutherford, Dan Dailey—they were all part of the new crowd hanging around my house. Swimming parties were very big that summer of 1938. All my friends were three to six years older than Pat and I.

Pat once told me—very hesitantly, but very convincingly—that my stepfather had made a pass at her. The way our house was set up, the focal center of the rear of the house was a huge playroom, in which I had installed my drums, a piano, a small stage, and some recording equipment, and to get from the playroom to the pool, you had to go through a dimly lit laundry room. Pat said that Bigelow had made his pass in the laundry room.

I was almost seventeen, and my mother felt that my romance with Pat was too serious. She was probably right. She and Chuck took me away for a month to Coronado, near San Diego, but he stayed only a few days. As usual, he provoked a fight, and angrily he packed up and drove home, back to the city by himself, in our house, ready and able to swing.

Incidentally that month in Coronado turned out to be great for me. At first, I was angry at having been separated from the true love of my life, but that wore off in a few days. I met a fellow there, a seventeen-year-old like me, who had a speedboat, and that was great. I also discovered sailboating, equally great. I think the Coronado time was what, when World War II came along, made me head toward the Navy.

Bigelow had lots of time alone in those days. My mother had bought a place in Palm Springs, too. I loved that, because I had a horse there—a good Morgan quarter horse—and he never came down there with us. I seem to remember an endless series of lonely nights for my mother, with her calling him (or trying to) at home and when she finally got him, asking, "Why haven't you called me?"

He was still grasping. He decided that the kids I had for friends didn't come from families with sufficient influence to suit him. He found men of substance—big Hollywood executives—who had sons or daughters my age, and he told me to invite them to my parties. Never mind, he said, those friends you have now. Those friends, he said, couldn't reciprocate.

Bigelow had dropped all pretense of being a buddy-buddy father. I was active, then, in things like music and boating and horse shows. He never came to anything I did, whether it was a jazz session I was in or a sailboat race or a stock horse show. Not once was Chuck Bigelow in attendance.

In 1940, when I was still seventeen, I woke in the middle of the night to the sounds of a terrible argument. I could hear my mother's voice, angry but sobbing, and his voice, angry and demanding. I went into my bathroom, which was closer, so I could hear better. But I still couldn't make out the details, only that it was the bitterest fight they had yet had. Finally, there was a crash and then quiet. I ran into their room.

I could tell, in an instant, what had happened. He had evidently thrown the telephone at her—it had a long cord—and had missed, and the receiver had struck and shattered a mirror-matted picture. He turned to look at me—I slept in my shorts, and that was all I was wearing—and he turned white. He knew what was coming. I hit him once, hard as I could, hit him in the face. (I damn near broke my hand, too.) He fell backwards, slammed the back of his head against the wall, and slowly sagged to the floor, leaving a trickle of blood against the wall to mark his downward progress.

My mother, sobbing, collapsed on the bed. I grabbed Bigelow, who was unconscious, lugged him into the bathroom, and held his head under the faucet in the bathtub until he revived. I helped him put some clothes on, put some on myself, and drove him to Georgia Street Receiving Hospital. We never said a word in the car. The doctors examined him, said he had a slight concussion, kept him for a few hours for X-rays, stitches, and such. Then I drove him back home again. That was the end of it.

My mother gave me a lecture about violence. That was the first time in my life that I had ever hit anybody in anger—I had never had a fight of any sort—and it made me realize that most movie fights are terribly phony. My swollen and aching hand testified to the fact that the slug-slug-slug pace of movie fights is totally unrealistic.

Bigelow and I succeeded in avoiding each other from then on. For a while I was much more concerned about my mother, whose health was steadily deteriorating. She went into the hospital for a tumor operation. I doubt Bigelow ever came to see her, and he was rarely at home in her absence. I guess he was just playing around. I didn't miss him. The doctors found a spreading malignancy in my mother. They should have just sewn her up, and she would have died in a month. Instead, they cut out what they could and let her come home.

For a while she felt fine. The doctor—Dr. Sam Herzikoff, a fine man I had come to know well—told me that the malignancy was sure to return and that my mother had, at the most, a year. So I was very solicitous of her.

New Year's Eve 1940 gave way to 1941. The whole family was together for once with friends and, as it turned out, for the last time. We went to the El Mirador Hotel to celebrate. As the midnight hour struck, my mother was so happy and feeling so well.

"I'll never be sick again," she said, raising her glass to mine, and smiled at me. "Isn't that wonderful?"

I almost broke down. Bigelow, across the table, laughed with our friends. He hadn't heard her. I felt like punching him again.

By March 1941 Mother was feeling bad again. She had to stay in bed. I think this time she knew that she would never recover. It wasn't only the way she felt. It was the steady stream of visitors, people like Bing Crosby she hadn't seen in years. She knew they were calling to salve their own consciences, and they would do that only with dying people.

Still, Dr. Herzikoff told me that she must not know, that she must always be told she was recovering. I don't know if that is the modern theory, but then it was strongly held by doctors that the dying must not be told they were dying. And I felt he was right, and I fought to keep her from knowing.

Herzikoff and I talked a lot, and one day I told him—there was nobody else to tell—of my suspicions regarding my stepfather. He had become our business manager, and I said how I suspected him of milking my income. I told Herzikoff how he kept the change when he cashed checks. I told him how every night he emptied his loose change into jars on his bureau and how the jars became full and then suddenly were empty again. I told him about the safe in the closet off the upstairs sitting room.

The doctor said I should see if I could find someone who could get into that safe without damaging it. That way, he said, I would know for sure and wouldn't be forced into making accusations that might be unfounded.

You can find anything in a movie studio, even a safecracker. I asked around and was directed to a special effects man who knew how to get into any kind of safe, quietly and discreetly.

One day I told my mother everything I had learned about Bigelow through all those months—years—of watching him. I told her everything, even the tawdry things like the pass he had made at Pat Stewart in the laundry room. She sighed, with what I took to be relief.

She said it was all right with her if I could get him out of the house. She said she had married him only for my sake and had stayed with him only for my sake, too.

■ ■ ■

BILL SMITH: When Mabel married Bigelow—we're good friends at this point—she says to me one day, "This fellow wants to marry me, what should I do?" Well, you can't go tell people stuff like that, I don't care who your friends are. You can't advise people. She says, "He wants to marry me, and I've got to have a father for Jackie." I said, "Well, I agree to that." After all, she knew that I didn't want to get married. I says, "I can't advise you, Mabel." She says, "Well, what do you think of him?" Well, at this point he's over there eating dinner every night. She was buying him stuff, and he was down charging stuff in every clothes store. I couldn't say, "I think he stinks." I said, "Mabel, you've got to decide." So she says, "I've got to take a chance," and she married him, which was the worst thing she ever did. And the only reason she did it was to give Cooper a father. As soon as they married, he changed his tune. She didn't even know what he was making a week. I know he wasn't making any dough because I knew some guys at Monogram, and it was a lousy studio, a two-bit place. A good friend of mine told me about him. What did he do there? I don't know, a stooge job or something.

Mabel bought him a big car and bought all his clothes, and he was living at the house. Ordering everybody around. I found out he took a lot of perfume—Mabel had a lot of perfume—and he stole it out of the house. I don't know where he took it. I said to Norman, "Norman, this is no good, Mabel lying there dying, and this is no good." I didn't talk to Coop about it because Bigelow was bullshitting Coop, and Coop was just a kid. Bigelow didn't like me. So I got him alone one day, and I said, "Hey, you're fucking this nurse, and you're fucking up the whole household, and I don't like it." I said, "I'm not running this place, but these are friends of mine." He says, "I'll do what I want," and I says, "No, you won't do what you want." Anyhow, we got him out of the house, see—he was a no-good son of a bitch. I guess Coop got hep to him later on.

■ ■ ■

I had the man come in and open the safe. I found several bags full of coins—about $500 worth—and an 8 x 10 manila envelope, sealed. I took it downstairs and steamed it open over the stove and found it contained approximately $10,000 in twenties and fifties, with a few hundreds.

I went out to the hardware store and bought a mess of lead washers. Back home I cut up stacks of newspapers in the shape of bills. I put the washers in the bags, in place of the coins, and the pieces of newspapers back in the envelope, which I carefully resealed. I put it all back in the safe, just the way it had been, and closed it. And waited.

When he finally came home, I took him down to the playroom—I wanted to be as far away from my mother's room as possible—and I talked to him very quietly and calmly. I didn't want my mother to hear a word of our conversation.

I told him he had to get out of the house that day, immediately. I told him he could pack a bag, whatever he needed for his wants for a day or two, and we would send the rest after him. He started to cry.

"You can't separate me from my wife," he said, wiping his eyes.

"She doesn't want you," I said. "You're getting out of this house tonight."

He kept reaching for me, trying to grab my arm, not in violence, but in supplication. I kept backing away. I said that if I had to split his head open again, I would do it, only this time it would be for good. I said it softly, however, because uppermost in my mind was the need to keep all this ugliness from my mother.

He went upstairs. As I watched, he packed his bag. He went into the closet and closed the door, but I could hear the safe opening and heard the clink of those bags of coins (he thought) as he tossed them into his bag and could almost hear the envelope full of money (he thought) going in, too.

I have often visualized the scene as he opened his bag and found that his stash had turned into pieces of newspaper and bags of lead washers.

I saw Chuck Bigelow only once more. That was years later, in New York, in the bar of a hotel where I was staying. He still had all his hair, but now it was white, not black. He reached out and stopped me as I tried to walk past him. I didn't want to make a scene. I stopped and exchanged a few pleasantries. I even shook the hand he held out to me.

They tell me he came to my mother's funeral, but I didn't see him. He didn't sit with the family.

After he left, my mother and I never discussed him again. That summer, 1941, we bought a house in Malibu. She thought she would like to look out at the ocean from her window. I thought she should have anything, everything, she wanted. But it was a long drive for Dr. Herzikoff, and anyhow, she soon got to the point where sitting up to look out the window was too much. So we came back, but because we had rented out our Beverly Hills house, Taurog arranged for us to rent a small house in Westwood. It was adequate for her to die in.

We had a wonderful nurse those last few months. She taught me how to use the hypodermic needle with my mother's medication. Pointedly she told me how much would be too much and would kill her. I thought about it. My mother was in terrible, unbelievable pain. I'd wake up in the morning and pray that she had died during the night. She often had convulsions, often was not lucid, always suffered. When the nurse wasn't there, sometimes I would fill the hypodermic to the point that it contained a lethal dose, but I couldn't inject it into my mother. I didn't have the guts.

I came home from work one day. I could hear my grandmother's voice. She was at the top of the stairs, talking to the nurse, arguing with her.

"She doesn't believe she's going to die," the nurse said. "That's peaceful, thank God."

"But just think," my grandmother said, "if she doesn't do something with her jewels and furs, Jackie will just give them away. We have to tell her she's going, so she will do the right thing with all that stuff."

She was trying to talk the nurse into letting her tell her own daughter she was going to die, so my mother might give her some of her valuable things. I practically leaped up the stairs and grabbed her by both of her arms.

"If you tell her she's dying," I said, "I'll kill you."

A few days later that same spot—the top of the stairs— was the scene of another confrontation on the same subject. This was during a period when my mother was not lucid, and the parish priest, a certain Father Donovan, had come and was just about to give my mother the last rites of the church.

I liked Father Donovan. Years before, I had even boxed with him at my home for fun. But now I was angry. I explained to him that my mother still did not believe she was going to die. He said that she wasn't lucid.

"So you see, Jackie," he said, "your mother will never know she's been given the last rites—but God will."

I knew that my mother's coma came and went, that she could regain consciousness and lucidity in a twinkling.

"Once in a while she wakes up, Father," I said, "and if she should wake up while you're giving her the last rites, it would really upset her."

But he insisted, and I had to stand there, with my body across my mother's door and my arms outstretched, to bar the way. I said that if I ever caught him trying to give my mother the last rites, I'd knock him down the stairs. He left and never returned.

A few nights later my mother died. Only the nurse and I were there. I tried to help the nurse give her a needle and bring her back again.

"Jack, she's gone," the nurse said.

I called my grandmother and Norman and Florence and Julie and Jack. They all came, stayed for a little while, then left.

The nurse and I sat up all night, polished off a bottle of booze, and said good-bye. I was nineteen when my mother died, that fall day in 1941.

She left a legacy of mysteries. There were the usual ones— life, death, and all that—and those are mysteries which some people find answers to and solace in religion. It didn't help me.

The family had been Roman Catholic. Yet at the same time they weren't. "Deathbed Catholics" they were known as. When I was a kid, on Sundays they would drop me off at church and then pick me up again when it was all over. I used to ask my mother why they did that.

"Jackie," she would say, "you'll grow up and make your own decision about religion. But now I think you should go to church and get some training."

So I did, and my mind was still open on the subject when my mother died. One of my uncles made all the funeral arrangements, and it was to be a big, old-fashioned religious funeral. My mother hated funerals. She always ducked them when she could, so I thought it was pretty hypocritical to make her the star of her own, but I was only nineteen, and I had no say in the matter.

I told Uncle Roddy and Uncle Norman that Mother didn't like the business of funerals, thought it was awful to have a dead body displayed, thought it was awful to have a lot of people crying and wailing, thought it was awful to be buried. She had wanted cremation. I told them that, but they brushed me off. If I had been a few years older or more mature, I would have insisted. But I wasn't, so I didn't.

They told me just to keep out of the way. So they had the rosary, and everybody was crying, just what Mother hated, and I cried, partly out of a boy's sadness when his mother died (and, God knows, I felt that, in spades) but partly out of frustration, knowing that my mother's wishes were being totally ignored.

They made me look at her body in the coffin. The funeral

people had daubed her face with a lot of makeup, and she seldom wore any makeup. I cried because she looked orange and she looked awful.

Then the next day there was the funeral, at the Church of the Good Shepherd, and hundreds of people, faces I knew, faces I didn't know, and maybe a lot of faces who were there just to see my face. The body and the parade of limousines wound its slow gray way to Calvary Cemetery. Another ceremony. Another bunch of priests to tip.

A priest I had never seen, and who had never met my mother, delivered a mechanical eulogy. I was never a rebel, and I'm still not, but I had had enough. I don't know where I got the nerve, at nineteen, but I got up from that front pew, knowing everybody there was watching me, and I walked all the way down the center aisle and out the door. I could hear my mother saying, "Good for you!" I knew the whole church had turned around to watch my exit.

"Take me home," I said to the driver of the first limo in line.

I never went back. I never visited the crypt. I went home and went to my room and locked the door. All day I lay on the bed, thinking about my mother, what a great lady she was, how I missed her, how the world had done its best to beat her down but had never quite succeeded.

When it was dark, I went out and took my car and drove around. Maybe I should have just gone to a bar and gotten drunk, but I was only nineteen, and nineteen-year-olds then didn't think in those terms. I didn't want to go anywhere where I would see anybody or where anybody could see me; I didn't want any good-hearts cluck-clucking their sympathy at me. I wasn't ready for that yet. Later I'd be able to smile and say, "Thank you very much," but it takes time to develop a shell.

So I drove. I found myself cruising along Sunset Boulevard. And ahead of me, just before I came to Vine Street, I saw the bulk that was the Church of the Blessed Sacrament. Mother had taken me there a time or two. I remembered the peaceful quality inside, the vast emptiness of the church that seemed so serene. A little serenity would be welcome. Maybe, too, I could find an answer. Others had.

I parked my car, walked to the door. By now it was, I suppose, close to eleven o'clock at night. I tried the front door, but it was locked; that angered and depressed me. I banged on it. No answer. Suddenly all my closed-in anger and rage at everybody for taking my mother away from me exploded. I smashed on the heavy door with both my arms. I can still hear the sound of the clanging I made as I beat on that heavy metal door until my hands were bruised and bloody. I beat on the door and I yelled and I screamed and I cried.

Of course, the police came. They were sympathetic. They knew who I was, knew about my mother's death. They talked to me, quietly, calmly. I was crying, trying to explain that my mother had died and I wanted to go in the church to pray or to talk to her or something. They told me it was too late, that I should go home and try to go to sleep. I got back in my car, and I drove home, and my kindly cops followed me to make sure I got there safely (and, incidentally, didn't cause any more furor).

That was my last experience with a church.

LOS ANGELES, Nov. 27 (AP)—Mrs. M. C. Bigelow, 36, died at her Bel Air home yesterday. At her bedside were her sisters, Mrs. Julie Taurog and Mrs. Florence Kenmore, her mother, Mrs. Lillian Leonard, her brother, Jack Leonard, her son, actor Jackie Cooper, and her physician, Dr. Sam Herzikoff.

She was born August 15, 1905, in San Francisco. When Jackie was born on September 15, 1922, his parents were a youthful vaudeville team known as Johnny and Mabel Cooper.

Lots of mistakes in that story. The home was Westwood, not Bel Air. My grandmother's name was not Lillian. My parents were never a vaudeville team. And my mother was thirty-nine, not thirty-six.

Still, it marked the end, and it was a release. I have never, before or since, seen such horror as the slow death of my mother.

Norman stepped in immediately and told me what to do. I was grateful. I needed somebody. He saw to it that I was out of that house in a few days and found me an apartment.

Less than two weeks later the Japanese attacked Pearl Harbor.

11.

There is a story in Hollywood trade papers, dated June 6, 1931. It tells how seven-year-old Jackie Cooper was in the office of Louis B. Mayer, the head man at MGM, to sign a new contract. (That story was wrong, too; I was eight.)

"What do you think of the Depression?" a reporter is quoted as asking me.

"I think it's fine," they have me saying. I can't believe that even at eight, I could be so dumb.

"How about the stratosphere?" another reporter tossed in. Apparently that was a new word and concept about that time.

"Aw," they have me saying, "I don't like them poet guys. I like football players."

I suppose I was quoted correctly, and I imagine the public liked me even more for my naïveté. I was, the stories (possibly planted by Howard Strickling or one of his elves in the MGM publicity department) pointed out, a regular kid. There was nothing sissy or uppity about Jackie Cooper. He was, after all, America's Boy.

The star treatment was mine.

I placed my footprints in the forecourt of Grauman's Chinese Theater.

I had a fan club, started by a woman named Anna Glance, from somewhere in the East, Ohio or Pennsylvania.

There was a Jackie Cooper newspaper.

We had someone handling my fan mail. I never saw it and never answered a single letter personally.

I began to meet other big names, who found it advisable, from a public relations standpoint, to be seen in public with me. I met President Roosevelt. I met Charles and Anne Morrow Lindbergh, pausing in Los Angeles on a round-the-world flight. I met George Gershwin, who came to our house, although that was not for publicity purposes. My mother, who still loved to relax by playing the piano, had bought a very special concert grand, and Norman Taurog had told Gershwin about it. One day the front doorbell rang, and it was Gershwin, who introduced himself and asked if he could play our piano. And he did, for a few glorious (for us) hours.

Clara Bow was a frequent visitor. She was a good friend of my mother's, and Clara and her husband, Rex Bell, often were dinner guests at our house.

Russ Columbo was around a lot. He had been a friend of Uncle Norman's and became a friend and, I think, an admirer of my mother's.

Some didn't come to see me but invited me to see them. Mary Pickford was one of those. After all, she was Hollywood's queen, and it wouldn't be seemly for her to come calling on anyone, even America's Boy. She said I should come visit her, and I did; as it turned out, she was doing her radio show at the same time, so she killed two birds with one visit, and I appeared on her show.

I didn't like Pickfair, the home Mary Pickford and Douglas Fairbanks had built. I might like it now, but it was no garden of earthly delights for a kid. It was cold, deathly quiet, uncomfortable both physically and spiritually to me. I had been in the White House and found that much more homey than Pickfair. I remember thinking, when I was shown into the living room, that I was the first human being who had ever set foot in the place.

I was invited out to see Harpo Marx, too, and I happily accepted that invitation. I guess, like all kids, I loved Harpo. I sensed that the kid in him had never grown up. And when I went out to his house, in Malibu, I quickly realized I was right. He *had* never grown up. He was a kid, like me, and we got along very easily. I met Chico, but I didn't take to him, and I knew Groucho only slightly in later years. The other brothers I never met, that I can remember, but Harpo remained a good friend.

I was very recognizable in public. Now I couldn't go out alone anymore because of the kidnapping scare which was rife in that era. Soon I had a bodyguard, accompanying me wherever I went. When I went with my mother or grandmother, shopping or wherever, inevitably I would be stopped for my autograph or to have someone take a picture with me.

An indication of how important an MGM property I quickly became in the Hollywood scheme of things was that I was one of the very few to get invited to spend weekends on L. B. Mayer's yacht. Some strange things happened when my mother and I were invited for those little cruises. At the time I didn't understand, but in retrospect, I came to believe that it wasn't so much me L. B. wanted on his boat, it was my mother. She was reasonably healthy then and a very attractive woman, and Mayer liked attractive women.

Mayer and his friends would push food at me to keep me quiet. Their idea of the perfect dish to bribe a kid with on a yacht was lox and bagels and cream cheese. That was my first meeting with those delicacies. I created some kind of a stir when I asked, in all innocence, "What is this red fish?"

When I was eight and a half or perhaps nine, I was part of an elaborate hoax which attracted much attention in Hollywood. Tallulah Bankhead, then the toast of Broadway, came to the West Coast for one of her first films. Joan Crawford was hosting a party for her and told Tallulah that she had a blind date for her—"a very attractive blond young man, a Mr. Cooper."

Joan, then married to Douglas Fairbanks, Jr., had a lovely home in Brentwood, and when Tallulah arrived, she was promptly introduced to her escort for the evening—Mr. *Jackie* Cooper.

Many of the greats of Hollywood were there that evening, and Joan's little stunt captivated and titillated them all.

It was a sparkling evening, capped off by a screening of the sensation of the moment, the Lunt-Fontanne film *The Guardsman*. I slept through it all. Miss Bankhead, as I remember, was charming and witty and called me "darling."

I did what I was told, then, always. "Be nice, Jackie," my mother would say, and I think those three words were pretty much a blanket dictum to me through the years before I began to assert myself. So I would be nice.

On the set, in film after film, I had to "be nice" and do what the director said. In the studio classroom or with my own tutor, I had to "be nice" and listen to my teacher. When I had some free time, it was always, "Be nice, Jackie," and don't get in trouble, or don't do anything that might hurt you, and don't cross the street. And so, dutifully, I led a life that was, in retrospect, a terrible one for a kid.

Children, we all know, can be cruel. Jealousy sparks that cruelty, and most kids I met were jealous of me. Jealousy was a concept they probably didn't understand and certainly could not articulate, and it was a concept that I couldn't understand either. I would ask my mother why the other kids, when I had one of my rare encounters with them, were always mean to me. She said they were jealous. I asked her what that meant. She said it was because I was a movie star and making money, while they were not. I don't remember what I said, or if I said anything, or what I thought, for that matter.

I was told, often enough, two things—first, that I was a very lucky boy and, second, that my job was to be an actor. It was put in that light: I had a job and a responsibility, and that was my lot in life. Naturally I didn't question it. I did what I was told, as all children do—until they reach the age when they begin to suffer the first pangs of independence.

I think my acting at the time began to improve. Certain directors, as I have mentioned, started to work with me, to indicate that I had to do something more than just say the words as I had always said them. I began to think, vaguely and childishly, about acting.

I did enjoy acting, the make-believe game that all actors play. The work itself never bothered me. In fact, I really loved it and was, I think, at my happiest as a child when I was acting. Maybe that is partly because my home life left so much to be desired.

Yet I was making what was then literally a fortune. I think, for a while I was making more money than the President of the United States.

LOS ANGELES, Sept. 3 (UP)—A petition for guardianship of Jackie Cooper, 8, was filed in Probate Court by his mother, Mabel Leonard Cooper, yesterday, with the request that she be allowed to spend $1,600 a month to support the child "in his profession as a juvenile actor."

Assets of the child are listed as a $50,000 13-year endowment policy, $8,000 in cash and a motion picture contract calling for a salary of $1,300 a week the first year up to $4,000 a week the third year.

Mrs. Cooper sets forth that she is divorced from her husband, John G. Cooper, and doesn't know his whereabouts, his last address having been the Cooper Music Shop, 432 South Broadway. She obtained her decree and custody of the child on Feb. 8, 1928, she declared. Attorney Adriance C. Stanton filed the petition.

Two years later, as was his continuing practice, and because of the Depression, L. B. Mayer talked my mother out of another salary raise due under the terms of my contract. I would have been earning $1,700 a week, but was now earning $1,300. MGM was—like everybody else—screaming poverty, and anyhow, in the Depression, $1,300 a week was not bad. Also, my agent at that time must have been beholden to Mayer. I was told they were friends.

I was luckier, in financial terms, than many child stars. Even before the Coogan Act was passed—named after Jackie Coogan, it requires a percentage of the moneys earned by a juvenile to be kept in trust—my mother had been very careful with my money, though she was no judge of good theatrical agents.

Whenever I had a new contract in my childhood days, I was required to go to court. It was a little ritual. The documents had all been read and approved by lawyers for both sides, but the legal traditions had to be upheld, meaning that a judge had to give his official approval to the arrangements. One phase of that ceremony was, as I remember it, always the same.

The judge would peer at me over his glasses and summon me up to sit beside him on the bench with a wag of his finger. My mother would pat me on my shoulder and send me on my way—"Be nice, Jackie"—and I would smile my way up to the bench and shake the judge's hand.

"Well, Jackie," the judge would say, "tell me. Do you like what you are doing?"

"Oh, yes, sir."

"Good, good."

And that would be that for another few years. I hadn't lied. I did like what I was doing. By and large.

I did all kinds of films in those early years, whatever they wanted me to do. There were the many rip-offs of *The Champ* story, set in all sorts of locales. One was a western based on the Will James book *Lone Cowboy*.

In 1933 I was cast in a big MGM musical, *Broadway to Hollywood*, which purported to be a history of vaudeville from 1886 to the time the film was made. I worked for the first time with Mickey Rooney in that. Mickey is two years and a day older than I am, but because he is shorter, he played me at five or six, while I was supposed to be my correct age, eleven. Russell Hardie was the star, and both Mickey and I were playing him at younger ages.

Through all those years I struggled with my schoolwork.

The board of education had assigned a woman named Carmen T. Holliday as my teacher, and she had excellent credentials—she had once taught Loretta Young. She taught me from the time I was ten until I was sixteen. By that time I had discovered that Mrs. Holliday, a large buxom woman, had interesting sights to look at if you could maneuver things just right. If she could be somehow persuaded to bend over and you assumed a certain angle, you could see down the front of her dress.

At about twelve, things like that were beginning to attract my attention. Mrs. Holliday, no dummy, quickly caught on. She spoiled my fun by attaching a large handkerchief to the upper reaches of her dress. My mother was no dummy either, and when I was sixteen, she asked the board of education to supply me with a male teacher.

The boy had become a youth.

PART TWO

The Youth

12.

For a boy like me, with very normal urges, Hollywood and the movie studios were a spectacular place to grow up. For example, when I was sixteen, and at Paramount, one of us kids discovered the Paulette Goddard scenic view. Pretty soon we all knew about it. Somebody had noticed that there was a vantage point with a direct, unimpeded, and total view into her dressing room. Furthermore—and this was the juicy part—Miss Goddard liked to loll around her dressing room topless.

You can imagine what sport a bunch of young teenage boys would have with that knowledge. Paulette Goddard was a lady of fantastic construction. I cannot vouch for my contemporaries, for Mickey Rooney and Jackie Searle and the others, but I know that I would find many excuses to take myself to that particular vantage point and just hope that she was there and in her usual state of astounding undress.

On any lot, too, there was a constant parade of chorus girls and dress (or undress) extras, for the lavish musicals and spectacular costume dramas that were being filmed there. Just a stroll around the lot, and an enterprising young lad could gawk at dozens of gorgeous girls, and since this particular enterprising young lad was well known, they gawked back. I was no longer in the cute and precious stage, so they had no excuse to fondle me, but I was a star, and they were almost always ambitious, so they would talk to me, and I quickly learned how to converse with girls.

I remember one day when I was eleven or twelve, on the MGM lot, watching with tremendous interest the progress of Jean Harlow down a street. She was wearing a gown so sheer that it was possible—indeed, probable—that everything she had was in almost plain view. And she had plenty. My mother was with me, and she noticed my interest, and she laughed. She didn't reprimand me for gawking, and she wasn't embarrassed or shocked by it. She thought it was normal and an indication that I was normal and, also, growing up.

I knew the facts of life. My mother was a very progressive and intelligent lady, and she had answered all my childhood and adolescent questions fully and without embarrassment. If she was, for example, talking to a friend about "labor" when I was nine or ten, and I would ask her what she meant, she would tell me. No hesitation and no detours. Yet she would never give me too much information. Some parents I know, in their desire to be forward-thinking, will answer a child's innocent question with an hour-long dissertation complete with slides. At that age, if I saw a pregnant lady and I asked my mother why she had such a fat tummy, my mother would say, "She's carrying a baby in her stomach." I would say, "Oh," and that would be that. No more, no less. My curiosity would be amply satisfied, but I would not be burdened with information which I did not need and could not, for that matter, understand yet.

My mother answered all my questions, and she would always give another bit of helpful information. She would caution me not to talk to the other kids about such matters. I guess she felt that they would give me the wrong dope—kids often having been given wrong ideas by other kids—which would only confuse me. I never did ask the other kids.

In my era the human body was pretty much a hidden commodity. Until Paulette Goddard's time I really had only seen one body—mine. There were no centerfolds in magazines for kids to moon over. The bikini hadn't been invented yet. There were no nude scenes in movies. And so girls, to me as I entered those exciting teenage years, were still a mystery. What was it they had, under all those clothes, which somehow stirred me? I knew, of course, and yet I didn't know. I knew intellectually, but I had yet to see for myself.

There had been one small experience when I was very young. It had been when I was so young, in fact, that it served only to disturb me, rather than excite me.

When I was seven or eight, we rented a beach house. This particular beach house had an outdoor shower. My aunt Julie— a year or so younger than my mother and the one with the family reputation of being the beauty—would get in the shower with me. It was an enclosed shower, so nobody else could see or even knew. We were both naked. I remembered looking at her. I remember being bothered by it. Nothing happened in the shower, but it was, to me, an unpleasant experience.

I was twelve or so when I went to some parties when we lived in Ocean Park. There was a little girl across the street whose name, if my memory isn't playing tricks on me, was

Farrell Minick. She was the first girl of twelve or thirteen—the first *big* girl—who paid any attention to me, the kind of attention a boy realizes comes because he is liked, not because he has a worm in his pocket. There were parties, and we went, and we played spin the bottle. My first real kiss was from Farrell Minick after the bottle had spun in her direction.

■ ■ ■

BILL SMITH: Cooper, as a kid, was a smart little son of a bitch. I'll tell you something else about him. He could always get the broads. We're on a [vaudeville] tour, and Mabel said, "Would you please go with me? I'm so sick and I can't handle it alone." Just to give you an idea on Coop. Now he behaved, and he was smart as hell; Jesus, he was smart. They talk about Shirley Temple, and I've been through all of these people, Jackie Coogan and all of them, and this kid is as good as any of them. Any rate, we're on the road, see. We're in Philadelphia and with this act, and there was four or five people in this act, a well-known act, I'll think of the name in a minute. Poor Mabel is sick as a dog, see; she never even went to the theater. And we leave Philadelphia and we're going to Baltimore and this act is going with us, too; a lot of times the acts go with you. In this act was this good-looking dame, see, little Jewish girl, cute as hell, and we're on the train, and I can't find the son of a bitch. He was only a little guy, thirteen or so, and I don't know where the hell he is. So I get down and I look in one of the act's rooms and then I knocked on the door and I open the door and he's in bed, stark naked, with this broad. And I says, "Get up," and I slapped him on the ass, see. He behaved with me, you know. And he gives me this, you know [the look with the lower lip out], and I says, "Come here. Put your pants on," and I slapped him on the ass. And I says to her, "You dirty cunt," and I'm bawling her out. And he's scared as hell. Then I turned around, and I kicked him in the ass easy out the door. I didn't tell Mabel.

■ ■ ■

I had known Judy Garland around MGM, but not well. Then we did a radio show together—it was hosted by Wally Beery—

and our mothers thought we looked good together. What's more, since we were both in the business and understood what it was like to be in the business, we had that in common. So Mabel Cooper and Ethel Gumm decided that Jackie Cooper and Judy Garland would be okay to go out a little. They both recognized the fact that their children were growing up and needed to consort with people of the other sex, and they felt that this would be a good thing. Judy was about nine months older than I was, but I was taller, so that was okay.

I cannot speak for Judy, but I was pleased by the prospect of seeing more of her. We had things in common besides acting at MGM. Music, mostly. I had begun playing the drums, and so we had a lot to talk about.

I was invited over to her house for a Sunday dinner. The dinner itself was a bore—too many adults, and I didn't know them—but afterward, in Judy's room, we played Benny Goodman records, and we held hands.

We had to reciprocate and have Judy over to our house for dinner. I learned that it may be okay for a girl to ask a boy up to her room, but the reverse is considered sinful. So Judy and I walked on the beach, and she said, "Can I kiss you?" and so I was in love. She said she was, too.

I hadn't yet reached my fourteenth birthday, and I couldn't drive, so when I asked her out on a date, I had to prevail on my mother to hire a driver. We went to a movie—holding sweating hands—and then somewhere for an ice cream soda. We had other dates, and I discovered the joys of necking in the back seat of a car, with a discreet driver who turned up the rearview mirror. And we talked, by the hour, on the telephone. She told me how mean L. B. Mayer was to her, how he continually picked on her appearance (when I directed the television movie *Rainbow* about her, I had the writers add a scene about Mayer and Judy, drawing on information she herself had given me). She told me about her family problems. I am sure I told her mine, although what I had to tell—mostly, I suppose, about my grandmother—paled when compared to Judy's accounts of her parents and their actions toward her.

Judy put an end to our relationship a few months after it began. She did it very nicely. It hardly hurt. She had fallen for an older man, Billy Halop, who was sixteen or so and just recently imported from New York. We remained good friends, although I seldom saw her after that. She did ask me to do her a favor once, a couple of years later. She had fallen—as many other women had—for Artie Shaw. But she knew he was forbidden fruit, too old, too experienced, so she could never let him pick her up. Instead, would I pick her up? I was still okay. Then I was to take her to wherever she was meeting Artie and just sort of hang around someplace else for a few hours, then pick her up and take her home. You know how it is with us shnooks. I said sure. I did that a few times. They weren't the greatest nights in my life, but I felt I had been a good friend.

I had also had a brief on-the-set fling with Deanna Durbin, when we did a picture together. It is an old Hollywood custom for leading man and leading lady to fall for each other. In *That Certain Age* I kissed her on screen, and I gave her a few off-screen kisses, too. We had problems finding privacy on the bustling movie set and finally took to a tactic which I imagine has stood romantically inclined couples on movie sets in good stead for many years. We would duck behind the backdrops and find a few precious—although musty—moments of quiet and togetherness. Then, when the call came for the first team to report back, she would go one way and I would go the other way. And we probably fooled nobody, with our smeared makeup and our perspiring bodies.

I was seventeen, and I began to go over to Joan Crawford's house to play badminton. She was a friend of my mother's and, over the years, had offered me the use of her court. She didn't have room for a tennis court, so had put in a badminton court, and I had learned to enjoy playing that game.

The court was right off the pool house, and one day, sweaty from an hour of exertion, I went into the pool house with Joan. I was thirsty, and she poured me a Coke. As she bent over, I looked down her dress.

"You're growing up, aren't you?" she said.

I was brash, fresh from some romantic triumph, I suppose, and I made some remark which I assumed was sophisticated, witty, and very sexually provocative.

"You had better get out of here, young man," she said.

But I didn't go. Instead, I made a move toward her, and she stood up, looked at me appraisingly, and then closed all the drapes. And I made love to Joan Crawford. Or, rather, she made love to me.

Over the next six months or so the performance was repeated

eight or nine times. After the first time, however, it was always late at night. I would set a date with her, then manage to sneak out of the house after my mother and stepfather had gone to sleep. I would roll my car down the street until I was far enough away so I could start the engine without waking them. And I would drive to Joan's house.

She was a very erudite professor of love. At the time I suppose she was in her early thirties. I was seventeen. She was a wild woman. She would bathe me, powder me, cologne me. Then she would do it over again. She would put on high heels, a garter belt, and a large hat and pose in front of the mirror, turning this way and that way.

"Look," she would say. I was already looking. But that sort of thing didn't particularly excite me. I kept thinking: The lady is crazy.

But I recognized that she was an extraordinary performer, that I was learning things that most men don't learn until they are much older—if at all. There was never any drinking or drugs with her. It was all business. She was very organized. When I left, she would put me on her calendar for the next visit. I could hardly wait.

One night, after one of our sessions, she said that was the last time. She said I should never call her again.

"And put it all out of your mind," she said. "It never happened."

And then she gave me one last kiss and added, "But we'll always be friends."

I was floating during that period. Fortunately I had enough sense not to blab my conquest all over town, but it was a magnificent secret to have. My friends might brag about some pimply-faced teenager or gawky sixteen-year-old they had had, and I would nod my congratulations. And I would think to myself: But I have been with one of the Love Goddesses of the Screen. Maybe I didn't say anything because I had enough sense not to. But maybe it was because I knew they wouldn't have believed me.

The last time I saw Joan Crawford was when I was doing a guest shot in Peter Falk's *Columbo* series. She was on the Universal lot at the same time, doing something, and the studio was buzzing with the news that Crawford was around. By accident, I happened to run into her, and she took my hand, looked in my eyes, and, I think, remembered.

Later in my teens I got to know Phil Silvers. He was, I

suppose, ten or more years older than I was. Sid Miller, who was four years older, Billy Tracy, five years older, Mickey Rooney, and I would often go over to Phil's place—he was such a New Yorker then that he refused to buy a house and had an apartment—and Phil would have us laughing our young heads off with his funny stories about the burlesque world. They were laugh-filled evenings, on Sundays generally. Rooney was funny, too, a great mimic who was famous for that gift. Rooney was quite a storyteller himself. Tracy talked about being a kid actor on Broadway, and Sid Miller usually played the piano while the stories and gags flew. And, with all that to get us started, we would always talk about girls and compare notes, names, and notions. One evening somebody had the bright idea of hiring a hooker—that word hadn't yet been invented; then they were just plain old whores—and spending a fun-filled night. There were five of us, and we all chipped in four bucks apiece and let Phil handle the negotiations. After all, none of us had any previous experience with such a deal.

Phil enjoyed the haggling over the phone. Apparently the lady wanted $20 apiece, rather than a group rate. Phil explained to her, with some degree of logic, that she would have to make only one trip, so her transportation costs would be negligible. Billy, Sid, Mickey, and I were listening to a ball game on the radio, but really were paying much more attention to Phil and his discussions, which proved to be successful. The party of the second part agreed to the $20 fee.

The five of us drew straws for position, and Billy was the first. He was in and out of the bedroom in three minutes. He came out a little unhappy-looking, and Sid, next in line, took no longer and also emerged grumbling. Phil and I spent about the same amount of time, and I found out why the long faces— she was no thing of beauty. Mickey was the last, and he went in, and we waited and waited and waited—the kid was in the bedroom with the girl for about twenty minutes. And he came out, with a big grin.

"Did I tell you guys or did I tell you guys?" Rooney said. And we were believers.

Then he left. The girl finally came out to pick up her money.

"Hey, little lady," Phil Silvers said. "You gotta tell us the truth. Was that kid in the saddle for twenty minutes?"

"Are you kidding?" she said. "Sixteen minutes of imitations and four minutes of fucking."

In my teens I had one professionally bad year, which turned

out to be a good one for me socially. That was the year when I was able to go to a public school for a whole school year. I was in Beverly Hills High School, and I loved it. I made friends—boy and girl—and I found out what it was like to be a normal kid for a while.

I had a romance with a Beverly Hills High coed, a girl named Jane. This was love again, a very serious crush, and we found ways—new to us, old to lovers—to have privacy. The car was one. There were others. My mother, for the first time, worried about me. Looking back, I cannot say that I blame her because I was only fifteen and didn't know what I was doing. But fortunately for my mother's fears it ran its course, as these things almost always do.

But my mother didn't know there was another source of worry she was totally oblivious to. That was a contemporary of hers, in a situation something like that which was later celebrated in the movie *The Graduate*. My mother had a friend, a lady named Mrs. Martin. She was a divorcée from New York, and she didn't drive. When she came over to visit my mother, she would take a cab, and then my mother would ask me to do her a favor and drive Mrs. Martin home. The first time I did so reluctantly. But on the way Mrs. Martin began groping me very seriously. And she asked me in. That quickly became a routine procedure. Mrs. Martin became a regular visitor at our house. And equally regularly I would drive her home, jump on her, then speed back home, murmuring something about "heavy traffic" to explain why a ten-minute drive had taken a half hour.

And so I passed from innocence to experience and had a marvelous time en route. In all the books that have been written about Hollywood, no one has touched on this one angle, which was, to me, a high spot of my early motion picture experience. A movie studio is a very exciting place for a red-blooded American boy to spend his adolescence.

My actual introduction to sex and its mysterious, magical workings had come partially from my enlightened mother's explanations and answers to my questions, but also from a practical course I had taken. My instructor had been a twenty-year-old girl who lived across the street from me during the brief time we lived in Ocean Park.

I was friendly with her younger brother, who was a year or so older than I. At the time I was being taught by a tutor, who would arrive at our house at nine in the morning. I was always an early riser, and I'd be up at seven. I'd see the brother go off to school at about seven-fifteen—he had a long walk—and I'd see his mother go off to work. There was no man around, for whatever reason.

That would leave the twenty-year-old daughter home alone. Innocently I would go over and talk to her. I was lonely; maybe she was, too. She was always in a nightgown at that hour. I was thirteen, and I started to look, and as I remember, she was a reasonably attractive girl, equipped with all the standard accessories, and in that costume they were frequently visible.

I have no idea how it happened, but we began to talk about sex. I suppose I brought it up, although maybe she did. She might have gotten a kick out of talking to a dumb kid who was too young to do anything. It was a subject which, naturally, intrigued me, and I asked questions, and she would tell me what she knew and laugh. I suppose she began to enjoy the effect her knowledge—and her body—were having on me.

Again, I don't know how it happened. Probably just a perfect example of one thing leading to another, but one of those mornings it did. She took me into her bedroom—I remember she shared it with her mother, but her mother was at work—and demonstrated a few pointers.

As you can imagine, that was pretty hot stuff for a kid my age. I was there every morning after that as soon as I saw her mother and her brother were out of sight. And for several weeks it was a little sex education before school.

I was always back in my house by eight fifty-five, so my tutor wouldn't have to ring the bell and wake up my mother. But my early-morning activities across the street began to tell. I began dozing off during my nine-to-twelve session with my tutor, and she quite naturally wondered why a healthy thirteen-year-old would fall asleep sitting up in the morning.

She asked me, and I shrugged it off. Then she asked my mother, who wondered about it—she knew I went to bed at a decent hour and seemed to be sleeping well. So my mother began to watch me, and it didn't take her long to figure things out.

I was forbidden to go across the street anymore. Anyhow, around that time I met Judy Garland, and that changed things for me. To me, seeing Judy at that point was a lot better than sneaking across the street.

■ ■ ■

JOHN FORSYTHE: Jackie was part of that group, Judy Garland and Mickey Rooney, and some of the things that he told me that they did when they grew up together were so ridiculously sophomoric. They had been funny to him then, but that crowd must have been impossible. For example, this is what they considered fun: If they were sitting around a living room, and there was a powder room close by, what those kids did one time because it set the girls' teeth on edge, because they were all proper, seemingly proper, they took a hose and—I don't know if it was Jack or Mickey Rooney—went into the bathroom and put the nose end of the hose into the toilet bowl and turned up the water very, very high and kept it going for about four minutes, and pretty soon there was a hush that fell over the whole place, and everybody was listening to what was going on in the bathroom as if he had been urinating for four minutes. But that's the kind of sophomoric fun they considered fun.

■ ■ ■

In some ways, I suppose, we did the kind of things all kids did at the same age. The only thing was that as stars we had to be more circumspect than most. I was always being cautioned, and I am sure the rest of my MGM pals were given similar warnings, that I had to be very careful because of who I was and what I was.

I was careful. I never really got into any serious trouble until I was in the Navy.

13.

My uncle Big Jack was always there when I was growing up. We weren't close. Ten years is a big gap for kids to bridge, and we couldn't manage it.

We got along all right, but that's about it. I guess he resented me, after I had become a star, the way I had earlier resented him because of the way my grandmother spoiled him. Although we were always civil and surface-friendly, we never did manage to conquer those resentments.

When we had money—from my working—he got his share. I used to think, when I was old enough to think about it, that maybe he got more than his share. They sent him on a trip to Europe once, long before I had ever been, on my money. He always had nice cars and clothes and things, and that was all because I was working; he hardly worked, steadily, that I can remember, until his middle twenties.

He used to be pretty arrogant about things, too, and demanding. I remember once he borrowed my mother's car—at the time it was new, and she was very proud of it—and proceeded to wreck it. I don't think he even said he was sorry. I used to wish I were big enough to—as the expression was then—knock his block off. But still, somehow, I loved him.

■ ■ ■

BILL SMITH: They didn't pay much attention to Cooper as a kid. He was a little guy; they lived on Yucca. He played in the yard. And the grandmother was bored with him, sort of a pain in the ass, you know? They'd go down to Ocean Park and play the game with the wheel. They'd gamble. Cooper was nothing as a baby, and the grandmother paid no attention to him. But when he got up there and was making money, then she was bleeding Mabel all the time for dough. And Mabel, being easygoing, would give it to her. When he became big, they were having a lot of trouble with the studio. Mabel was having money trouble all the time. She was having money and tax trouble. Grandma and Jack pumped her for dough. The only one that didn't bother anybody was Florence. She was very quiet. Mabel—they browbeat her all the time, the grandmother and so on. The old lady, she was a bitch. She never picked on me.

■ ■ ■

Just before she had her final bout with cancer, my mother went into the interior decorating business. She had always had a knack for that sort of thing and had decorated the homes of family and friends for years. The job she had done for the Taurogs in their mansion had attracted a lot of attention, and maybe that was the impetus for her to start a formal business. In fact, my studio biography at Paramount in 1939 identified my mother as "Mabel L. Bigelow, who won prominence as a stage pianist and also as an interior decorator."

One of Mabel's passions was Lucite, which was very new at the time, in the late thirties. She was one of the first to use it in any quantity in her work. She used to buy almost all of the output of a small factory, and eventually she acquired the factory itself. I think perhaps she was at her happiest during that short period, running the plastics business and decorating homes and watching me grow.

She found a spot for Big Jack in the plastics factory, and I think maybe that was his first regular job. He liked it, too. And my grandmother, still doting on her only son, evidently decided that was where he belonged.

I remember waking up one night to the sounds of a yelling match, a big argument between my mother and grandmother. Queenie was saying that Mabel had the decorating business and the money from what I was earning, and she didn't need the plastics business, too. She wanted my mother to hand the whole business over to Jack, so he would have something.

My mother kept saying no. She said that my career was hardly guaranteed, that I was a teenager now and I had leveled off, that I wasn't going down maybe, but I sure wasn't going up either. She wanted the plastics business to be for me, in case the bottom dropped out of acting.

But my grandmother was nothing if not persistent. So, as

I listened, the argument raged for a couple of hours. And my grandmother wore my mother down.

"All right, all right," she finally said, capitulating completely. "For Chrissake, take the damn business, and I hope you both choke on it."

And Jack took it, and for a while he lucked out. When the war came along, Jack Leonard was in the right spot at the right time with the right product—plastics. He got some fat government contracts, including one biggie, making telephones for the Army. His only problem was that he couldn't outguess history. When the war ended, he was stuck with thousands and thousands of telephones nobody wanted. He went under because of that.

Poor Jack. Whatever he did, he loused up. Even that European trip that bothered me so much—he lorded it over me that he was going to Europe—he came home with a dose of the clap.

Yet he was a charmer. He had a way of smiling that people liked, that I liked. We never were really close, but I genuinely liked him, and I think he liked me, despite the resentment. He married a very nice girl—Dale—and they had three children. When the war and that telephone fiasco put an end to the plastics business, he decided to do what I think he had always really wanted to do—write.

He and a friend of his, a movie actor and writer named Frank Fenton (the brother of the late director Leslie Fenton), collaborated and hit it big. They wrote a movie for Robert Mitchum in 1950, *His Kind of Woman*, and they were quickly established as a writing team. Jack then signed a nice contract with MGM, for (I think) $1,250 a week as a writer.

But he loused that up, too, and it was tragic to watch it happen. He had always drunk pretty well, but now, with the pressure of a high-paying writing job on his back, he drank more and more. He died very soon of cirrhosis. I don't think he was at MGM even a year. He was only forty-two when he died.

14.

I had my fourteenth birthday while I was shooting a movie called *The Devil Is a Sissy*, with Rooney and Freddie Bartholomew. That was a big birthday for me—I was allowed to drive, for one thing—because it marked a major turning point in my career.

Until then things had gone along fine. Picture after picture. Some good, some bad. I remember them for reasons which often have little to do with the actual movie. For example, there was one called *Tough Guy*. I was twelve then, and about all I remember about that was that my fourteenth (driving) birthday was less than two years away. So as my mother drove me to and from the studio, she would let me sit on her left behind the wheel, so I could work the clutch and the brake and steer the car.

I worked in *Dinky*, with Sidney Miller and Mary Astor. That one is memorable because while we were shooting, all the fuss about Mary Astor and her flaming hot diary came out. I had liked her, and she had been nice to me, but all the newspapers pictured her as a vixen.

I asked my mother what a "vixen" was, and for once she didn't give me a direct answer. She just told me not to think about it.

And then came *The Devil Is a Sissy*, and I was fourteen and began driving my car and having a great time. I drove myself to and from the studio for the first time. The picture was a rip-off of *Dead End* with Freddie Bartholomew as a rich kid and Mickey Rooney and me as waifs hanging around near where he lived. Freddie and I were the stars. Mickey, until then, had been playing bit parts. But he had a great scene in this film when his father, in jail for a murder, is electrocuted and he knows the exact moment because all the streetlights dim.

That was the first time I felt one of my peers was stealing a scene from me, and I didn't like my reaction to that. But there wasn't much I could do about it because I didn't have the weapons—my part was simply not that strong—to fight back. So I just watched Rooney go to town and steal the scene and the whole picture.

That ended my MGM career. They—and by they, I mean Louis B. Mayer himself—felt that I had become a rather bland juvenile, and I think they—he—were right. Mickey, because of his size, had more versatility. The *Hardy* series would be coming soon for him, but they never would have put me in that anyhow. I had been known for drama, not comedy.

My mother and I were summoned to meet with Mr. Mayer. We knew this was going to be a difficult session. My mother, ordinarily sweet and accepting, was determined to fight for her son.

Mayer started out by saying things I couldn't believe. He said that I was going through puberty and that puberty disgusted him. He said, "Adolescence is repulsive." He told my mother, and he acted as though I weren't even in the room, that adolescence and puberty reminded him of two things—pimples and pubic hair—and he found both those things revolting.

This was after six years of what was supposed to have been a seven-year contract. My salary was around $1,900 or $2,000 a week then. (My mother had been talked out of just about every other raise that was supposedly coming to me.) Mayer, after all that stuff about how "repulsive" I would be during adolescence and that nonsense about puberty (I am sure this was all designed to weaken my mother's negotiating position), said he was prepared to offer me a new seven-year contract. The salary would begin at $250 a week. He said he would find bits for me to do—playing bellboys and waiters—for the next few years, until I got through my adolescence. After that, well, it would all depend on what I looked like when I had grown up a little.

My mother said no. She tried to bargain, but Mayer wouldn't. It was his deal or nothing. My mother was just as unyielding. We walked out. I was out of work.

Hollywood in the thirties was a lot different from the way it is today. Then the studios ruled the town—MGM, Fox, Warners, Columbia, Paramount—and woe to anyone who defied any of the studio moguls. We had defied them by not agreeing to take Mayer's offer. So woe to us.

Nobody would see us. No agent would talk to us. Casting directors were out. Producers wouldn't return calls.

Jackie Cooper, untouchable. A has-been at fourteen.

My mother thought it was unjust, and she was right about that. There was this tacit understanding among the studios, and everybody in town abided by that unwritten law. The studios, like Chicago gangsters, split up the territory. They respected each other's possessions, so that Jackie Cooper—who had dared to defy Boss Mayer—was not to be received by Boss Zanuck or Boss Warner or Boss Cohn or any of the other bosses.

Meanwhile, I had a great year, but my mother felt my career was being jeopardized, so she knocked her head on the closed studio doors repeatedly. She finally got me a part in a picture at Monogram—the dregs—in a film called *Boy of the Streets*, and I went back to work. It was the same old story, only now, at fifteen, I was allowed to play a little older, to have a girl friend, and the whole thing was on a slightly more mature basis.

Then I got going again. The year of penance was over, and studios would hire me, and I did that film with Deanna Durbin, and then I worked at Warner Brothers in *White Banners*.

That was directed by Edmund Goulding, who was the next director to give me constructive advice. He talked to me as though I were a man, and I appreciated that.

"Stop whining and leaning on your old tricks," he said to me. "You're a leading man!"

I looked at myself in a new light then. Leading man! It definitely had a ring to it. From then on, I think, I no longer thought of myself as a child actor. That may have been the first of a long series of turning points in my life. I was closing in on sixteen and prepared to be an adult actor the rest of my life.

We took a four-picture deal at Universal. The pictures were nothing special—things like *Newsboys' Home* which gives you a rough idea—but at that point in my life acting was a job, while my interests were elsewhere. I don't believe I was taking my work very seriously when I was sixteen or seventeen. Girls and cars and music were what I cared about, pretty much in that order. And I think for those couple of years I was pretty much of a pain in the ass to my directors. I didn't rebel—I didn't care enough to rebel. It was just that my mind was elsewhere, and I would walk through my part, or maybe run through it, to get the hell out so I could go out with some new girl. I was often called on the carpet in those days; it didn't bother me, except that I didn't want my mother to know.

Somehow, I think, I managed to keep her in the dark about my sins. Maybe when she saw those pictures, she'd know I surely wasn't Laurence Olivier, but I don't think she ever knew about how often I was reprimanded for just going through the motions.

After the Universal deal came a three-pictures-in-a-year contract with Paramount. These films were of a little higher quality. *Seventeen* was one of them. I remember shooting that one particularly because about halfway through it Judy Garland sashayed back into my life, saying how wrong she had been to leave me, how she really loved me, how it was meant to be. It lasted a week, I think.

I did the movie version of *What a Life*, playing Henry Aldrich. My leading lady was Betty Field, who was twenty-seven but was playing a seventeen-year-old. She was a little self-conscious about it, but she looked young enough, and I enjoyed our love scenes.

They wanted to make that into a series and offered me a contract to play Henry Aldrich in a bunch of pictures. I think it could have knocked Andy Hardy out of the ring, but my mother decided to turn it down. She felt—I believe she was absolutely right, too—that a series was a kiss of death for an actor. I did one more as Aldrich—*Life with Henry*—and then bowed out. Jimmy Lydon took over as Henry, but they turned them into B pictures after that. My mother was right. A series was the kiss of death. The only exception, later, was Rooney and the Andy Hardy pictures.

I went back to Metro as part of an all-star cast assembled for *Ziegfeld Girl*. Mickey was now a big star. I played Lana Turner's brother, who was Judy Garland's boyfriend. Among the others in that biggie were Jimmy Stewart, Hedy Lamarr, Tony Martin, and Charles Winninger.

I went there figuring it would be a lot of fun, working opposite Judy. It wasn't. Maybe it was because of our past relationship, but she was acting differently. She was cold and distant and an entirely new, and unlovely, person. It could have been pills, as I think back on it, but that never occurred to me then. I just knew that the five weeks of pleasure I had anticipated had turned into many weeks of unpleasantness.

Five weeks had been the deal, at $5,000 a week. But it turned out to be longer than that. The ladies, bless their temperaments, caused problems. First it was Lana; she decided she wouldn't work when she had her period. So, of course, neither would Hedy or Judy. Then there were script changes, production problems. Delays, delays. My five weeks, at $5,000 a week, stretched out, longer and longer.

In the tenth week Mayer called my agent, Charlie Feldman, and said he wanted to cut my salary. I had worked twice as long as I had been originally contracted to work. Since all the others in the cast were MGM contract players, it turned out that I would be making more on the film than any of them—more than Stewart or Lamarr or Turner or anybody. Feldman said no, a deal is a deal. I kept on getting my $5,000 a week.

One morning I was called to work early. I reported as ordered. I had one brief scene, which I did, and I was through in ten minutes and dismissed. As I was leaving, I said to the director (Robert Z. Leonard) jokingly, "Hey, next time if you only need me for ten minutes, call me later, so I can get some sleep." It was only a small joke. Nobody thought twice about it. What I didn't know, and what I doubt if more than a handful of MGM employees knew, was that Mayer had almost every sound stage bugged. There was a little room somewhere in the administration building (now called the Thalberg Building) where Mayer's brother, Jerry, was stationed with earphones on his head. The open mikes in all the studios were fed into this secret room, and Mayer tuned around, hoping to catch somebody saying something terrible. I was unlucky; he happened to be listening when I made that small joke about getting called so early.

I left the stage that morning, went to my dressing room, changed, and got in my car to drive home. When I reached the gate, the officer on duty said, "Jackie, Mr. Mayer wants to see you."

I have never been chewed out so thoroughly as I was that morning by Louis B. Mayer. He really let me have it. How dare I make a joke about working so hard when I was earning more than anybody else on the picture? Just who did I think I was to make light of gainful employment? Did I not realize that there were dozens of actors in Hollywood—as good as or better than you, Cooper—who would gladly have done my work for half my salary or less?

On and on it went. And it had only been a very small joke.

15.

The first time I appeared in a play, after the war, in 1947, the producers and the directors and everybody worried about whether or not I could handle it. They somehow lumped me with all the Hollywood people who were strictly creatures of film. They wondered how I would be affected by a live audience.

I told them not to worry. I practically grew up on stage. From 1932 on, when I first became a name, I went on the road for a month or so every year. Vaudeville was still big then, and it kept demanding new personalities. In those days everybody who achieved any fame would go on a vaudeville tour—prizefighters, aviators, murderers—and so there was certainly a demand for the child star of the moment.

I went on the road for the first time in January and February 1932, just after *The Champ* was released. *Skippy* had made me quite famous, and *The Champ* solidified that fame. The public would want to pay to see me. Fortunately I could do something besides just stand there and talk about myself—that's what the fighters, aviators, and murderers did. I could sing and dance a little.

Norman Taurog got a writer, and he and that writer and my mother put the act together. It was about twenty minutes plus a couple of encores, a big finish to get them excited and a smaller one so I could get off. It was easy for me to learn, and I never recall any nervousness about either the act or performing the act. I liked vaudeville. My mother made it easy for me.

I opened wearing my Skippy costume in a pantomime bit. I came out from the wings—applause, applause!—eating an ice cream cone and carrying a big loaf of bread under each arm and a newspaper. I would drop a loaf of bread and bend to pick it up, and the bending would cause me to drop the other one. Every time I'd pick one up the other would fall. Finally, I'd get the two loaves of bread firmly positioned under my arms—and the ice cream would fall. That would cause the audience to laugh, and I would then make-believe I noticed them for the first time.

"Oh, hi," I would say, and then start a brief monologue, talking to the audience about working in pictures. Taurog had it written so I didn't sound too egotistical. It wasn't all me-me-me; it had a lot about how important the director was—of course.

Then the curtain would part behind me, and my mother would be there at the piano. I would introduce her, and I'd climb up on the piano and sing. While I sang, I took out a pocketknife and whittled the piano, or that was what it looked like. Actually there was a piece of wood attached to the piano for me to whittle, but the audience was always laughing, thinking I was putting something over on my mother by whittling the piano. Finally, my mother would catch me and scold me, and I'd stop whittling. But then I would take out a little tin can and—still singing, of course—get out a turtle from the can and play with it. That was from *Skippy*, where the character had a pet turtle he kept in a can. I would put the turtle on my head, lie on the piano, and let the turtle plod across my chest.

And all the while I'd be singing. Then I'd get down and do one number—"Exactly Like You"—at the mike, just singing it straight, no gimmicks. I would do a short tap dance and a monologue from *Skippy* and go off the stage.

Then I'd come back for an encore, the jail scene from *The Champ*. It was all done in the first person, as though I were talking to Wallace Beery, and I worked in just a pinspot, the tiny circle of light on my head. There was very quiet background music as I went through that maudlin but always effective scene, and there wasn't a dry eye in the house. And that includes my own—music always made me cry, and I am still sensitive to certain kinds of music.

Then I'd come back for one more encore, a brief song, which let me get off. It all lasted roughly twenty-five minutes, and I would do it three or four times a day, and I did it for a few years, with slight variations. Later on, as I grew older, the act changed considerably, but that first one set the format the others invariably followed.

That first tour also established the tone for life on the road. It was always a successful act. That first year was the most successful, however, because I was new and audiences were curious about me. We opened in St. Louis, moved on to Kansas

City and then Chicago. They had to have police outside the theaters where I played and the hotels where I stayed because of the crowds. This wasn't long after the Lindbergh baby was kidnapped, so the police forces in the various cities were apprehensive and assigned plainclothes police to serve as bodyguards for me all day long. We invariably had a suite in the best hotel in town, and there was a bodyguard sitting in the living room of those suites all night long.

■ ■ ■

BILL SMITH: We were staying in New York, playing Newark. He and I would go over on the tubes every day and come back, and we had two cops with us 'cause you get a lot of crazy mail from fags, you know. They had to watch him all the time. He doesn't know this to this day, but I had a thirty-eight in my belt.

■ ■ ■

The first crowd that shoved around me frightened me a little. I didn't know what they wanted. My mother said nobody wanted to hurt me, they just wanted to see me. That was a concept you might expect a child would have difficulty in understanding: Why did all the people want to see him? But to me, it was all part of the same package which my mother and grandmother had been selling me for the past few years. I had a job to do, and it was all part of that job. I was different from other kids—not better, just different. And the key to that difference is that I had a job. I couldn't play because I might get hurt. I had to work at the studio; that meant I couldn't go to regular school but had to study with my tutor at home or on the set. And this was simply another facet of that same situation. I shrugged it off. That was just the way things were for me.

I liked to talk to the cops assigned to guard me. They would show me their guns. A few would carefully take out the bullets and let me hold the gun and even pull the trigger. In Chicago the cops talked about Al Capone. This was in the days when he ruled Chicago, and the cops talked about him as though he were a hero. I had always thought of him as a gangster, a bad guy, and I couldn't understand how these cops could talk about him so favorably.

My mother, when she had been touring with Edith Clifford, had played Chicago and had, in fact, played some of the joints Capone owned or controlled. She had even met him, a fact she mentioned to those cops in our suite. I was stunned. She had never said anything about that to me. I think I was a little confused by that because I still couldn't get the idea out of my head that Capone was a bad guy, and I didn't like the thought that my mother had consorted with bad guys.

One day, between shows, the telephone rang, and one of the cops answered. I could see an amazed expression on his face.

"Mrs. Cooper," he said. "It's for you. It's—it's Al Capone!"

And it was Scarface Al, calling my mother. My mother talked to him very calmly, and it was apparently a very pleasant and very polite conversation. She didn't say much except little pleasantries like "Thank you very much" and "How nice of you, Al," and "We certainly will," and she gave a few polite laughs.

When she hung up, she told the cops and me that Capone had said that we wouldn't need a bodyguard in his city, that nobody would harm a hair on my head while we were there; all we had to do was name it, and we could have it.

The last stop on my first tour was New York. And an event occurred there, as I played the Capitol Theater, which has become almost a legend in a certain show business quarter. That is because I told the story once, and only once, but to a very select audience. I told it in Las Vegas, in the late fifties, one night after what is known as a professional show. Frank Sinatra had performed for the public, and then there was this special show, mostly for other entertainers playing Las Vegas who had had no chance to catch Sinatra's magnificent act because of their own show schedules. So the cream of show biz was in the room, and after Sinatra performed, everybody else came up and did something, too. Milton Berle had gone up and—as he usually does—taken over and become the unofficial MC. Berle had been sitting with us; his wife, Ruth, and my wife, Barbara, are old friends, and Milton and I have been friends for many years, too.

Anyhow, eventually Milton got around to introducing me. And I got a very nice hand. I obviously couldn't do the things that the rest of that starry crowd could do, so I hoped they would just let me take a bow and sit down. But the applause continued, and Berle insisted I come up onstage. As I walked up, wondering what the hell I could do (it wouldn't make much impact to sit in with the band and play drums), the sight of Berle standing there made me remember the Capitol Theater in 1932. And I told this story.

In those days Berle was a legend in vaudeville—and a scourge. Maybe equal parts. He used to take great joy in, and receive tremendous ovations by, crashing theaters, heading up onstage, barging in while the entertainers were working, completely ruining their acts, and leaving the place a shambles. And woe to any comic onstage who tried to ad-lib with Milton. Milton could out-ad-lib anybody, and he had left more comics lying in ruins on the stage than anybody else. He often began by heckling from the audience, then coming onstage and carrying on. And he would bury anybody who tried to exchange ad libs with him.

As a child star, however, I was immune. The public wouldn't have any sympathy for a grown man who tried to break up a kid's act. At least that was what some people thought as I did my act at the Capitol Theater in New York in 1932. Berle was playing in town, too; I forget now if he was at the Palace or maybe working a nightclub like the Martinique. The act was a hit in New York, as everywhere, and I was making a lot—it varied between $7,500 and $10,000 a week, compared to the $1,300 or so that Metro was then paying me. And the public jammed every show.

One day I was doing my *The Champ* monologue when I noticed a commotion in the theater. Somebody was walking down the aisle. It was, of course, Milton Berle. He just couldn't resist trying to upstage a kid. This time he was making believe he was a newsboy.

"Wuxtra, wuxtra," he was calling. "Get your paper here, the latest news! Jackie Cooper is a fag! Read all about it here. Jackie Cooper caught in the back of a cab with Wally Beery!"

I didn't know what was going on. I just knew that something was happening and that the audience loved it. They were screaming with laughter. My mother was behind me, at the piano, waiting there to accompany me in my final encore.

The stage manager knew that I couldn't compete with Berle. He turned on the houselights, and everybody now could watch his passage down the aisle. He was really rolling now. He stopped to chat with the ladies, sitting on a lap here, putting on one of the ladies' hats there, kissing another one. And all the while I stood there on the stage, confused and perplexed. What should I do now? Nobody had told me about this kind of situation. I had never heard of Milton Berle. I watched the man as he reached the front of the theater and began to make his way up the stairs. The applause began to build from the audience. My mother was an experienced vaudevillian, but I was only nine, on my first tour. My mother apparently forgot that difference, and as Berle climbed onstage, I felt her tug on the back of my Skippy coat. I leaned back a little, and I heard her whisper in my ear, "Don't ad-lib with him!"

That was the story I told in Las Vegas that night, and I will be immodest and tell you that it got the biggest laugh of anything that was said by Sinatra or Berle or any of the other show biz greats.

16.

I learned to love vaudeville, including Berle. I found that I loved watching from the wings and learning routines, and I particularly liked watching the pit bands and the drummers.

Music was something I suppose was born in me—my mother and father were both musical, and if there is anything to genes, I have some that like music.

In 1935 I persuaded my mother to take me on a ship, and she booked passage for the two of us on a banana boat that sailed down the West Coast from Los Angeles to the Panama Canal and back. That three-week cruise changed my life—again. There were three wonderful attractions for me aboard the ship. The pool—I loved the idea of going swimming in a pool aboard a ship. A girl—I had a crush on a fifteen-year-old (I was thirteen), and she was the first girl I danced close enough with to feel the lumps on her chest, and that was pretty exciting stuff. The third thing was a revelation—the drums.

I had learned ballroom dancing through the courtesy of that nice lady on *Treasure Island*, so I danced every night with the lumpy girl I was desperately in love with. Night life! I stayed up, I imagine, until a sinful 11:00 P.M. One of the great advantages of shipboard life, particularly on a relatively small vessel, is that you know everybody, crew included. So I got to know all the band musicians, and I was absolutely enthralled by the drummer. I watched him night after night, and I began asking him questions, and he was nice; he would show me how to hold his brushes—he wouldn't chance letting me use the sticks themselves because I might break something. I guess I had a pretty fair sense of rhythm already—I'd done some tap dancing, and I'd sung, and I had taken four years of piano lessons, which for the rest of my life I've been sorry I quit.

By the time we reached the Canal I knew I wanted to do some serious drumming. A week after we got back home, the drummer from the ship (obviously at my mother's request) showed up at our house with a small set of drums. They weren't toys, but regular drums. I taught myself, drumming to a steadily increasing library of great jazz records. I played for two or three hours a day and eventually got to be pretty good.

■ ■ ■

SIDNEY MILLER: The jam sessions at Jackie's house on Crescent Drive—I lived just down the street—were a place to go, a thing to do. As I recall, it was almost every Sunday. The invited guests were the kids like Jane Withers and Bonita Granville—Jackie was going with Bonita then—and Leonard Sues played trumpet, and Buddy Pepper played piano, and I once in a while played my six flats. The sessions were marvelous. We did everything. Later on there was another time that was a very strong era with Jackie and me and music. There was a man I started writing with named Sid Kuller. It was during the *Colgate Comedy Hour* days, with Donald O'Connor. Maybe even before. Yes, before—it was in the early forties. Jackie was then playing terrific drums. He was really a top drummer. Sid Kuller used to have a house right here in the Hollywood Hills, and his door was always open. He loved most of the jazz bands, and his closest friends were Duke Ellington and Duke's son, Tedesco, and Hal Borne. He knew seven or eight pianists and two or three harpists and a lot of musicians that used to play in the band over at the—you know, it's now the Aquarius Theater, but then it was Earl Carroll's. Sid Kuller's girl was a show girl, and after show time everybody would come up to his home, and a jam session would start at midnight and maybe end at four or five in the morning. People would just pour in there to sit and listen. Duke sat at the piano and played; then he moved up to the treble, and Nat Cole moved to the bass; then Duke would get off, Nat would move to the treble, and Hal Borne would take over bass; then Hal would move up, and Tedesco and Inez James, who I used to write with—and always Jackie was on the drums, and Buddy Rich was on the drums, and Mickey [Rooney] would try to play drums and couldn't—Mickey was nowhere with the drums, he thought he could, but he couldn't—but Jackie would come up there, and we would all just sit and listen to him improvise. He was professional caliber. Absolutely. It was always a surprise to me that he didn't form a band.

■ ■ ■

In my teens drums were an entrée into another world. As we toured, I'd see many of the big bands of the era because our tour would coincide with theirs. I got to hear and see— and eventually to meet—Krupa and the Dorseys and Goodman and Shaw and Miller and all of them. They knew who I was, too, of course, and the word spread that I wasn't just a duffer on the drums, so they would invite me to play a little with them. What a thrill that was for this kid!

Drums and music were an entrée, too, into a fast world that I had never even known existed. Through music I met Anita O'Day, perhaps the finest band singer of them all, especially when she was with Gene Krupa in 1940. Anita was the first person to turn me on to pot.

Krupa was playing in L.A., and as usual, I was there every night, watching, waiting for the chances Gene gave me to sit in with the band. I'd usually end up backstage, talking, listening, absorbing that atmosphere, which was, to me at that time, magical.

One night I was depressed, for reasons which I cannot recall, but Anita noticed my down state and said, casually, "Hey, Jack, want to light up?"

I guess I looked so dumb—I didn't really know what she meant—that she expressed herself more clearly.

"Do you want to smoke some tea?"

I was game; at eighteen kids are stupidly game for anything. I said sure. I brought my car around, and we both got in, and she lit up, and I had my first experience. It was pretty good. We sat there for a while, puffing away, and then she said that, after the job, we should go to her place. She had a little rented apartment, nothing elaborate, but nice. When we got there, she asked, "Do you want to light up again?" She was, I would estimate, twenty-one or twenty-two at the time, not beautiful but attractive. She lit up another joint—they were called that even then—and I said, "Oh, yeah," although my enthusiasm was less for the effect than for the experience. We drank a half bottle of wine, finished the joint, and I passed out.

That was all. Anita was very nice. She covered me up, let me sleep it off. When I finally woke up, I found myself on the couch. Anita was in her bed. I was so embarrassed I just put on my shoes—that was all she had bothered to take off—and sneaked out. I didn't see her again until I was doing *Mister Roberts* in Chicago, almost ten years later, and she came by to say she had enjoyed the play. She wasn't in too good shape at that time and didn't remember that she had initiated me into pot smoking. Now she's fine again and looks and sings as well as ever.

The first year I drummed in my act, we were in New York and there was some kind of musicians' benefit, and we went. Bunny Berigan's band was playing at the club where the benefit was held, but all the great musicians who were in New York at the time showed up. In one number Berigan was joined up front by Tommy Dorsey and Benny Goodman. They invited me to sit and play the drums, and they set up my drums in front with Berigan, Dorsey, and Goodman. And they played the Dorsey arrangement of "Marie," with Jack Leonard (not my uncle Jack Leonard) singing the vocal. I just played the arrangement—one of the many I had committed to memory. There was no drum solo, but that made me feel even better, because they had entrusted me with playing one of the regular arrangements, not just something flashy. I played it, note for note, without a mistake. I was floating.

Each year after that I'd add more music to my act. By 1941 I was doing numbers with the theater band. I had a four-minute drum solo, too, and the whole musical segment consumed about eight minutes. I liked that—the more music, the less talk and recitations and all the rest of the stuff. I preferred music. The fact that there was now music in the act made it more attractive to theater owners, too. They liked names—I was still a name—who could do something besides just stand there, mumbling. The other star kids of my era had nothing like that—Mickey did a lot of things musical, but none of them very well, and Freddie Bartholomew did nothing, and MGM would never let Judy do a vaudeville tour.

Once, on tour, my natural craving for girls got me in an almost serious jam. It began in New York. My mother and I had gotten friendly with a reporter named Ted Lloyd, and he began going out with us after our show. We often went out to see other shows and mostly, as my interest in music grew, to catch whatever jazz artists were in town. Ted maybe had an interest in my mother because he suggested our always being three was awkward, and how about it if he got a date for me? That way we would be a foursome, and wouldn't that be a better arrangement? I was fifteen and all for it, of course, and my mother went along, so Ted Lloyd showed up the next night with a twenty-year-old chorus girl in tow. I was tall enough at the time, so it didn't look too peculiar for me to be with a mature chorine. The four of us went out for several nights then, after our show, to other theaters, to clubs, to jazz joints. Sometimes they'd ask me to sit in on the drums, giving me a little chance to show off for my date.

One night I picked the girl up—I remember she was at the Plymouth Hotel—and met Ted and my mother at some club, and I played the drums and the girl applauded, and we went someplace else, and it was midnight. My mother said it was time for me to go home. I said it was too early. She said she and Ted were going up to Harlem, which was then the in place for people to go late at night, and I should take Kathryn (I don't remember her last name) home and then go home myself and go to bed. She was firm. I said okay, I would.

My mother and Ted left for Harlem, but I took Kathryn to the hotel where my mother and I were staying. It didn't take much persuasion. There was some booze there, and we had a couple of drinks. We hopped in the sack and out again, and I had her back to the Plymouth and got back to our hotel before my mother returned from her nightclubbing in Harlem. Actually Ted Lloyd had even taken her out after the Harlem excursion to a private club and then Reuben's for a late snack, so they didn't get in until almost five-thirty in the morning. He was keeping her away from the suite, so I would have plenty of time. I was sound asleep when my mother got home. She came in to see if I was tucked in.

"Did you have a good time, Jackie?"

"Yes, Mom. I put her in a cab right after you left."

"Good."

But I didn't see Kathryn again the rest of that stay in New York. My mother arranged for me to be very busy. We left as our tour moved on. I wrote Kathryn some letters, and I said how much I missed her and how I sure hoped we would see each other again. She wrote pretty much the same thing. I wrote back again and said maybe she could come out to Detroit when we played there. She wrote back that it sounded like a great idea. Somehow I persuaded my mother to go along, and she even sent the girl a train ticket. But she fixed it so the reunion would be in Flint, Michigan, not Detroit; she felt Flint was a little smaller, and that meant fewer reporters, and maybe we'd luck out and nobody would hear about the tryst. As the big day drew near, I was excited. I wasn't in love; this was just an adventure, and I knew that if I could maneuver everything just so, I could maneuver Kathryn into the sack again.

On the day of her arrival the newspapers came out with headline news: JACKIE COOPER GETTING MARRIED: CHILD STAR, 15, TO MARRY CHORINE, 20.

My mother arranged to meet Kathryn at the railroad station, and she coldly and efficiently transported her to our dressing room and coldly and efficiently kept the press away from both of us. She questioned Kathryn, who simply said, "I just assumed that we were getting married." My mother did some assuming, too—she assumed the young lady was solely interested in getting some publicity. I never even saw her, much less got her to bed. She was on the train back to New York that day.

But I must say I was pleased with myself. The little escapade had given me a new image, and I knew that back home my friends were thinking: Hey, Jackie's not a kid anymore. I was right about that, too. They treated me with a little more respect after that. It was my first taste of machismo.

17.

This will be very hard to grasp for anybody who hasn't been there, but it is true. Child stars aren't taught anything about money, and that is one of the unsung tragedies of the child star trade.

I grew up knowing absolutely nothing about money, the value of a buck, how to budget, how to save, how to balance a checkbook, any of those basic economic lessons. From the time I was a $2-a-week allowance kid until suddenly I was on my own and once pretty damn near flat broke, everything was done for me. Not a bit of practical experience. Just the opposite, I was deliberately shielded from money talk and money concern.

When I was a child, my mother (who recognized the dangers of her son's being a child star and tried to shield me from them) gave me an allowance. The theory was that if I had the allowance, then I would know what money meant and would have to save up if I wanted things. A dandy theory that simply doesn't work in practice. At the time the system was inaugurated, I was so young that there wasn't anything I wanted that I couldn't get for a nickel or a dime. So two bucks were just two pieces of paper. I stacked them up in a bureau drawer. Every week two more were added to the pile. My young friends would come in and enjoy riffling through the stack. I didn't understand their awe.

A few years later, when I was a well-known kid star, many executives felt it would be politic of them to give me presents at various occasions. Some of them, with no better idea, would give me $5, $10 or $20 gold pieces. I accumulated a lot of those coins. My mother thought they were safely stowed in a chest at the foot of my bed, but they weren't. I had a tree house, and those glittering coins were great playthings up in the tree house—pirate gold or cowboy poker chips or whatever. That's all they meant to me. They were toys.

At fourteen, when I started to drive, I was given $5 a week to pay for my gas and any expenses I incurred on a date.

Supposedly I was learning to budget. Again, a lovely theory that was impractical. Ordinarily I'd take my date to a modestly priced restaurant, and my allowance would cover it. But if I had a big date or there was a special occasion, there was always extra money forthcoming. I didn't even have to ask. It wasn't so much that I was being spoiled as the fact that they recognized I needed more money, and they felt it was part of my professional image (a word nobody used then, thank God) to be seen in the top places by the top people. So if I said I was going to take a girl to the Victor Hugo, to dance to Skinnay Ennis and his orchestra, or to the Wilshire Bowl or the Coconut Grove, I'd always get an extra $10 or so. No questions asked.

I remember only once embarking on a careful campaign to save money. I wanted to modify my car—have the cylinder heads polished, get a second carburetor and twin exhaust pipes—and so I carefully squirreled away part of my allowance each week. It worked, too, and my mother was very proud. She told me that I had been very sensible, and she was sure that I would be okay about money when I grew up.

But then I'd see Chuck Bigelow, my stepfather, spend twice as much as those car modifications had cost on some trifle, and I'd wonder about it. Why had I busted my butt all those weeks to save when Chuck just went out and bought something—and I knew it was mostly money I had earned he was spending?

I was making great money. My Metro days—1930 to 1936—had me on salary and going up from $1,000 a week to about $2,000 a week when I left the studio. Plus the thousands and thousands the vaudeville tours had brought in.

It was all just numbers to me. I knew enough about salaries, having lived through the Depression, to know that I made a lot more than most people. Even so, it was just numbers, not real money, not even its equivalent in purchasing power. It was a concept, not an actuality.

Of course (and I didn't learn about this until much later), those big salaries were eroded by percentages: 10 percent to an agent, 5 percent to a business manager. And my stepfather had pretty much taken care of my mother's share of my earnings.

I never gave money much of a thought. Obviously I never was in want or never really craved anything I didn't get. I always had a few bucks in my pocket, and all the bills went home, where my mother took care of them.

Then she died. Norman Taurog took over things. I was on my own—my own apartment (rent, utilities), my own car (garage, insurance), my own life (clothes, necessities, luxuries). And suddenly, my own checkbook.

That was a strange instrument to me. Norman told me just to write on the stub how much each check was written for and who it was made out to. I said, "What do I put down in the place marked 'balance'?" He said not to worry about that. They (presumably the "they" were Taurog and his accountant) would take care of that.

So I went along, not worrying about the balance. I really didn't give a damn, then, about how much money I had, I was concerned only with how much money I could spend. Once in a while Norman would call me and say that I was spending a lot. So I'd back off for a while, not write any checks, and then I'd start in again. I always felt, in those years, that if I didn't hear anything, then everything was okay.

All through the war years money was no concern really. I had my rent paid by the Navy, and it supplied food and clothing. Once in a while I'd spend some extra, and write one of my checks, but I never heard that I shouldn't, so I just assumed it was okay.

When the war was over, I came back home to my wife, June. There was reality to be faced. I was twenty-three, but I still had absolutely no idea how much money I had. I assumed that since I had made so much for so many years, and because I was sure my mother had been frugal, there was a pretty hefty sum left somewhere.

But I didn't ask. I had been taught as a child that my business was acting, that other people would take care of my money for me, and I had it so ingrained in my mind that—even when I was twenty-three—I didn't have enough sense to ask anybody how much money I had. And nobody told me. Besides, I think I was scared I might find out there wasn't much.

June and I wanted to buy a house. When I started looking with her, the real estate people's first question, properly, was what our price range was. I had absolutely no idea what our price range was—because I had absolutely no idea how much money I had.

Later Taurog and my business manager, a man Taurog hired named Myrt Blum, set a $30,000 limit. We found a house that had a $32,000 price tag. Since it was $2,000 over the limit, both Taurog and Blum had to inspect it before we were allowed to buy it.

I asked them how much I would be allowed to spend on food each week and what to do about all the other house expenses. Blum said I should send him all the bills, and he'd pay them. So I was again shielded from the cold, hard facts of economic life. I never had an inkling about what things like utilities cost until later, when I moved to New York and was totally on my own.

While June and I—and then our son, John Anthony—lived in that house, I was back where I had always been. I was on an allowance. They sent me $50 a week, which was to pay for everything out of pocket. If June needed something special for the baby or the house, she had to call up Blum or Taurog and request it. It was degrading for her, and of course, she didn't like it. She said I should do something about it, but that was the way I had always lived, and I didn't have it in me to break away.

Once I wanted to buy June a dog for a present. She had her heart set on a standard poodle. I think it was $150, which was expensive for a dog in those days. I couldn't make it out of the allowance, and I knew that Blum and Taurog would never okay that expense. So I borrowed the $150 from Bill Smith and bought the dog.

Blum, the business manager, was not exactly what you would call shrewd. Before the war my mother had bought us a 110-acre spread for $10,000 out in Camarillo, then pretty remote from Los Angeles. That was where I kept the horses I had at the time—I rode my quarter horses in stock shows in those days—and it was a nice little ranch. When the war came along, Blum and Taurog got scared and made me sell everything—the house we had had in Beverly Hills, the Palm Springs and beach houses and the Camarillo acreage. Got peanuts for the ranch, too—and our next-door neighbor out there, Joel McCrea, sold his 1,000 acres for almost $6 million after the war.

After the war I said I'd like to get a ranch like that again. Blum said no, buy a car. He said all my money was in the bank and should stay there, so buy a car. He even had a friend who was a car dealer, so I not only had to buy a car but had to buy a car from this dealer. It was a car I hated, too, but I bought it.

I never had any idea of how much money there was left, but I just surmised there was a lot. When June and I separated, I had a shock. I found that all I had to my name was the house in Cheviot Hills where June and I had lived and two insurance policies with a cash surrender value of $39,000 each. I wasn't exactly destitute, but I was hardly wealthy.

New York was a lesson. I learned about money there—to a degree. I supported myself and paid my own bills and got by. Then, when I came back to TV and had two hit series in a row—*The People's Choice* and *Hennesey*—I made a second fortune.

By now Blum was out. I was married to Barbara by this time, and we had an accountant instead of a business manager. But I still had an agent (10 percent) and now a career manager (20 percent) and the accountant (2½ percent), and we had a good life—three children, a nice house, a lot of entertaining and trips and good clothes. But we saved very little. My early training was still working for me: If nobody yells at me (my mother or Taurog or, in this case, the accountant), then everything is okay. And nobody was yelling, so we kept on spending.

I had learned a new trick: how to live beyond my means. I figured I'd save later—after all, with a couple of hit TV series, there was never any more question about not having a great income forever and ever. But the year between the two hit shows had been expensive—we kept on living high, but the income was low, and that ate up a lot of the reserves. And the *Hennesey* thing wasn't as lucrative as it should have been. Don McGuire and I had a partnership on that show, and we took the advice of my accountant and Don's lawyer, who got together and urged us to form a Swiss corporation. We would have been better off with the cheese. About two years from the time we incorporated, the government changed its laws in regard to Swiss corporations, and we wound up not making anything close to what we might have.

But once again, I didn't know about it—the accountant kept the figures to himself. It wasn't until later, when we checked all our juicy profits, that we found they weren't juicy at all.

The second fortune disappeared at a stroke of the IRS—we had to pay a 50 percent corporation tax as it turned out, and that pretty much decimated those *Hennesey* earnings. Between that and our expensive living, the second fortune went quicker than the first.

During that period there was a silver lining. Barbara insisted, over the protestations of our lawyers, that we buy the house on Rodeo Drive in Beverly Hills where we wound up living for twenty years. We bought it for $125,000 in 1960, and when we sold it, in 1980, it brought $1.7 million.

That was fortune number four.

18.

I think the war probably saved me.

There is only one way to say it, and at the risk of sounding corny and a cliché user, I'll say it: The war made a man of me. I think that if there had been no World War II and hence no cause for me to go into the Navy, I would be a drunk and a total loss today.

But there was a World War II, and there was Navy service for me, and I had to take a lot—maybe more than most guys, because of who I was—and it was hard at first and caused me pain and grief, but here I am.

Like most young men my age, as soon as Pearl Harbor came, I was all for going down in the morning and volunteering. Because I had fallen in love with small boats while playing around Coronado, I thought immediately of going into the Navy and playing around with PT boats. I guess, like the average guy, I thought of war as fun and games. Oh, I knew people got killed, but you never think of that; you think only of the glamour.

Soon after Pearl Harbor, by coincidence, I was part of a Hollywood contingent that went to Washington, to help Roosevelt celebrate his birthday. We had lunch at the White House with FDR and Eleanor. After I was introduced—Robert Montgomery, wearing a lieutenant commander's uniform, presented us all to the President—I had a chance to talk to Bob, and he said he was going into motor torpedo boats. Wow! That was what I wanted, too, and I said so, and he said he'd see what he could do.

I got back from Washington all excited about it, and right away I told Norman about my plans. No, he said. It was far too dangerous. The boats were wooden, and they might catch on fire. I was certainly old enough to have just gone off and enlisted on my own, but there was still that vestigial trace of obedience to my elders in me. I knew my mother would have said, "Jackie, listen to Norman; he knows what's best for you." So I said, "Okay, I won't enlist right now."

And I must admit Hollywood had changed and was a lot of fun for me. The war mentality quickly swept away a lot of inhibitions. People lived for today and, just as often, for tonight.

I was still making pictures. Just before Pearl Harbor I was in *Syncopation*, which I finished a few days before my mother died, with William Dieterle directing. Bonita Granville was in *Syncopation* with me. It was at the height of our romance, and it was great to be working with the girl I loved.

I was rushed into a war story, then, a little dandy called *The Navy Comes Through*, which helped me solidify my intention to join the Navy. George Murphy, Desi Arnaz, and Max Baer were my fellow sailors in that one, a remake of a World War I story which had starred William Boyd and was all about a merchant marine ship battling a German U-boat.

I was still itchy, wanting to get into uniform. It began to feel strange to be in civvies with so many of my friends already serving. But Norman said wait, and I didn't even have to register for the draft yet, so I waited.

Then I did a western, *Men of Texas*, with an old friend, Bob Stack, and a new friend, Broderick Crawford. It was the old cattlemen versus sheepmen story, a western made on the Universal back lot. Brod was the first older man I ever drank with. At the end of the day we'd sit in his dressing room and have a few belts, then go off to the Cock 'n' Bull, where the friendly neighborhood bartenders would slip a little rum into my Coke. I learned then I had a capacity; I'd go drink for drink with Brod Crawford, and at the end I'd have to drive him home.

One day I came to work with a bad cold. I tried to work, but I really felt rotten, and at noon the director sent me to the studio infirmary. The nurse on duty took my temperature, found I had a fever, and said I had the flu. She sent me home. Soon after I had gone to bed, the studio doctor came to my apartment, according to studio rules and regulations, to confirm the diagnosis. He wrote out a prescription for me, which the studio driver immediately went out and had filled.

I was lying in bed, later in the afternoon, when the front desk of the apartment house called. The doorman said that the nurse was there, was it okay for her to come up? I figured the studio had sent her, so I said sure, send her up.

I was in my pajamas, of course, and I let her in, and she looked very official, in her uniform, cap, badge.

Skippy was always the regular guy.

Left: Mabel in front of Johnny's record shop, where love blossomed or a deal was made.

Top right: My own "mother dearest" before Joan Crawford got the idea. *Right:* Bill Smith and Mabel about 1926. Bill was the closest thing to a father I ever had.

With the other **Our Gang** members.

From silent films to talkies in the **Our Gang** days.

With Wallace Beery in **The Champ**. Everybody wanted to know what he was like.

In **O'Shaughnessy's Boy** with Wallace Beery. There was everything but warmth.

With Chic Sale in **When a Feller Needs a Friend.** Some of the grown-ups were nice.

Top: With Robert Coogan in **Sooky**. Robert's big brother drove a Rolls. *Middle*: With George Raft in **The Bowery**. Did he really wear a girdle? *Bottom*: With Wallace Beery in **The Bowery**. Four films together, and I never had a comfortable moment with the man.

For years Uncle Norman Taurog controlled my life.

With Mabel and Chuck Bigelow, when we seemed to be a happy family.

Left: Buster Keaton visited the set. *Right:* In **Tough Guy** with Joseph Calleia and Rin-Tin-Tin, Jr.

They laughed when I shot Wallace Beery in the leg during the making of **Treasure Island.**

Off on a vaudeville tour with Mabel.
In Chicago, Al Capone called.

Harpo, the Marx Brother who was my friend.

With Freddie Bartholomew and Mickey Rooney in **The Devil Is a Sissy**. Rooney taught me what it was like to have a picture stolen.

With Judy Garland in 1935—my first real love.

I met Judy on Wallace Beery's radio show in 1935. An older man broke it up.

After the exile, with Robert Warwick in **Gangster's Boy.**

While Jane Withers and I were making **Her First Beau**, Rita Hayworth came by to visit.

On the drums for jam sessions and
pool parties.

With Gene Krupa in **Syncopation.** The
musicians had plenty of dope and girls.

Claude Rains in **White Banners.** Bonita Granville was in the picture, too, but I didn't notice her then.

Right: I thought it would be fun to be with Judy Garland in **Ziegfeld Girl**, but it wasn't. *Below:* With Lana Turner in **Ziegfeld Girl.** Older women were interesting, too.

In **Gallant Sons**, with June Preisser, Gene Reynolds, and Bonita Granville, whose mother was always watching.

Right: June Horne. Was she the only one who would miss me? *Below:* On the drums with the Claude Thornhill band in Honolulu in 1945—an island behind the war, an island ahead of the mail.

"Have you had your bath?" she said.

"Bath? No, I haven't had a bath."

"Oh, you must have a bath."

She trotted right into the bathroom, and I could hear the water running in the tub. It sounded like a strange treatment, but who was I to question a trained and experienced nurse? She ran a very, very hot tub and helped me in and out. When I reached for the towel, to dry myself off, she said she would do it. I was a little groggy from the fever and the medication, so I let her do it, but it seemed strange.

Then she helped me back into bed—and before I could do or say a word, she was in with me, and she was masterful. I drifted off to sleep, thinking of the wonders of modern medicine.

In an hour she woke me up.

"Time for your bath," she said. And damned if the same process wasn't repeated—the hot tub, the drying off, back into bed, with her on top of me.

An hour later she woke me up again. I was groggy, but game. But just as I was about to put my foot in the hot tub, through my foggy mind drifted a suspicious thought—Brod Crawford. I went right to the phone and called the studio, and when I was connected to the stage, I asked to speak to Brod Crawford.

Over the phone I could hear him in the distance, saying, "Who is it?"

The man who had answered the phone yelled, "Jackie Cooper!"

And I could hear the whole stage burst out into gales of laughter.

They had hired a hooker, sent her to wardrobe, had her outfitted as a nurse, rehearsed her, and she had done a job on me. So I said to the lady, "Do I owe you any money?"

"No," she said, "they gave me a lot. Hey, while I'm here, can I have an autographed picture?"

She didn't even empty the tub. But you know, I got over that flu faster than any other case I've had.

Norman Taurog arranged another tour for me, a tour that was part USO, part vaudeville. The people at my agency, William Morris, said it would look good on my record to do a USO tour and might get me a deferment. I worked up an act, used an old skit I knew, and they got Phyllis Brooks to work in it with me. We toured bases in Oklahoma, Kansas, and Texas, and then they wanted to extend it. Phyllis had to go home, but they sent another girl to replace her, and we went on. Then I did a few more weeks of vaudeville—pitiful because that was the beginning of the end of vaudeville and it was sad to see how low it had sunk—and then came back.

I did one more picture—*Where Are Your Children?* with Gale Storm. Norman had asked Abe Lastfogel to get me deferred to do that film because they both felt it was important. It dealt with delinquency, and thus they insisted to the draft board that it was for the public good, and I got a deferment. By now, and this was well into 1942, I was ashamed to be still out of uniform, but there was little I could do about it. I was still doing what people told me to do.

When that picture was finished, I worked on Norman again to let me go into the Navy. By then I had read *They Were Expendable*, the story of the men who fought in the Navy torpedo boats, and that had fired me up again to enlist in that branch. Norman still said no.

Then he told me I should be nice to a sergeant we will call Jones, who would come to my apartment on a certain day, and that I was to take him out to dinner and wine and dine him regally. I didn't ask why, I just did what Norman said.

At the appointed hour Sergeant Jones came. He proved to be a master sergeant, a short, bald man who looked like an agent at the William Morris office. He was not a very nice-looking person. And he had a real East Side New York accent. I immediately disliked him, but Norman had said be nice to him, so I tried.

Norman had said he would get me another deferment. I didn't really want another deferment.

At the time of my meeting with Jones, Norman was living in the same apartment building as I was. He and my aunt Julie had split, and he was batching it. He had come down, a little while before Jones was to show up, and had given me a sealed envelope.

"Here's some money," he said.

"How much?"

"Never mind. Just give it to Sergeant Jones when he comes."

I didn't want to do it, but I was still following orders; that was my life. Norman told me to slip Jones the envelope only in the car, only when I was sure that nobody could see what was going on.

Jones picked me up, that summer night in '42, and we went out to drive to dinner. As we drove, I waited until there were no cars abreast of us, no cars immediately behind us, no cars immediately in front of us. I quickly whipped the envelope out of my pocket and shoved it at Jones. He just as quickly took it and, without stopping talking for a second, stuffed it into his own pocket.

"Yes, sir," he was saying, "we are going to find a very nice, very comfortable spot for you, Cooper."

Taurog had told me that Jones had connections, the right connections. He did, as it turned out. Pretty soon I got an official notice that I had a new draft number. I could tell that I was now safe until December 1942, at the earliest.

But now I was miserable. I hated what I had done. So I kept after Norman to let me enlist in the Navy, and eventually I wore him down. He said okay, but I had to be an officer. He got me an application for the V-12 program, which entailed taking young men, giving them an accelerated college education and then a Navy commission.

19.

At the time I made *White Banners*, I was fifteen. I played a brainy kid, the illegitimate son of the housekeeper (Fay Bainter) in the home of a scientist (Claude Rains). Bonita Granville played Rains's daughter, and my character and Bonita's became very chummy.

But we didn't. Not then. She was a year younger than I was, and after all, I was almost a man, I thought. I had watched Mickey Rooney palling around with twenty-year-olds, and I watched Judy Garland dating thirty-year-olds, and I'd been friendly with Lana Turner and Ann Rutherford. At the time, too, I was very involved with Pat Stewart, who was a year older than I was, so I didn't give fourteen-year-old Bonita more than a friendly hello.

My date throughout much of that period was Pat Stewart. I liked, throughout my entire life, to be with one girl. I got very serious very fast. There is something in some of us that wants a steady girl, for whatever reason, and I had a lot of whatever that something is. Maybe it is the need for attention. Maybe the need to possess someone. Or to be possessed. Whatever it is, that was the way I was. My mother knew me well enough to know that about me, and finally, she decided I was just too deeply involved with Pat. She went to Pat's mother, and that lady was apparently as concerned about her daughter's involvement as my mother was. The two mothers, as they did in those days, came to an agreement—that we could see each other, but we also had to see others—which they passed on to us. We were not rebellious; both Pat and I agreed to the new terms.

And so when I ran into Bonita Granville again, I was available, after a fashion. I began taking her out, and within a couple of weeks I was in love with her, and Pat was history.

I had to be considerably more careful with Bonita than I had been with Pat. She had a mother who watched every move she made. She and her mother were very religious, and they both took their religion very seriously.

We had fun together. There were the Sunday jam sessions at my house. There were the parties at Forrest Tucker's. Some of those were a bit wilder than the ones at my house. In fact, the action at Tucker's would often start late. I'd take Bonita home after a date, come home, and go to bed at a decent hour so I was in bed when my mother came by to see that I was okay. When she and my stepfather were asleep, I'd quietly ease out of the house, using my old roll-the-car-down-the-hill trick. Then I'd drive over to Forrest Tucker's, and we'd go at it until very late—or very early. I'd get home, especially on Sunday mornings, at eight or so, and my mother would wake me up at eleven—"Come on, lazybones, get up, you've been sleeping twelve hours."

There was a lot of booze around. There was some marijuana. Some of the boys and girls had Dexedrine—we didn't yet call it speed—and if we were planning to be up all night, we loved those little green pills. Maybe we were wrong, but it seemed to us that they deterred premature ejaculation—in fact, we learned, to our dismay, that two of them would make you impotent for the night. So we'd break one in half, take half early, the other half later, and, with booze, you'd get pretty stoned. I never bought the pills, but the other kids had no trouble getting them. They'd just buy them from their friendly neighborhood druggists, but I was always afraid to ask because it had been drummed into me that careers got ruined by people doing chancy things. In those days Bonita never drank or smoked—not even cigarettes—and I doubt if she'd even heard of Dexedrine.

■ ■ ■

BONITA GRANVILLE WRATHER: When Jackie and I dated, I'm sure plenty of the kids drank and did things they weren't supposed to do, but there was no dope, there was none around, you never really heard of dope and you really looked askance on anybody who got loaded regularly, falling down drunk; that was not the thing to do. We had fun—I basically would call it good clean fun, which young people in motion pictures, and out of motion pictures, don't seem to have much of anymore because it has to involve PCP or angel dust or something which makes people go crazy and you're a square if you don't smoke marijuana. Alcohol seems tame now compared to all these other things.

■ ■ ■

Bonita and I ordinarily dated only on weekends because she either worked or went to school during the week and couldn't go out. We saw each other regularly on Friday and Saturday nights for a couple of years.

Some Saturday nights she would insist that I take her to her church, so she could go to confession. I'd sit in the car and wait for her. I wanted to be with her, and she wanted to go to church. I'd take her so I could be with her, although it wasn't exactly my idea of a fun evening.

I believe that during that time I was the only boy she dated. We did all the usual things—house parties, bowling, swimming, dancing, out to the premieres and studio parties, ice skating, roller skating. And always there was her mother. If we were going to somebody's house for a party, she'd check to make sure the host's parents were going to be there, too. We always had a curfew—be home by one was the usual— so we'd get home by twelve-thirty and spend a half hour necking around the corner.

Bonita was a great source of comfort to me during my mother's last illness. She would come to Malibu to visit my mother—and me—but she was not allowed to stay overnight. I would have to drive her home.

After my mother died and I got my apartment, Bonita's mother sat me down and lectured me one day. She said she understood about young men and all that, but I had to realize that Bonita would never—NEVER—come to my apartment. And no matter how I tried to persuade her, she never did.

I had a grudging respect for her for her principles, but I was a terribly frustrated young man.

We talked about getting married as soon as I was twenty-one.

We talked on the phone every day. We began seeing each other more during the week. As she got older, her mother permitted her to go out during the week, too, and we saw each other four or five times a week. Then her mother sat me down for another talk.

She said she realized that a boy of my age craved the sexual experience, "and surely you are not having any sex with Bonita."

"Oh, no, no," I said.

She suggested that I see other girls. I shook my head no, but of course, I secretly did once in a while. Although honestly not very often. I was really in love.

We'd go to the Palladium to catch the big bands as they came through Los Angeles. They knew me and would invite me backstage, to smoke a little grass with them and talk about music. Buddy Rich, who was my idol, never smoked or drank anything that I saw. Tommy Dorsey was the wild one; he drank quite a bit, and with him then he had Pat Dane, who was his equal at wildness. (Once Tommy said to me, "Jackie, you want to see what I consider a real fan?" He lifted Pat's dress, and she had no underpants—a fact which was well known—and Tommy pointed to where Pat had shaved the initials T. D. in her pubic hair.) When I told stories like that to Bonita, she was shocked and turned crimson and said I was awful. I guess I enjoyed shocking her; it was a way for me to appear older and more worldly. She didn't like the language the musicians used either.

■ ■ ■

BONITA GRANVILLE WRATHER: Jackie and I did very glamorous things together. We also did a couple of very funny things. One of our special dates—we did this quite often, I might add—he would pick me up, and we would go to the Hollywood Palladium, and we'd get seated at a very nice table, and then Jackie would proceed to go up onstage, and Buddy Rich was the drummer, it was the Dorsey band. Buddy Rich was the drummer, Ziggy Elman played trumpet, Joey Bushkin played piano, and for a while I think Skitch Henderson played piano, and Sinatra was with the group, and Jo Stafford and the Pied Pipers and Connie Haines—it was a super thing. But I used to spend the evening with Buddy Rich at the table and Jackie sat in at the drums. I must say after a while that caused a little upset and friction. I think it's funny now. He did love to play the drums.

■ ■ ■

Bonita didn't like musicians. She kept talking to me, very seriously, almost as a mother would, about "the company" I was keeping. Especially after my mother died, she began to adopt a very maternal attitude toward me and my life. She felt that I was frittering away my talent and that "the company" I kept was dragging me ever downward.

I wanted to win her approval, so I thought seriously about doing what she said. And yet I liked musicians, and Buddy Rich was a particular friend. I was torn. She didn't like them, and they thought she was square. They also had the musicians' basic philosophy—namely, that a woman was a woman, and no more and no less, and that one woman was pretty much like another woman. That idea infuriated her because she was very much a liberated woman, in the days when liberated women didn't march about it.

It was a dilemma, and so I was pleased to be able to escape without having to make a choice. That was when the USO tour came up, which Taurog had arranged so I would get in good graces with my draft board. It was a three-week trip, followed by a four-week vaudeville tour, and then, while I was away, they added another three weeks of USO shows. So I was gone about two and a half months.

During those two and a half months Bonita and I wrote. We didn't call because in those days kids used long-distance telephone pretty much for emergencies only, not for simple conversations. But we wrote. My letters were passionate. Hers were reserved. She talked of her work mostly, and she was doing a movie called *The Rising Sun*, for director Edward Dmytryk, with a good-looking actor in his twenties named Tim Holt.

When I got home finally, I took her out to our favorite restaurant, The Players. And strange things began happening. A lot of people drifted over to our table and began talking to Bonita—men, mostly. That hadn't happened before. She said they were people she had met through Tim Holt.

One of them was a cheerful Irishman named Bud McTaggart. He was a bit player trying to make it as an actor, and I liked him. (He didn't live much longer, unfortunately.) Bud sat with us and said he needed a place to live. I found him a small apartment in my building, and we became chummy. He said he wanted to introduce me to some girl. He said that in the ten weeks I had been away, Bonita had blossomed and was now dating the world. He told me she had even gone out with Bill Smith, who had been my mother's friend and contemporary. Bill later confirmed that.

As far as I was concerned, that was the end of my romance

with Bonita. I suppose it was wrong of me to expect total fidelity since I had hardly been totally faithful myself.

There had been one night, for example, when I was out with Bonita at a party at the home of Barron Polan, the agent. I was eighteen then; my mother was still living. Judy Garland was at the party. She was Barron's date. She whispered to me that she was bored, and she said that I should get rid of Bonita and come back and take her home. I couldn't resist her, although I knew what Judy was about and what her proposition meant. So I took Bonita home and came back to the party and got Judy and took her home. She was still living at home then, but she didn't get along with her stepfather, so she had a separate entrance to her own part of the house, and she could literally lock herself away from the rest of the place.

We had a rowdy old time that night. She was a big girl, and I was a big boy, and it was a great night. But I knew, and she made clear, that this was all it was, and I didn't even try to call her again. I never told Bonita.

I should have understood. Ten weeks apart is a long time. I had hardly been celibate when I was on that USO/vaudeville tour—I had worked some with the Charlie Barnet band on that trip, and there had been a lot of girls and grass and not what you would call the constructive life, and it had been fun. But the double standard was around then, and I expected Bonita to be sitting at home, waiting for me, and she had, instead, done the natural thing and had gone out and had fun.

That was the end. We drifted apart.

■ ■ ■

BONITA GRANVILLE WRATHER: Jackie was really my first romance. Mother had always been kind of strict, and I never had a chance to date and go out and do things like that like everybody else; they all started a little earlier than I did. So this [dating Jackie] was when I was about seventeen. I think Jackie had a couple of serious romances [before me]. I look fondly back on it because it was very glamorous.

■ ■ ■

20.

I saw vaudeville die. At the very least, I watched it on its deathbed, gasping for breath and not getting any.

It was 1947, after the war, when Hollywood had no need for me and I tried Broadway, which didn't immediately accept me either. So I signed on for one last fling of vaudeville, on a decrepit old wheel called the Fineberg Circuit, playing places like Binghamton, New York, and Pottsville, Pennsylvania, and Springfield, Massachusetts.

I didn't do any of my old act this time. I talked some about my childhood in pictures and then got into some Army and Navy jokes, and I sang "Oe Marie" in English and Italian.

There were the pitiful old vaudevillians, unaware that their world had crumbled, who did the same beat-up act they had been doing for decades. And they didn't realize that that box in the living room—television—was making them anachronisms. I met a few young people—like Alan King and Gary Morton, who later married Lucille Ball—who used vaudeville then as a training ground. And a few acts, like me, who were just biding their time until something else came along. So we all trouped around those towns, where the pit bands were awful and the hotels were second-rate. We survived.

That same year MCA, for whom a client must earn money, tried to make me into a nightclub act. I played the Town Casino in Buffalo and a place in Rochester. In the latter spot I shared the bill with Jane Russell.

We weren't exactly knocking them dead. Her act was dying, and she was drinking some. I was bombing, too, and I think one reason was that they expected blue material—they expected anybody who talked in clubs then to do blue material—and I wouldn't.

Jane would sing, and I played drums in her backup band. She would often forget the lyrics, and I'd have to prompt her.

After the show she and her pianist and I would go to our hotel and drink beer together. She was all right. It was a hard time for her. It was a hard time for me. It was a hard time for show business.

I had been part of vaudeville in its glory years, and it was tragic to watch it fall apart. I owed vaudeville a lot—not only the money I earned but the things I learned. Later, when I did comedies on the Broadway stage, I realized just how much I owed to my vaudeville years. I had developed an instinct about audiences; I could read them within less than a minute of walking onstage.

It helped me, later on Broadway, recognize the audience for what it was, and what it wanted, and alter my performance accordingly.

My last few years on the road, in the prewar days, had been difficult. In 1940 I traveled alone, because my mother's health was going downhill, and she couldn't make the trip. So that year I did only four weeks, and I'd call home every day to ask how things were. I'd generally say that I was just about to go to bed, but I wasn't, and she knew I wasn't, and I knew she knew I wasn't. But for both our sakes, we kept up the fiction, and she would say, "That's good, Jackie, have a good sleep."

It was a wild time, those prewar years, because everybody knew the war was coming, everybody had a feeling of living for the moment, the defense industry gave everybody jobs and money. Nobody wanted to know names or histories, just whether or not you were alive and capable of love. The people in our business, who traditionally were less frustrated than the general public, loosened up even more.

In Hollywood, as the war approached, there were endless processions of shows to raise money for this war charity or that one. I worked in several—my guilty conscience showing through—and in one for *Bundles for Britain* I did a skit with Rita Hayworth. I also did a dance number with Bonita and an adagio number with Simone Simon, but the skit with Rita brought down the house. We had material from an André Charlot revue, and it worked out well for us. Rita was only a starlet then, but certainly a beauty (although later they did things with her hairline that enhanced her beauty), and the skit was good material.

That last tour, in 1942, between the USO engagements, was the wildest of all. Because of the war, we had to do more and more shows. I remember in Boston, with Louis Prima, doing six shows a day during the week and eight on weekends. And

I loved it. I played New York, too, working at the Strand, down the street from Tommy Dorsey at the Paramount. I played the drums and did the Charlot skit and enjoyed it. But always there was that feeling that I should be doing something more, that there was a war going on, and what was I doing in a silly skit on the vaudeville stage?

21.

I think maybe the only time I really regretted being recognizable was during the war. It was tough on celebrities then. The officers wanted to show everybody they didn't play favorites, so they were twice as hard on us. The men wanted to show us they were as good as we were, so they would go out of their way to pick fights with us, to prove they were our equals or betters.

Mickey Rooney had it tough, and he tried very hard to get out. Dan Dailey told me this story and swore it was true. Rooney was assigned to latrine duty by some officer who got his jollies by saying that he had assigned Mickey Rooney to cleaning toilets. Rooney did it awhile, but when he kept getting it again and again, he naturally wanted out. One day he knew there was a big inspection coming, and he cleaned his latrine until it shone. Then, in one bowl, he spread a few big blobs of peanut butter just about the water level.

During the inspection the inspecting officer noticed those brown blobs.

"What's that, Private Rooney?"

Rooney stepped forward, scooped up some of the brown stuff on his forefinger, put it in his mouth, tasted it, then gave the officer a smart salute.

"Shit, sir," he said.

He got his discharge very shortly after that incident.

In my time in the Navy I'd get into fights in any bar with guys who saw me and would immediately start razzing me about all the pictures I'd done. The Shore Patrol would usually say it was my fault, no matter how many witnesses said the other guys had started it. Like all the other celebrities in uniform, I had to work twice as hard to get half as far. Any tiny slip-up, and they would always say something like "This isn't Hollywood, Cooper; you can't get away with that stuff here."

And yet for the duration I wouldn't have wanted to be anyplace else. It would have been worse outside, getting the sneers from women wondering why you weren't in uniform.

Besides, there was that patriotic consideration—my country was in a desperate war, and I wanted to do my part, corny as that might sound, so we would win.

I had registered for the draft in California during a USO vaudeville tour and I was in Massachusetts when Norman Taurog called me and said it was time to report to the nearest draft board. I began by taking my pre-Navy entrance test to see if I was mentally qualified for the Navy's V-12 program. I remember that one part of it required me to write a 500-word essay on myself, my life, my capabilities. I wrote it all very seriously. In 1962, when as a reserve naval officer I went to the Bureau of Personnel, they let me see my service jacket, with all my records in it. That 500-word essay was in it, and I read it in amazement. Almost everything I had thought in 1942 had changed in the subsequent twenty years. I doubt that I would have recognized myself, but it was in my handwriting.

Then I had to go down and take another test at a recruitment center. This was really my first brush with the rank and file of the military, and I got my first taste of being elbowed around and the first of many times hearing that belligerent whine "I bet you think you're somebody, don't you?"

In due time I received the word that I had passed all my tests and that I was to start the new semester somewhere in Montana. It sounded okay to me, but not to Taurog. He didn't think I was ready to be on my own either socially or academically. I agreed with him about the academic part—I had had only a couple of years of classroom instruction in grammar school (kindergarten and first grade) and a year in high school in the public school system. Everything else had been under private tutors. Taurog said I'd never be able to keep up at the college level, especially with the accelerated system of the V-12 program. He convinced me he was right. He also felt that I would have too many problems getting along with the other guys on a social level; I recognized that there would be problems, but I felt that I would be able to handle them and to adjust to Navy life.

Still, Taurog decided that Montana was not for me. He pulled more strings, and even before I was sworn in, I was transferred. Now I was told to report to Loyola, in the Los Angeles area. I think he told the Navy I was Catholic and should go to a Catholic institution, hence the Loyola assignment.

Taurog was right about one thing. He had looked into the

V-12 program and concluded it was trying to do too much. He said that very few kids would be able to finish four years of college in two and a half years, which was the aim. He said young boys just could not go to school steadily, six days a week, for thirty months and hope to learn very much. He was right, and the government soon realized it had made a mistake. The V-12 program developed problems when many of the kids began failing. Eventually they would change the system, but not soon enough for me.

I was having my hands—and my mind—full at Loyola. So Taurog hired a tutor for me. As a Loyola undergraduate I was not required to wear a uniform and could live at home. This was great for my social life, which flourished as before, but it was hell on my studies. So Taurog hired a USC professor to tutor me. His main job was to teach me good study habits, of which I had none. I had always scored okay in IQ tests, but I had never learned how to study, and now it was essential.

I liked English, and I got good grades in that. The rest of the stuff was very tough, and my marks reflected that. I'd not been to school in almost five years and had had no math in seven years.

In my defense, I had distractions. We all did. Most of my classmates were, like me, young and excited about being in the Navy, and this was just something we had to get through before we got our ensign's stripes and began winning the war. So we all had a lot of fun.

My fun was a continuation of the pre-Loyola fun. I had my apartment, peopled with girls and friends, full of booze and laughter. I'd be partying until one, then up at six to go to school. Taurog was trying to check up on me, so I'd call him every night at around ten o'clock and tell him that I had finished my studying and was turning in. But then I'd really turn out, instead of in, and off I'd go.

We finished our time at Loyola and were all transferred and put into uniform. As a "Catholic," I was shipped to Notre Dame, in South Bend, Indiana. Overnight things changed for me. It was the end of the gay life: formations; bugle calls; march to class; march to the mess hall; calisthenics every morning at five-thirty; the obstacle course every afternoon. I was having academic problems, as usual, so I would sneak into the head at night to study late, and frequently I'd get caught, and that meant demerits and more trouble.

It was not a happy time for me. I was in with strangers and

had a hard time making friends. The officers and noncoms kept after me, of course, leaning on me twice as hard as on the rest of the men. So I'd try twice as hard. The result was that I soon developed a nervous cough.

I was in a room with two guys who had been Regular Navy and had wangled transfers back into the V-12 program. They were veterans and never let me forget it. I kept them awake at night with my coughing. They kept telling me to get up and get a glass of water or something, and I'd get up and get a glass of water, but as soon as I lay down, the cough would start up again.

I'd go to sick bay with my cough, and the Navy doctors would give me a pill or some cough medicine, but it didn't help. All it meant was that I'd have missed something—a muster or a class or something—and get in more trouble.

I made a few friends. There was, I remember, a guy from Aurora, Indiana, and another from Niles, Michigan, and a third from Cincinnati. On weekend pass I'd go to their homes—but it turned out to be a bore. I'd get a good home-cooked meal for a change, but also a procession of their friends and relatives would come in to gawk at me and get an autograph and ask me what Wallace Beery was really like. I soon learned that those weekends would be grim, but I felt obligated to go home with the guys because they at least had been nice to me.

I made one friend in South Bend—the local FBI agent. We would go to quiet restaurants for dinner and talk. I wondered why an FBI agent was on a college campus and asked him, and he gave me a story about how there always was an agent around a Navy base. But later, when the atom bomb was dropped, there was a picture in the paper with all the men who had had anything to do with its development, and one of those men was a Notre Dame physics prof. My FBI friend sent me that picture, with the Notre Dame prof's picture circled, and he wrote, "Now you know why I was there."

I soon learned what I could—and couldn't—do in town. There were a few clubs in South Bend, favorite hangouts of the servicemen. If I went there, I could guarantee trouble. The girls would come over to talk to me—just innocent talk usually—and their boyfriends wouldn't like that. Almost automatically, try as I might to avoid it, a fight would break out. I had my lip cut often, my head cut. I could take care of myself, but the odds were usually against me. So I soon decided it wasn't worth the effort, and I'd stay away from those clubs.

There was a small contingent of WAVEs in town, yeomen, which meant they were doing secretarial chores. One of them was kind of sweet and did me a few favors. I dated her a few times, and we got along nobly, and she was cute and didn't drink. I'd be able to get her in the sack and out and back to her base by midnight. As far as I was concerned, it was a pleasant arrangement. No strings, no commitments, no talk of love on either side.

One night I was in my room, and an officer came in and said I had to report immediately to the Oliver Hotel, to the officer in charge of the WAVE detachment. I asked why.

"He'll tell you when you get there," the officer told me.

They drove me into town, and I got to the hotel and found the officer, and she said that this WAVE—the one I knew— was locked in her room, drunk, screaming and crying, saying she was in love with Jackie Cooper but that he didn't love her, and threatening to jump out of the window and kill herself. I couldn't believe it—I had never seen her drink, she had never said a word to me about love, and I always thought she was a particularly well-adjusted girl.

As soon as I got there, the Shore Patrol broke down the door. She was sitting on the window ledge and said she'd jump if anybody came closer. I tried to talk to her. I went into the room only a few inches because I didn't want to frighten her, but I began to edge my way across the room, talking all the way. I don't think she really wanted to jump—psychologists say that suicides who want to do it usually don't kid around, but do it quickly—because pretty soon she put her legs back over the windowsill, and I grabbed her, and the Shore Patrol were right behind me. They took her away, gave her a shot, and I never saw her again. I don't know if they transferred her or discharged her. I had known a couple of other guys who had been in the sack with her, so I never could figure that one out—what had triggered that outburst?

Things had been bad for me. That incident made it worse. Word got around that a WAVE had almost killed herself over Jackie Cooper, so suddenly they all called me Great Lover and whistled as I walked by. The whole thing hurt me and embarrassed me.

I should have learned from that incident that South Bend was not my town. But I didn't. Worse was yet to come.

It was a hard, austere life at Notre Dame. Reveille at dawn or thereabouts. Calisthenics outside every morning, even if the temperature was twenty-two below zero. The toilet down the hall. The locker that held nothing. The daily inspections. The lineup and march to chow. The lineup and march to classes. Then the noon meal. Then the afternoon classes. Then the gym period, the obstacle course, and the evening meal. A half hour of free time, study, lights out at nine.

Saturdays were the same except there was no gym period and no obstacle course. Instead, there was a white glove inspection in the barracks, followed by a major inspection outside on the drill field. Liberty was from noon Saturday to midnight Sunday. On Sunday it was noon to 6:00 P.M. Once a month we could earn an overnight liberty.

They called us cadets. Supposedly, when we finished, we would then move over to the V-5 program and study some more, and ninety days after that, we would be commissioned officers.

When I transferred to Notre Dame, I had the usual forms to fill out. Where it said religion, I had put down "none." But the eager-beaver young Jesuit priests sniffed a backslider and decided it was their duty to save me from myself. Every evening in study period one of them would come around and start talking to me about some religious subject, and the conversation would almost always end with a discussion of my soul. I had concluded that my soul was my own property and my own business, but these pink-cheeked Jesuits seemed to be more concerned with my soul than with their own.

Finally, I went to the dean, Father Cavanaugh, to complain. I told him I knew that the priests meant well, but they were causing me trouble. Their preoccupation with my soul meant that I was unable to study, and I was losing ground academically.

I told Cavanaugh of my academic struggles. Math, for example. I had only had beginning algebra in high school. But now, at Notre Dame, in my first six months I was expected to go through algebra, trigonometry, and on to the higher mathematics of physics. I had a good memory, fortunately, and memorized formulas and logarithms and got by, but my head was spinning. I told him that those six months had made me very nervous, and I didn't need any distractions, such as his well-meaning young priests.

He was nice about it. He said his young priests were like

young insurance salesmen. They had studied all about their product and believed in it, and now they were all avid to sell. He said I should simply tell them that I was busy and had no time to listen to them. I took his advice.

The Navy people discovered that I had advanced skills in sports, and they had me teaching classes in boxing and wrestling and swimming. There was a great deal of competition among the various sections, and my boxing section won—I had taught them all how to move by dancing the schottische—and that endeared me to the officer in charge. Through that, I was able to get a few extra liberties.

Not that there was much to do with my liberties. June and I had become increasingly serious, and we corresponded regularly, and she came east a few times. Otherwise, I'd mainly go off to Chicago by myself, rent a hotel room, rest up, eat at good restaurants, listen to some good jazz. When I traveled from South Bend to Chicago on the train, I didn't want to have to talk to people, so I'd slip into the mail car and sleep on the mail bags for the duration of the trip.

Most of my passes, though, were spent in South Bend. I had abandoned any thought of patronizing the local clubs: too much hassle, too many fights. So I'd rent a suite at the Oliver Hotel, South Bend's largest and finest, such as it was, and throw a party. I'd invite a few friends, a few local girls, a couple of the more friendly officers.

On the night of July 22, 1944, I had such a party. As a matter of fact, Father Cavanaugh, the dean, was among those present. My date was a girl named Pauline, a pleasant young lady from town I had come to know. All Navy personnel had to log in by midnight, so most people, including Cavanaugh, left by eleven. I was just sitting there, having a drink with Pauline and a sailor whose name was George Bender. Bender was with a young girl in a shiny black dress. I figured her as sixteen, maybe seventeen. She drank a lot in the few minutes I watched her, and then she passed out. Pauline said she'd take care of her. I ran down and rented the room next door, and we moved the girl in the black dress into that room and put her to bed.

We left the other sailor, George, in the room with her. Pauline and I went back to my suite. I knocked on the wall to signal George when it was time we got back to the base. He signaled back that he understood.

Pauline knew the score; we had been that route before.

Everything was paid for; just make sure all the cigarette butts were out. I asked her please to see that the girl in the next room got home okay. She said she would.

George and I grabbed a cab and checked in on the base before the midnight curfew. But back at the hotel, the girl in the black dress was out cold. Pauline couldn't get her awake. She didn't know who the girl was, so she couldn't call the girl's home. The girl's mother had missed her daughter and called the police. The cops checked around and somehow found out that the girl was with Jackie Cooper at the Oliver Hotel.

SOUTH BEND, Ind., Aug. 5 (AP)—Jackie Cooper, the former child star now in the Navy, has been arrested here and charged with contributing to the delinquency of two teenage girls, aged 15 and 16. The arrest of Cooper and several others followed a drinking brawl on July 22 in a local hotel.

Also accused are George Bender, 24, Sheffield, Ill.; Miss Pauline Frederick, 19, South Bend; and Olie Lowery, a Negro waiter at the South Bend Hotel.

The girls said they had been approached by Miss Frederick and asked to go to a party. At the hotel, the girls were "plied with liquor." The sixteen-year-old excused herself and disappeared. The younger girl said she had three scotches, some bourbon and a bottle of beer.

Miss Frederick and Cooper are accused of helping Bender convince her to go upstairs with him to a room the movie actor had rented.

The case parallels the story of Cooper's last prewar movie, "Where Are Your Children?"

HOLLYWOOD, Calif. Aug. 5 (AP)—June Horne, 25-year-old movie bit player and daughter of director James W. Horne, and fiancée of Jackie Cooper, says she still believes in her fiancé despite his current difficulties.

"He just isn't that kind of boy," Miss Horne said today.

The only thing I was actually guilty of—or even accused of—was contributing to the delinquency of a minor because I had rented the room where George had supposedly fooled around with the girl.

Nobody accused me of anything else, yet the headlines were all painting me with a very heavy brush: JACKIE COOPER INVOLVED WITH 14-YEAR-OLD GIRL ON MORALS CHARGE.

But they wait for movie stars, you know. The slightest infraction is immediately made into a *cause célèbre*. Celebrities have to be much more careful of their behavior than anybody else because of that very thing.

Taurog called up, very concerned. He said he'd get Jerry Giesler, then the top Hollywood trial lawyer, and have him on the next plane. I said no, thanks. I somehow knew that if I needed a lawyer, I should have a local one.

So I went to see my FBI agent friend, and he got me a very good South Bend attorney. The trial didn't come up until the fall—October—so I had two months of sweating and thinking.

For the first month I was restricted to the post. Then I could get out, and I tried going to South Bend, but that proved to be a mistake. The local folk yelled terrible things at me. So I went to Chicago. No better. A woman came up to me in a restaurant and spit on my uniform. She said she had a son in Guadalcanal.

For a while I kept up my academic work. But my heart was no longer in it. The combination of the emotional trauma of being arrested, the ostracism of the people, the crank letters which flooded in, and the studies themselves piled up on me until I couldn't handle it.

So one day I said the hell with it. I went to sleep and let my studies go. And I didn't give a damn after that.

The trial was nothing.

SOUTH BEND, Ind., Oct. 4 (AP)—Jackie Cooper, ex-actor now a Navy trainee, 22, has been returned to his base in Notre Dame after being found innocent of a morals charge. His co-defendants were also cleared.

The judge ruled that if the one girl had gone home—I had never even known *that* one was there, incidentally—then the other one could have gone home, too. She stayed, obviously, because she wanted to stay, not because anyone had forced her to.

A combination of incomplete grades and a lot of demerits got me transferred out of the V-12 program into the inductees' Navy. They put me in boot training at the Great Lakes Naval Station.

Everybody told me that if I thought Notre Dame was tough, I should be prepared for something REALLY tough—boot training. But it was just the opposite. Compared to Notre Dame, boot training was a breeze. I actually enjoyed it.

The first time I went to Chicago after my arrest, I went to see a newspaper friend of mine at the Chicago *Herald-American*. I wanted to show him something. I had a copy of the paper reporting my arrest with the headline SKIPPY JAILED, and I compared it to a framed headline in his office that read WAR DECLARED. I measured them both, and they were exactly the same size. I said that it seemed to me that the two stories were not of equal historical significance. I said to him that I was only twenty-two years old and had a whole life ahead of me, a life that he and his colleagues apparently did not mind ruining.

"What are you trying to do?" I asked him.

"I'm selling newspapers, son."

The whole thing did affect my life. It was the straw that made me quit my V-12 studies. If I'd gone on, who knows what might have happened? It affected the girl, Pauline, too. She was a very decent young lady, and the publicity ruined her, and she, too, quit college.

As soon as I reached Great Lakes, I was called into the office of a lieutenant who had me stand at attention while he delivered the lecture I had heard so often: "Just because you're Jackie Cooper, don't think you're going to get away with anything around here."

This time, however, I had revenge. A couple of days later the base commander invited me to his home for cocktails and dinner. He even drove me to his home and back again. I told him about the lieutenant and what he had had to say to me. Within a week that lieutenant was transferred to some unpleasant overseas assignment.

Four thousand miles away my future was being decided, although I knew nothing about it. Claude Thornhill, the bandleader, had been part of the band Artie Shaw had put together in the Navy. But that band had broken up, and Chief Petty Officer Thornhill was reassigned to the staff of an admiral. His assignment was mostly to play piano for the admiral when he entertained. That was okay for a while, but Claude quickly got bored with that, and he asked the admiral—Vice-Admiral Calhoun—if he could form another band. He wanted to take it on a tour of remote South Pacific bases. The admiral gave him the okay and a carte blanche to get any musicians he wanted who were in the Navy.

I had played with Thornhill once, at the Palladium, early in 1942. I guess he knew I was in the Navy because of all the publicity from South Bend. He was in Hawaii, and he called me and asked if I wanted to join him. He said he already had a drummer but thought I could entertain a little and play a drum solo. It sounded magnificent to me. He said he had a good band and entertainers such as Tommy Riggs and Betty Lou (a great act—Riggs was a ventriloquist) and singer Dennis Day, who used to be with Jack Benny, as part of his group. I said that he could count me in, and I asked him what did I do next. He said to sit tight, and he'd have all the arrangements made.

The transfer eventually came through. I was put on a troop train, bound for San Francisco. The trip from Chicago to the West Coast took five and one-half glorious, fun-filled days. One of the officers slipped a Shore Patrol armband on my arm and told me my job was to exercise the men in my car. Every time the train stopped I had to take these men outside—even in the snow—and put them through calisthenics for ten or twenty minutes. That endeared me to one and all.

The troop train ride across the continent was long and unpleasant. There were lines snaking through the train for all meals. If I hadn't found a private sleeping sanctuary, I would have been in one of those four-high tiers of bunks, and I'd have to have been very tired to sleep under such an arrangement.

When we reached California, I was given a two-week preshipping leave. And it was during that period that June and I were married. I think I wanted somebody to miss me in case I never came home.

22.

LOS ANGELES, Dec. 11 (AP)—Jackie Cooper, the former child star, married June Horne here today. William J. Smith was the best man. Only Miss Horne's mother, the widow of director James Horne, and Norman Taurog and his wife, and a few friends were in attendance at the ceremony at the Beverly Hills Hotel.

After the Bonita affair broke up, I was really alone. The military was breathing down my neck, and I began seriously thinking about that question: Would anybody miss me?

So I guess I was very susceptible when I met June Horne. She had been working as a film extra mostly because she and her mother needed the money. Her twin brother was in uniform, serving in Africa. Her father had died not too long before I met her. James W. Horne had directed some Laurel and Hardy features, and his death had been a terrible blow to June for several reasons. First, she loved him very much. Theirs had been a close family, and the loss of the husband and father was felt deeply. Second, he had left an estate that was in disorder, and June had to go to work, literally, to save the old family homestead so her mother would have a decent place to live.

We had that in common—the recent loss of a parent that we each loved very much. And, of course, a familiarity with the movie business. There were other things that we didn't share, but you don't think about those when you are first exploring each other. It was only later that they loomed larger. She was older than I was, by almost five years. She had already been married and divorced. And she had a tendency, even then, to drink more than was good for her.

But at the time everybody was drinking more than was good for him. There was a war on! Here's to the Army! Here's to the Navy! And so we had a gay old time, night after night, day after day, as 1942—and my civilian life—wound down.

Even after I started at Loyola, I was still living in my

apartment, still going out every night and mostly with June. The old one-girl-at-a-time thing operating.

■ ■ ■

JUNE HORNE COOPER: It's funny. My dad was a director. And I remember quite a while before that we were somewhere having dinner, my father and mother and myself, and he saw Jack come in, and he said, "Oh, he wouldn't remember me, he was a little teeny kid, and I used to direct him." My father did most of the Laurel and Hardys. And they used to have directors, and they'd skip them around, and he did a couple of the *Our Gangs* with Jack.

Many years later Jack's mother died the same year my father died, just by coincidence. And so a friend of mine said, "I got a guy who's got to meet you, he's real down, he broke up with his girl, and his mother died." And I said, "Who is it?" And he said, "Jackie Cooper." And I said, "That little kid? You got to be kidding." He said, "No. You got a cute sense of humor, you'll make him laugh." I said, "Oh, come on." He said, "No, you'd be surprised, he's pretty adult." So we went on a blind date, and we just started going together.

■ ■ ■

Suddenly I was transferred to Notre Dame. Loyola hadn't been the real thing, but this was. Now I was going away, and it hit me then, forcefully: Would anyone miss me? Who cared about me really? It came to me that in the whole wide world maybe only June Horne really would miss me when I was gone. I told her I loved her. You always love the only person who might miss you; that is only natural. She said she loved me, too.

I believe at the time we both meant it.

She came out to visit me in South Bend whenever she could, and it wasn't a fun trip for a girl, not in the early forties, not on those grimy wartime trains. She would stay in the room I had gotten for her in the Oliver Hotel and wait for the few hours of liberty I might get on Saturday night and the few more hours I might get on Sunday afternoon. Her fidelity impressed me. Her willingness to go through hell for a few hours of my company impressed me even more.

When I got into that trouble in South Bend, she called me and said she believed in me. She said that if it would help, she would come out to South Bend and marry me tomorrow. I think that was the first time the word "marry" was used between us, but I had been thinking in that direction.

For those few desperate months when I was facing criminal charges in South Bend, she was the one straw I could cling to. Over and over again she would write to me and tell me that she loved me, that she was sure I would be cleared, and that it was all nonsense. She would come to see me, and I would cling to her and say how frightened I was, and she would reassure me that it would all be okay.

She was virtually the only person who wrote to me. Norman never wrote to me. My grandmother never wrote to me. None of my aunts ever wrote to me. I did get a letter from my uncle Roddy, Florence's husband, and I was very touched by that. But regularly there would be a letter beginning "My Darling" and ending "All my love, June," and I don't know if I could ever have made it through that period without those letters.

Then I was cleared, and things happened rapidly after that: boot training; the contact from Claude Thornhill; the knowledge that I was headed overseas.

We talked about ourselves and our future very seriously then. June said she would rather be my wife for the short time we might have together, if that was what fate had in store, than never be my wife at all. I quickly called Norman and said I was coming home on leave and I was going to get married, and would he arrange everything? He grumbled about my being too young, but when he sensed my determination, he agreed.

And so, on December 11, 1944, we were married. I tried to figure out somebody I felt strongly attached to who could be my best man. The only person was Bill Smith, and so Bill was my best man.

23.

I said good-bye to June—Mrs. Cooper!—and went back to San Francisco, and then I was put aboard a Liberty ship for the trip to Hawaii. I was assigned a bunk in the depths of the ship, but I had just about found the place when a merchant seaman, part of the crew, came to me. He said he had seen me come aboard, and he knew who I was, and since he had a cabin with an extra bunk—he turned out to be the ship's commissary steward—he thought I'd be more comfortable bunking in with him. He said he'd fixed it with the Navy brass for me to move in with him. I was delighted—I crossed my fingers that he wasn't a fairy, and he wasn't. It turned out that he was just crazy about Hollywood and Hollywood stars, and this was the only chance he'd ever have in his whole life to get the inside scoop from somebody he felt he really knew. So for the five-day voyage he asked me questions, and I answered them, and those I didn't know I made up; he never knew the difference, and it made him happy, and he gave me a lot of good extra rations, and that made me happy. Most of the time when I wasn't being Mr. Information Please, I ate and slept.

Claude Thornhill's troop had been assigned space at the Aiea Naval Hospital on Oahu. It was a strange place for a band to rehearse, but that was all that was available. I was promoted to seaman third class and started working. I put together a little act—a few old jokes, a little talk about Hollywood, a few minutes of drums—and Thornhill also asked me to be part of the band's vocal quartet. I would have liked to have been the regular drummer, but Thornhill had asked a kid from Coffeyville, Kansas, before he asked me, and he couldn't go back on his word to the other boy. It was unfortunate because Thornhill had always been a swing band man, and the drummer was more at home with Dixieland, so he didn't fit in too well. But Thornhill was loyal, and he knew he'd break the kid's heart if he bounced him, so he kept him and found room for me, too.

It was a good small band, ten men, almost all out of the top bands in their civilian days. We also had Dennis Day to sing, a dance-comedy act, the Graziano Brothers, and Tommy Riggs, the comedian-ventriloquist. And we gradually worked our way into putting on a damn good show.

For us, life in Hawaii was ideal. We had permanent passes, so we could go anywhere we wanted to go. We had it made, but the Navy brass, speaking through Thornhill, let us know very plainly that the first guy who abused those privileges and screwed up would be shipped out to some unpleasant combat station the next day. So we all had fun but drew a line considerably this side of screwing up.

We whipped our troupe into shape, and by January 1945 we were ready. For the next eight months we crisscrossed the Pacific, via Navy Air Transport, playing, as I remember, twenty-eight islands in that time. Our first stop was Kwajalein. When we got to an island, such as Kwajalein, we didn't just play one grand, glorious, gala show and expect everybody on the island to come to us. We were sent to them. We went to wherever there were guys stationed, and stayed on each island until every last man on that island had heard us. Bob Hope, bless his peripatetic heart, would usually play once per island and have audiences of thousands, but lots of guys would not be able to see him because they were stationed too far away or were on duty or whatever. And most of the USO troupes operated that same way. But Thornhill's position was that we would play to every last GI, marine, and sailor on whatever island we were on if he had to drag him out of a foxhole to hear us.

Our table of organization was odd. Thornhill was definitely in charge, but he was a chief petty officer, which is noncommissioned. Dennis Day, our vocalist, was an ensign—a commissioned officer—and hence Day outranked Thornhill. Pretty soon Day began to think along those lines. On every island we visited, there was always an officers' club, and Day would head directly for that, and I think he got infected with officeritis. He began to try telling Thornhill what to do—he wanted to change the order of the show; he refused to sing in some of the smaller places; he finally came right out with it and said he thought he should be in charge. Thornhill didn't take him very seriously.

Thornhill did, however, take his assignment seriously. He was very gung ho about the whole job, and most of us caught that spirit. We dressed in green fatigues and called ourselves Thornhill's Raiders and even had those words stenciled on our bags and equipment. It was just musicians' fun, but on some little islands the troops thought we were real commandos, and it got embarrassing.

Inevitably Thornhill and Day had a falling-out. It happened on Tarawa. Day said since he was the officer, he should be in charge. Thornhill's admiral, who had given him his orders, was far away, and I guess Claude didn't quite know what to do. He was in the Navy, after all, and he just couldn't fight a commissioned officer, not without risking a lot of trouble.

So, on Tarawa, Thornhill said he had a bad earache, and he went into sick bay. He never came out until we were gone.

I think the poor man had just had it with the hassling with Day, and decided he wouldn't take any more. Years later I ran into him and asked him what had happened back there on Tarawa.

"I had an earache," he said to me. Maybe he believed it.

So Dennis Day was in charge. I never knew if he ever received any official orders to that effect, but he just assumed command, and none of us questioned him.

Dennis and I were the only two men in the unit that the troops recognized, and it evidently galled him that he had to share the spotlight with somebody. They knew him from the Jack Benny radio shows, and he had made one movie with Jack—*Buck Benny Rides Again*—before the war. I sensed his envy when I came out to do my spot, and the soldiers (or marines or sailors) would always cheer a lot when they saw me. I was a contemporary, of course, and many of them told me that the first movie they had ever seen was *Skippy* or *The Champ* or, with the younger ones, *Treasure Island*. So they automatically identified with me. Day didn't appreciate that.

I didn't want any hassle or friction. I guess I had had an ego, but the problems I'd had in the Navy had all but amputated it. All I wanted at that point was to do my job, and I told myself that my job helped the war effort somewhat by boosting morale. I don't know if it was true or not, but that's what I told myself. It's what we all told ourselves, and we all felt a little better for it. So I didn't need any problems with any commanding officer, no matter how dull a tenor he was.

So one day I went up to Dennis and said that I would be happier (and I knew he would be happier, too, although I didn't say it) if I was just the drummer in the band and didn't have a solo spot. Our regular drummer—the kid from Kansas—wasn't very good, but part of it wasn't his fault. Part of it was that he had terrible equipment. He had scrounged a set of drums in Hawaii, and they were pretty shoddy. Even before Thornhill left, I had suggested that he could send for my own drums, and he had said he would. I had written to June, and they were shipped out. I reminded Dennis that my drums were coming, and I said that God and the Navy Air Transport willing, they would catch up to us soon. (It eventually took them six months to go from L.A. to the Pacific and find us.) I suggested I play drums only as a member of the band and forget my solo bit, and the kid from Kansas, who also played a little trumpet, could sit in the brass section.

Dennis immediately implemented that idea. Now I was in the back of the band, and he had the center stage to himself. He introduced me once—only once—and I took one quick bow and then sat down and played my drums. I actually was happier, too.

Day was the prototype of the caricature of the officer. He took his one stripe terribly seriously. On most of the islands we would play for the enlisted men in the daytime and play at the officers' club in the evening. Day was very selective about where he would show up. If we were, for example, set to entertain a bunch of black infantrymen in a remote camp, he would beg off. But he was always there, smiling away, when we did our stuff for the officers.

He was, unfortunately, a rotten conductor. He simply could not keep a proper beat. So it was my function, as drummer, to start us off. I'd set a clear tempo, but he could never stick to it. When a number ended, we generally had a long chord, and it was his job as conductor to cut the chord off. Too often, however, Dennis would be basking in the warm glow of applause and forget that job. So usually I'd do it, with a rim shot to tell the boys all right, stop, enough already. But once in a while, just to be mean, I wouldn't, and that last chord would go on and on, while he took bows or smiled at some pretty nurses. After one such chord, which lasted for what seemed to be a half minute, he had a long talk with me. The upshot was that I was ordered—and he put it on that basis, an order from an officer—to cut off all the final chords after a decent time.

Our morale went downhill. It had been pretty good under Thornhill, but it changed. Maybe it was the new officer in charge; maybe it was just a matter of time, and it might have happened anyhow. We were usually only an island behind the war, and while we were never shot at by anybody, the war was often very close. We never got any mail. We really never had a comfortable billet. We scrounged food from whatever mess hall we were near.

Gradually our tight little group fragmented into several loose little cliques. There were fights. So the Shore Patrol on one island ordered us to give up the knives and .45 pistols that had been issued to us. I hid my pistol in my bass drum, carefully opening the drum up and taping the gun to the inside of the shell.

When we traveled from island to island, we took whatever transportation we could get. I knew we often flew over bypassed Japanese-held territory, over parts of the ocean where, if we had to go down, there was no doubt that the enemy would get to us first. I followed the suggestions of an old Navy hand and sewed a rubberized map of the South Pacific waters inside my flight jacket.

We often played in hospitals, where we were asked to walk around the wards afterward, a painful but important duty. I remember there was one kid who had been blinded in combat barely eight hours before. They told him that Jackie Cooper was standing next to him, and he felt around on his bed for a pencil and paper so he could get my autograph.

The war was just out there, and you could see what it did. You knew that the public was being fed pap (we saw the newspaper reports on Tarawa that 1,500 had been killed, and we had no trouble counting 5,500 graves), and you knew the war would last ten years more, and you wondered if you were helping much by playing music. Yet you also saw what happened to so many good guys—dead, dying, blinded, horribly mutilated—and so your patriotic fervor was muted by self-protection. We often talked about it. Were we doing enough? Generally, we had to admit we weren't. Well, then, should we request transfer to a combat unit? Unanimously we rejected that idea as the height of folly. We compromised. We played louder and better.

We did see action once. It was on Ulithi, which had a naturally perfect harbor. When we were there, that harbor was home to some 5,500 ships of the U.S. Navy—carriers, gunboats, and supply vessels. That was too good a target for the remnants of the Japanese Air Force to pass up, so while we were there, they launched a suicide attack from a bypassed island. They first flew around the fleet, dropping planeloads of nails and tin foil—anything metal—in a successful attempt to confuse our radar totally. Our antiaircraft guns were popping off at thumbtacks, at anything that showed up on the radar screens. They were even shooting at the puffs of smoke from other antiaircraft guns. Then the kamikazes came in. I saw one dive at a battleship and miss and go right into the water. Another one hit the small nearby island of Mog-Mog, which had only one thing on it—all the beer rations for the sailors on those 5,500 ships. The whole contingent at Ulithi moaned in unison when they saw the beer storage building on Mog-Mog blazing away. Then one of the enemy crashed his plane into the fantail of the carrier USS *Randolph*, all the ammo aboard its aircraft blew up, and hundreds of sailors were killed.

The day after, we went aboard what was left of the hangar deck of the *Randolph*, and there were ankle-deep puddles of blood. From that moment on I recognized how artificial war movies are. They never convey the true horror of war. That day I was glad I was a musician.

When the war ended, we were on the French island possession New Caledonia. It was at the time loaded with Americans. The admiral in charge asked us if we would do a show for the local French, and we said yes, but then four of our guys were hurt in a jeep accident, one seriously, so we couldn't play. Without those four, our arrangements made no musical sense. We had a long wait for their bodies to mend.

I saw an Armed Forces Radio Service station not far away, and I wandered into it one day and asked if there was anything I could do for them, take a shot at being a disc jockey, anything. Sergeant Hy Averback (today a successful director) was there, working for a fine man named Bob Lamond, an Army lieutenant. Jack Paar was part of the unit, too, but they didn't like him much. Later they bunked me in with Paar, and I didn't like him much either.

■ ■ ■

HY AVERBACK: I was on Nouméa, New Caledonia. He came there with Claude Thornhill's band, and I was with the Armed Forces Radio Service. There was boredom in his band, and I kind of got him over on special duty with us, and he and I became very close friends. That was the period of VE Day and VJ Day and all of that, so anyway, after VJ Day those of us who had been at the station for a year—I'd been in the Pacific for a couple of years—were sent up to take over Radio Tokyo and left a complement there to run that station in New Caledonia. The complement was Jackie, Jack Paar, who had been with a special service company, and a guy named Bruce Collier, who is a distributor in Texas now. We left the station with them.

■ ■ ■

We were sent to New Zealand, on a goodwill tour, after our four buddies recovered. The New Zealanders knew about us, and they had been starved for entertainment during the war. They gave us our own plane and pilots and set up a thirteen-city tour, and we played both islands, north and south, that make up New Zealand. We played in concert halls, in parks, in Army bases.

It was winter there then, July, and I still believe that I have never seen a place as magically beautiful as New Zealand in winter. It has a range of scenery that is extraordinary—from gentle farmland to rugged mountains, from sandy beaches to snowy slopes, a little bit of everything.

At the time we were there, it also had a horde of young ladies, eager and inviting. I don't think they had seen any healthy young men in several years, literally. They were outside our stage door every night, by the bevy. All you had to do was point your finger and say, "You, you, and you."

I had one weekend there to myself, and by then I had discovered the beauty and charm of the Maoris, the native New Zealanders. So I spent my one weekend with them, and it was a delight. They were happy people, and all the women looked like Merle Oberon.

That was the end of the war, really, for me and for our unit. After that New Zealand trip we were sent back to New Caledonia, and then, in October 1945, we were shipped home. After a long, forgettable trip, we reached Hawaii. I sweated out a ship back to the mainland, but the sweating-out period was pleasant. I had met a lot of people there on my way out, and I was invited to nice parties, dinners, all that. It was a relaxing stay. Our band was still intact, and sometimes I'd get them together, and we'd play at one of the lovely Honolulu homes to which I was invited.

Finally, after a couple of weeks on Hawaii, I got my shipping orders. They were sending a parade of battleships—five of the glorious old fighting ships—back to California, with Admiral Bull Halsey in charge. It was to be his last command. I was lucky, and they put me—me and some 6,000 other guys—aboard the USS *Colorado*, and Halsey's flagship, the famous USS *Missouri*, led the parade. I slept in a 40 mm gun turret; that was cozier than it sounds. But the lines for the mess were so long that I ate only once a day.

In San Francisco I managed to get a private plane ride to the L.A. area. We landed in Burbank, and there was June, still driving the old red Plymouth she had had before I left. We ran into each other's arms. It was good to be home. It was December 1945. I stayed with June and her mother for a while.

I was still in the Navy, however, and still shy some points before I'd get discharged. There was always the danger I might be shipped out again. But somebody put me in touch with somebody at MCA—the big talent agency—and he told me that if I signed with them, they'd get me out in a month. Naturally, I signed, and the next thing I knew I was stationed around the corner from Vine Street on Santa Monica Boulevard. I was with an all-service band, led by Sam Donohue, and its assignment was to make what they called V discs, which were canned shows that were sent overseas. Ours was called *Jubilee*, and we made it at the old NBC radio studio, and it was a damn good show. We had guests such as Ella Fitzgerald, and it was great to be the drummer in a topflight band, considered a good musician, backing topflight artists and playing topflight arrangements.

In January 1946 I got the word that my time had come, and I had to report to San Diego for a one-day physical and a discharge.

24.

I came home, like millions of other servicemen, with high hopes. All we wanted was a little love and a chance to start our careers again.

I had June. Oh, there were Uncle Norman and Aunt Julie and Aunt Flo, too, of course. And my grandmother was still around, but I had given up on her, and I guess vice versa.

Soon after I was out of the Navy, June and I went to Palm Springs. Julie had invited us down, and my grandmother was living with Julie then, so, of course, we talked. But it was merely proper, icy talk, no warmth on either side. And then, once in 1955, when I came out from New York to talk to the man who was writing my first television show, *The People's Choice*, I stayed with him, and he lived in Palm Springs. So, simply as a gesture of courtesy, I stopped in to see Julie and my grandmother. Again, it was hardly worth the effort.

I never had any good thoughts about her. Even now, when I think about my grandmother, it is a hard thought. I remember her sweeping, when I was a little boy, and pushing me out of her way with the broom, and saying, "You're more bother than you're worth."

I remember her pulling me by the ear. Slapping me. Pinching me. Hitting me with whatever she happened to be carrying. Once, as a child, at the dinner table, I wasn't sure what was on the plate, so I sniffed it—and she pushed my face into the plate of food.

When I did something wrong, my mother would defend me to my grandmother. She would almost always say to me that I should forgive my grandmother—"She's had a very hard life," my mother invariably said—and maybe I did forgive her for the first few years. But later, when I could reason, I concluded that hard life or not, the woman exceeded the bounds of decency and morality with the way she treated both my mother and me.

I didn't even go to her funeral.

■ ■ ■

BONITA GRANVILLE WRATHER: Queenie! What can you say about Queenie? She was a character, just a character. A good old Italian grandmother, who thought she ruled the roost. I never felt she really did, but she thought she did. She was very intimidating, I might add.

■ ■ ■

BILL SMITH: Incidentally, I never said this to Cooper. I haven't seen him in years, but I was with him all the time then. At any rate, when she [his grandmother] died, he didn't go to the funeral, which he should have done. I never said anything. What the hell, you know, why be involved?

■ ■ ■

FLORENCE KENMORE: Julie brought her in from Palm Springs, in to me. We were living in Cheviot Hills then. She was eighty-one. She wasn't smoking towards the end. Towards the end she really couldn't talk. I fed her soup. I was feeding her broth when she died, the eyes rolled back. Julie kicked up a big fuss.

■ ■ ■

I spent a lot of years ridding myself of the family. And more years after that ridding myself of my guilt because I never saw them.

I always liked my aunt Florence best of all. She never pushed, never tried to force herself on me or at me. She went her way, and I went my way, and I think we were both happy that way.

But Julie was different. Even after she divorced Norman Taurog, she was different. Maybe my feelings for her—about her—go way back. The time when we were in the shower together—that always left an unpleasant taste in my mind. Later, when I was a teenager, she was carrying on with our dentist. I came home one night and found Julie and the dentist making love on the couch in the living room. I am probably guilty of a double standard because by then I was doing that sort of thing myself, and yet the idea that my own aunt! And in the living room of our house!

As my mother lay dying, my aunt Julie would be on her hands and knees in the hall outside her door, saying her rosary, and at the same time she was systematically knocking on wood. She always was a little ding-y.

Years later my mother-in-law—Barbara's mother, Charlotte—who is a lovely warmhearted lady, cluck-clucked about me and my family and decided she would reunite us all. To her, family is family is family, and she could not abide the thought of a family that never spoke or saw each other. So she took the bull by the telephone, called Julie, invited her over, called me, invited me over, and we both showed up. I wasn't hostile.

Actually Julie and my mother-in-law got to be pretty good friends, so something nice came of that.

Then Julie, nourishing that faint spark of family togetherness, instigated another reunion and invited me. I went. There were a whole flock of cousins there. It was quite a bore.

■ ■ ■

JOHN ANTHONY COOPER: I really know very little about Dad's side of the family, the people that are my relatives and so forth. He's been fairly private about that. I knew there was an aunt, Julie Taurog, and so forth, and she would always remember me at Christmas and my birthday with a card or something, but I hadn't seen her in years. And then I got this thing—won't you come to such-and-such—and I felt, I've been ignoring this lady for years, I should go. So I went. This was about 1970 or 1971. And I went. And I met all these people—I'm your cousin so-and-so, I'm your great-aunt. I did not know these people existed. I did not even know they existed. And probably would not know they existed today had they not taken that kind of initiative. Since then we have lost touch again. But I met all these relatives I never knew I had. I know my father has some feelings about them, but to this day I have never said to him, "Why didn't you talk to me about these people? Why didn't you say, 'You have a right to know you have relatives; maybe you'll want to meet some of them'?" Obviously he has strong feelings about why he doesn't see these people.

■ ■ ■

25.

When I got back home after the war, I was very anxious to see Norman. He had not written me one letter during all those months I had been overseas, not a single word. Still, he was the closest thing to family I had, except, of course, for June. And we had business matters to discuss. I wanted to talk to him about my career, money, the house June and I wanted to buy, all of that.

After one day of being a civilian again, I decided the time had come. During that period there was no phone service available—there was a phone strike—so I couldn't call and say we were coming. June and I just got in her little red Plymouth and drove over to the Taurog mansion.

It was late afternoon, about five-thirty or so. We were going to go out later for dinner, and I felt this would be an hour when Norman would almost surely be home. He was. So was his new wife, Sue.

Norman seemed to be happy to see me. He said they were just about to leave for some cocktail party, but he sat down and offered us drinks.

Then Sue came downstairs with her coat on. Norman introduced us. Sue didn't even sit down. She said they were late and would have to go, right away.

Norman got up to leave, looking a little embarrassed. We said that we had a dinner date to go to and tried to make it easy for poor Norman.

Norman and June walked together to the door, and Sue made a point of grabbing hold of my arm.

"We've got a nice marriage, Jackie," she said.

I said I was glad.

"But don't ever call me Mama," she said. Then she laughed, as though she had made a joke.

I saw Norman a few times in the weeks that followed, as I tried to get my career moving again. That was the time when I should have pressed him about money matters but didn't, and when he should have educated me about money matters but didn't.

After we bought the house and decided we wanted to have a child, June worked hard at achieving pregnancy, going through all the routines she had heard about. And pregnant she became, a state we naturally, and naïvely, assumed would automatically cement our relationship and head us into happily-ever-after land.

The few times I saw Norman—mostly for lunch, although there were one or two dinners—were uncomfortable sessions. We simply didn't get along. We seemed to rub each other the wrong way without even trying.

When June was sure she was pregnant, I rushed off to tell Norman. I was so excited about the prospect of parenthood that I was bubbling over.

Taurog growled his reply to my enthusiasm. "I think the timing is all wrong."

I imagine he meant that because I wasn't working and was having a tough time finding a job, I shouldn't take on new burdens. Maybe he was right, but it was the way he said it that annoyed the hell out of me.

"What do you want me to do? Take it back?"

And I walked out. That was the last time I saw him for many years. In the interim, I went to New York for a few years. Then I would come out to do guest shots on filmed TV shows, but I never saw him. I moved back to California in 1955, nine years after that scene about June's pregnancy, to do the TV series *The People's Choice*, and I never saw him even then.

In recent years our contacts have been very few and far between. For a while we had to talk occasionally, for business reasons. But after I went to New York and broke with the business manager and agents and all that in California—people Taurog had hired for me—even that ceased.

He was always a hard man for me to talk to. I suppose a psychologist would have a field day analyzing both of us—was he jealous of me, was I afraid of him, did I want him for a father, did he want me for a son, were we both in love with the same woman (my mother)? All sorts of questions, all sorts of human passions and doubts and inhibitions.

I don't know the cause. But the effect was plain. I found him uncomfortable to be around. Temperamental. Narrow-minded. Bitter about his daughter, about his declining health, about his failing eyesight.

Yet he could be compassionate. In 1970 he read that I was producing and writing and directing and starring in a TV pilot. He called me and said he was concerned for me, that I was doing too much, that I should take it easy. He was right, and I appreciated his concern.

Despite everything, I have no hatred for him. Actually I feel sorry for Norman Taurog. I think he tried to do his best for me, but his idea of what was best was simply wrong.

I don't know where I get it. But I just have never been beaten by anything. I've tripped and I've stumbled and I've fallen, but I've never been beaten by anything. Not even by an uncle I long secretly suspected of being my father.

■ ■ ■

BONITA GRANVILLE WRATHER: You want my opinion about something? I remember Mabel so fondly. I remember someone else very fondly, and I have seen him through the years a great deal, and that is Norman Taurog. He's a very sick man, and he's blind, and he's very bitter, I'm sure, but then I also think that Jackie was bitter. When I look back, in retrospect, that's one of the sad things, because it's just—well, sad. I've seen him through the years. Sometimes he's talked about it, and I'm sorry that he won't see you [Kleiner], but he's old, and he's very tired now, and he's very sick. If I wished for anything, it would be that before Norman died, they would reconcile. And I have no idea of the problem or what was wrong because it's so long ago. I see Norman's wife, Sue. I'm very fond of her; she's a wonderful woman. She was Louis B. Mayer's secretary and a top person, next to Ida Koverman, and it's too bad that Jackie never had the opportunity to know Sue because she is such a sensational human being, I mean a fine human being.

■ ■ ■

The postwar period was tough on everybody. It is hard making an adjustment like that, coming back from assorted types of hell and trying to fit in smoothly to the old, civilized routine. It's twice as tough an adjustment when that old civilized routine really doesn't want you.

I had been in the service a little over three years, and I thought I had definitely grown up. I had gone into the Navy a youth; I came out a man.

PART THREE

The Man

26.

I was twenty-three, and there was no doubt about it now—Jackie Cooper wasn't a kid anymore. I even tried to tell people that from now on I was to be called JACK Cooper. I figured that that would effectively and totally kill the little-boy image, but nobody bought it. It was as if Jackie Gleason had suddenly told the world he wanted to be called Jack Gleason. I think I was Jack Cooper for maybe a month; then I gave it up as a useless exercise. I guess I'll be Jackie Cooper when I'm eighty-three. My friends all call me Jack, of course, but the public always calls me Jackie.

It really didn't make much difference what I called myself then, in 1946, because nobody was hiring me anyhow. To producers and casting directors I was an ex-kid star, and who needs one of those?

I wasn't the only one who wasn't working, however. I ran into my old friend Dan Dailey one day. He was crying, literally with tears on his cheeks.

"They just told me at Metro," he said, "that they're going to let me go."

Under the law, when a GI—like Dailey—came back from the service, any company that had had him under contract before the war was required to rehire him for a minimum of a six-month period. (I hadn't been under a term contract to any company, part of my problem.) Metro had dutifully rehired Dailey, but the six-month period was up, and the studio had said that was it.

He thought it was the end of the world. I did, too. And I figured if they would drop a player like Dailey, there wasn't much hope for me. As it turned out, Dailey prospered. A little while after Metro let him go, he signed with 20th Century-Fox and began doing those happy Fox musicals with Betty Grable, and he was a bigger hit than ever.

When we met after the war, it was work, or lack of it, that had him bothered. That troubled me, too. Especially after my son was born, I grew more and more frustrated by the conditions in postwar Hollywood.

It was those frustrations which made me accept a few parts I knew were no good. But I had reached the point where I felt that I had to do something, to show Hollywood that I still could work and would work.

Mary Pickford was trying to turn her husband, Buddy Rogers, into a producer. She financed a Grade B quickie called *Stork Bites Man*, and I got the lead role. It wasn't bad, just not very good, just a type of film called, in those days, a programmer.

I worked and made a little money, but it did nothing for my reputation. Neither did the next two pictures.

I met another would-be producer. This was Sid Luft, who had the notion of teaming me and Jackie Coogan—the two Jackies, two of the biggest former child stars—in one film. We had never worked together, and Luft figured the public, who must certainly remember us both fondly, would pay good money to see us together. There had long been unfounded rumors that we had feuded, and furthermore, there had been other rumors that because of the similarity in our names, we were really the same person. So with all that Luft figured it would be commercial for the two of us to costar in a film.

He tried for months, but nobody else thought much of the idea. But then he had another idea. That bit of World War II graffiti "Kilroy Was Here" had captured the public imagination, but surprisingly nobody had registered the title for a movie. So Luft did. And he got Dick Irving Hyland to write a script, based on nothing but those three words. With that title, and the two Jackies as his stars, he was able to get together enough money to make the movie. Monogram—the last chance then among studios—made it for somewhere around $100,000. The shooting schedule was ten days, about the same as a ninety-minute filmed TV show today. It was a dumb picture, but it made some money—I don't know if it was the title that dragged the people in or the names of Cooper and Coogan together on the marquee, but something did. In fact, Monogram and Luft were so happy that they quickly rushed us into another one, *French Leave*, which we made in early '47. That did absolutely nothing, except maybe hurt me and my career a little more.

I realized that there was nowhere for me to go after doing films like *Stork Bites Man*, *Kilroy Was Here*, and *French Leave*. I didn't want to spend the rest of my life in D pictures, and that was what they were. In the past I had known what it was like to be in really first-rate films, and it was degrading to be seen in such schlock.

I knew I had pretty nearly reached the bottom of the movie barrel when I was offered the chance to play Wild Bill Hickok in a series of westerns that Republic was going to do. Financially it was a good deal. I was to get $10,000 a picture, and they said they would be doing ten a year. A couple of weeks per picture meant that I would work less than six months and wind up with $100,000.

June was ecstatic. She felt it was the answer to our prayers. But I knew that bugaboo about being in a movie series. I knew enough to say no. I knew that if I took it, it would ruin my career and probably turn me into a drunk. It would be a bore and a trap. I would not be allowed to do anything else, and the work itself would be so boring and repetitious that I could not stand it. So, even though acting jobs at my age were impossible to get, I turned the offer down. Later Guy Madison did it, and he played Hickok for five years—and he became a drunk.

June thought I was crazy.

I was insecure and frightened by this time. I still had no idea of my financial condition. It was still the period when Norman and the business manager controlled my finances. But I did have enough sense to be scared. When nothing was coming in, then obviously things were not good. Yet I had to keep up the front, play the Hollywood game. I still had my shirts tailor-made, still wore the gold cuff links, still strolled casually into Romanoff's for expensive lunches, to be seen. I was seen, but not hired.

It began to affect my health. Before the end of 1946 I couldn't sleep. I had trouble breathing. I finally had to sleep sitting up in a chair, but that didn't help very much.

In those days one honored institution was the junket. That was a device whereby some film studio, in order to promote a picture, would invite a bunch of Hollywood celebrities and take them on a trip to whatever city was involved in the film. Generally, we would travel by train, and we'd get to the city and appear at whatever function was sponsoring the junket, then take the train back home. If we weren't working, it was fun—first-class treatment, generally some gifts, or even a little money, a chance to be seen.

For me, who wasn't working, those were the oases in the desert that my life had become. I enjoyed meeting people I hadn't met and palling around with them for the duration of the trip. It was a curious phenomenon. On the train we would become bosom buddies. Once back in Hollywood we would barely nod at each other.

I went on one designed to promote the new film *Ramrod*, and the stars—Veronica Lake and Joel McCrea—headed the contingent that left Union Station for some town in Utah. As usual, the hosts had thoughtfully provided a bunch of starlets for the use of the stars. That trip I met and palled around with Richard Conte—most people called him by his real name, Nick—and that was good for me. I wanted to project a mature image, and Nick Conte was certainly mature.

Art Linkletter was on the train, and he was doing a live interview show. Conte and I were barreling down the car when Linkletter grabbed us.

"Stay here, fellows," he said. "I'll talk to you next."

He was interviewing June Preisser, a cute, bubbly blonde, part of an act with her sister, Cherry, in vaudeville before she became a semistar in films.

"I'm June, and my sister's Cherry," June was saying.

I guess Linkletter was only half listening because he suddenly turned to June and said, "Your sister's what?"

June said, "My sister's Cherry," meaning, "My sister's name is Cherry," and certainly not implying the possessive.

But Linkletter, feeling he was getting into very deep water, turned to Conte and said, "And now here is Richard Conte," and Nick grabbed the mike and said, "Thank you. My name is Richard Conte, and leave my sister out of this."

Another junket took me to Chicago, to attend the Harvest Moon Ball, and my friend on that trip turned out to be John Garfield, or Julie as everybody in Hollywood knew him. We had a good group on that one, including Danny Kaye and Keenan Wynn and Ava Gardner. Keenan taught Ava and me some old burlesque routines to do on our appearance at the ball.

Every morning, while I was in Chicago for that junket, I'd go downstairs for breakfast and would meet Julie Garfield. Like me, he was an early riser. We would eat together and walk from the hotel to the lake and back. We'd been on enough junkets to know we'd probably never see each other again, and so we told each other things we would never tell anybody else. I told him all my troubles with work since I'd gotten out of the

Navy. He listened and then said, "You're lucky."

"How do you figure that?"

"Look, Jackie. Warners owns me. I'll have to work for them the rest of my life. You, though, you can go anywhere."

We walked some while I mulled that over.

"Have you got any money, Jackie?" he asked.

I said I thought I had some.

"Go to New York," Garfield said.

And he began telling me about New York. About the theaters. About the actors, the actors' workshops, the actors' traditions. About the restaurants, the hotels, the apartments, the stores, the mood, the whole New York scene. He said I should go right away. I shouldn't even go back to Los Angeles on the junket but should buy myself a train ticket and go to New York.

It sounded like a good idea. I knew that I could make the transition from film acting to stage acting easily because of my vaudeville training. Audiences wouldn't scare me. I knew I could project. That would be easy. I was a little worried about getting a job there, but Garfield had said I wouldn't have any trouble. I might have to start in a road company or stock, but I'd get a job.

I didn't go back to Los Angeles on the junket train. But I didn't go to New York either. I was desperately torn. The concept of New York intrigued me, and yet there were my wife and son back in California to consider. There was also the conflict between the old and familiar (California) and the new and unknown (New York). As someone has said, the danger you know is less frightening than the danger you have not yet met.

I stayed in Chicago two days by myself, walking along the lakefront, trying to make up my mind. In the end the call of my family was too strong—at that point. I knew June wouldn't want to move to New York because she was a strictly California girl, so I knew a move to New York would mean almost a certain end to my marriage. It wasn't a great marriage even then, but still, I wanted badly to make it work.

27.

I had to do something because I was going sideways, and I was too young for that. I came back from Chicago, from those talks with Julie Garfield, and had New York on my mind. But my friends and June talked me out of that. Peter Lawford was almost violently anti-New York. He said that in the first place I was a movie star, and it was only a matter of time until something turned up. Besides, he said, New York was a cesspool, and the people in New York were just waiting for Hollywood types to try Broadway. He said I'd be eaten alive there.

June was vehement about New York, too. It was all on a personal level with her. Her mother was in California, her friends were in California, and New York City was no place to bring up a baby.

Okay, I would stay in California. But I had to do something. Then I came up with what I felt was a bright idea, a gambling idea, a new and different idea.

I went to see Louis B. Mayer.

Ida Koverman, my mother's good friend, was still his top secretary, and she made an appointment. I don't know what she told L.B., probably something about seeing me for old times' sake. He was a sucker for the old family approach, and I had been part of that old MGM family for a long time.

I told him I wanted to talk about my career. I had an idea, I said, something that was unheard of, but something I felt he would understand and appreciate. Then I went into my speech:

"Mr. Mayer," I said, "as you know, I never had any formal acting training. I just grew up acting for you. I have no certificate on my wall that states that I am a licensed anything. But you know that I can act. The problem is that right now I am not working. I think you, more than anybody else in the world, know that I know my business, that I can act when I have the opportunity. And you, more than anybody else in the world, know that I have a name that still means something to the American public. People who are buying movie tickets now

170

grew up going to see me in your films.

"Mr. Mayer," I said, "I have an idea. Now, I don't want to go back to school. Fortunately [I figured I could lie a little] my mother saved my money, and so I have money, and that's no major problem for me at the moment. What I want to do is have you put me back under contract to Metro. I know the studio has an acting school. I know you have Roger Edens teaching music. I know you have Chuck Walters teaching dance. What I want to do is to be under contract to you and the studio, to go to those classes, but also to haunt all your producers, to read every script that comes through, to find parts I think I'd be right for—even if they are just a line or two.

"Mr. Mayer," I said, "here's my proposition. Put me under contract, but put my salary, whatever you want—three hundred a week or three thousand a week—in escrow for a year. After a year is up, review what I've done in that year for you. If you agree that I have contributed to the studio, then I'll get the money. But if you say I haven't earned my keep, then all the money in escrow reverts to you. It'll cost you little, if anything.

"Well, Mr. Mayer," I said, "that's my proposition."

And I sat back and watched him. As he always did, he took off his glasses and carefully puffed on them, wiped them with a handkerchief. He mopped his forehead, then stood up and paced awhile, giving the distinct impression of being a man thinking about an idea that has been presented to him. It was his mulling posture.

He said that he thought the idea had merit, but that he had to talk to some others about it before it could be implemented. We shook hands, a warm smile, and I left.

I was floating. I thought my presentation had been direct and forthright. And I thought the idea was sound, one that he would accept because it would cost him nothing. I felt that besides being a capable performer, I still had name value, and Mayer knew that, and so the whole arrangement would be of benefit to the studio.

It simply never dawned on me that I had misunderstood Louis B. Mayer. Later others explained my mistake to me. Mayer was a proud man, and he would not let anyone work for nothing. So that facet of the deal was useless. That left only the fact that I was, in effect, asking to be hired, and not for anything specific. Again a mistake. Mayer would never pay anyone a salary unless there was a definite task to be performed.

So my suggestion was one which he could not buy because of his nature.

But as I left his office that day, those negative ideas had not yet crossed my mind. I was thinking very positively. So I sat by the telephone—literally—day after day, waiting for Mayer's call. It never came.

After two weeks I called Ida Koverman. She told me he had been terribly busy lately, but she was sure I would hear from him.

Two more weeks. Another call to Ida.

"Jack," she said, "you're never going to hear from him. I'm very sorry."

And I never did hear from him. I suspect that may have been the low spot of my life. For the first time, ever, I had some doubts about the quality of my future. Acting, everybody knows, is perhaps the most insecure of professions. Even terribly successful actors worry about where their next job is coming from. Unsuccessful actors worry more, and with more justification. I worried very well at that time, in 1947. I had a young son, a wife, and no job, no money coming in, and no prospects.

At home, things weren't so hot either. June drank a lot. So did I, but she drank more. We had a lot of arguments about that.

Then a ray of unexpected sunshine. Paula Stone and her husband, Michael Sloane, were going to produce a play. It was called *Sleep It Off*, and it starred Ann Corio, the stripper, and the idea was to rehearse in Los Angeles, then take it to a few cities to break it in, then to Chicago for a long run, and then on, in triumph, to New York. Ann had put up the money, Paula was going to direct, Michael was going to be the producer, and they said that they thought I would be just right as Ann's costar.

Just the very thing. I recalled Garfield's words, the romantic portrait he had painted about the theatrical life in New York, the camaraderie of Broadway show folk, all that. Here was an opportunity to get to Broadway without the trauma of having to go to New York cold and look for a part. The part had come looking for me.

I said yes to Paula and *Sleep It Off*. We rehearsed, and in time we cheerfully trooped off to Yakima and Minneapolis and then Chicago. I kissed John Anthony and June good-bye, and they would join me in Chicago (June was unhappy about that, but still, now there would be money coming in) when we opened there.

But we fell on our collective asses. The long run in Chicago turned out to be eight grim performances. We closed on March 20, 1948. The triumphant New York run was canceled before it began. June and the baby never had to come to Chicago.

And so, for the second time in not much more than a year, I found myself alone in Chicago, contemplating an invasion of New York. The first time, after the Harvest Moon junket, I had slunk back to California. Not this time. This time, even though the play had folded, I continued on to New York, as I had been planning to do, as Julie Garfield had told me to do, almost two years before.

This time I made it. But New York didn't exactly run up the flag to signal my arrival. For a year I made the rounds like all the other out-of-work actors. For a year I lived in small hotels, sent almost every penny I could back to June, as I did little parts in summer stock or whatever, and barely existed. I did my last, sad vaudeville tour. I was beginning to make some friends, and that was exciting because this was a different breed of people from the people I had known in Hollywood. They were bright, stimulating, enthusiastic. They were interested in things other than show business. Through them, for the first time, I began to take an interest in politics, philosophy, books, art. And I was delighted to find that I could hold my own in that sort of conversation.

It was, for me, a time of tremendous growth. My career was spinning its wheels, but my inner soul was sprouting.

■ ■ ■

RUTH COSGROVE BERLE: When I knew Jackie in New York—that's over thirty years ago—he wasn't working; things weren't going well for him. But he was always very up about it, he wasn't given to depressions or breast-beating or feeling sorry for himself in any way. We would go out to dinner or go to the Copa, which was the going place then, or the Little Club. He was very honest about the fact that it was a point in his career where nothing was happening, but he was out hustling; he was trying to get something and always very up about it. Not up like "I know the right thing will come along," but "Something will happen, I'll make something happen." I didn't just go out with Jackie—Bobby Condon, Dick Condon, those guys. In those days we were all friends, Jackie and Bobby, and if Dick was around, we would always either have dinner together or meet for lunch or go to some jazz place that they had found.

It never occurred to me then to ask Jack what he was living on. I just assumed that he had some dough and was using it up. He never discussed that part of it.

■ ■ ■

JOHN FORSYTHE: He matured exceptionally well. He was a very young twenty-seven. He knew nothing about politics. He knew nothing about what went on in the world. To give him full credit, he always asked questions, and he asked what books to read, which I gave him. I was fairly progressively oriented at that time and still am, and if there's such a thing as a left-wing Democrat, that's what I was, and he was very interested in that, and he got very excited and enthusiastic about all these things that were brand-new and fresh to him. And he subsequently took them all and became a very, very important worker in the Democratic party for one thing. I guess he became an intimate of a lot of very important people in Democratic politics. And I would watch and see, and I was very proud. For example, when he became the head of Columbia Pictures Television [Screen Gems], he did a remarkably good job. If anybody had told me, in 1949, that he was going to be the head of Screen Gems, I'd have said that's impossible. But he did. He matured well.

■ ■ ■

In 1948 I heard there was a play that was casting, called *Magnolia Alley*, starring Jessie Royce Landis, and I wangled a copy of the script. There was a part in it—a prizefighter with a plate in his head—that I knew I could play. I recognized the fact that it wasn't a great play—by this time I had read enough scripts so I was becoming discerning—but it was a flashy part, and I felt that if I could play it and the production was even halfway decent, I could make an impact with the part.

I auditioned. The producers told me I was fine—I had no problem, but the producers had a problem. They weren't sure if they could even open. They were short $15,000. In 1948 a straight play in New York cost roughly $50,000 to produce.

I put up the $15,000. I called Myrt Blum, my business manager, and asked him if I had that much. He hemmed and hawed but finally said yes and sent it to me. I invested in the play, and obviously the part of the prizefighter with the plate in his head was mine.

That decision did two things for me. It made me positive that New York would be home for a while, so I rented an apartment (on Park Avenue, for $400 a month) and I sent for June and John Anthony. June didn't like New York from the first minute she set foot in it. She arrived while *Magnolia Alley* was in rehearsals.

The second thing the decision to invest in the play did for me was to turn my career around. Even though it was, as I had suspected, a poor play, it was also, as I had trusted, a good part, a part that attracted critical attention. Fortunately that critical attention was positive. I got good reviews. The play lasted only a few performances, but it had done for me what I had hoped. It was worth $15,000. In effect, I had purchased a new life for myself.

When *Magnolia Alley* closed, June started packing her bags. She said there was nothing in New York for me—surely I must see that—and nothing for her. I would come home, after rehearsals or after a performance, to be greeted by a baby-sitter and a note, telling me that if I wanted to find her, she would be around the corner at the Little Club. Sometimes I went looking for her. More often I didn't. I knew that if I did find her, there would only be the same old argument—about New York versus California, about her drinking, about all the old problems—and there was no profit in that.

A break in a marriage is always hastened when one of the parties believes he has found someone more suitable. One of the cast members in *Magnolia Alley* was a young actress named Hildy Parks. At the time she was everything I thought I wanted in a woman. She was so thoroughly New York, and I had fallen totally in love with the concept of New York then. June was California; Hildy was New York. Hildy was books and museums and the theater and intellectual discussions and wine and cheese and politics and walks in the park. I had a crush on her, or believed I had.

June hated all that. She packed her things and John Anthony's things and went back to California.

■ ■ ■

JUNE HORNE COOPER: After the war he was offered jobs in B pictures, but he didn't like them, so he thought he'd try New York, which was actually the start of television. And he did two or three Broadway shows which were quite successful; one wasn't. And he was in on the start of television. I moved to New York, but I didn't like it, not really, but that was his life. But he met someone else, you see.

I was in New York three or four months, is all. And he did this *Magnolia Alley* with Hildy. We had actually been apart so much—we were only married two, three weeks when he went overseas, and when he came back, you know, it's like somebody you don't know. We bought the house, then I got pregnant, and everything was fine, and then work was pretty slow out here at that time, so he went on to New York, and he liked it, so he said, "Sell the house and bring the baby and come back," which I did. In the meantime, his whole life is a lot different. And all my friends are here; I didn't know those people. My mother was still living. It was just one of those things. We just grew apart, that's all.

■ ■ ■

JOHN ANTHONY COOPER: I have very vague memories of New York. I have memories of sitting in his hotel room, the Madison Hotel in New York, when I was five, and drawing pictures of skyscrapers and things. They [his mother and father] really didn't say nasty things about one another or about the difficulties with their relationship, and of course, as far as I was concerned, it was over as far back as my memory goes. They split up when I was three or two or something. If there were difficulties between the two of them, I really don't have a memory of it. I don't recall any yelling or shouting, none of that, ever, up to the time maybe when I was in my first couple of years of high school, when I was a little bit older and both of them permitted themselves to say some things around me, but they were both very good about that when I was a kid. I never heard unkind things about one from the other.

■ ■ ■

After June and John Anthony left, I was, temporarily at least, frightened. Even though I had begun accumulating friends and had plenty of acquaintances, I felt alone. I had always been family-oriented, and with June, despite our difficulties, I had felt that we were together 'til death us parted.

Yet more and more I was seeing Hildy Parks. Through her I was getting in with her circle of New York actors. It was a tremendous wrench for me, as it would have been for any Hollywood-raised product, to fit into the New York theatrical crowd. Maybe times have changed, but in those days there were two distinct civilizations, the New York stage scene and the Hollywood movie scene. In *Magnolia Alley*, I had run into some of the most flavorsome of New York's Broadway actors.

■ ■ ■

HILDY PARKS: I honestly don't know the reason why he came to New York, but I think it was one of the smartest moves he ever did. I think it was in New York that he was able to convince people that he was more than just a five-year-old with a funny face that millions knew. He came into an area of actors in New York that was—it was during a period of ferment here, the Actors Studio had just started, and there were exciting young people working here—Anne Jackson and Eli Wallach and Maureen Stapleton and Marty Balsam and Johnny Forsythe—and he was lucky that he came into a situation that was in that kind of ferment. I had nothing to do with changing him. We met in a play [*Magnolia Alley*] that had Julie Harris in it, that had Anne Jackson in it, that had Bibi Osterwald in it, that had a wonderful man named Fred Stewart who was very influential with the Actors Studio. So he luckily fell into a situation with a lot of people who were fascinated with developing their craft, who were also politically very aware because I have always found that—forgive me— New York is more socially and politically aware. It must have been an enormously stimulating and confusing period of his life, and with all of that to be recognized when he walked down the streets and to be recognized in restaurants as something that he had been.

■ ■ ■

28.

I suspect that perhaps the biggest break of my New York life was *Mister Roberts*—which took me out of New York.

The play was a gigantic hit in New York, with Henry Fonda as Roberts and David Wayne as Ensign Pulver. They had already sent one company to Chicago, with Richard Carlson as Roberts and Murray Hamilton as Pulver. Now the producer (Leland Hayward) wanted to send the Chicago company on the road, but Carlson didn't want to go on the road. So they hired John Forsythe to take over the Roberts role in this national company. Hamilton moved to New York, to replace Wayne, who wanted out. So that left an opening for an actor to play Ensign Pulver in the road company, and I wanted that part very, very badly.

I read for the part, at the Alvin Theater in New York, with seven or eight other aspirants. Hayward and the director, Joshua Logan, sat in the back of the theater, saying very little. But I got word to come back later in the day, and I met with Hayward and Logan, and they said they liked me.

I said how happy that made me. But I asked if it might not be possible for me to play the part in New York, with Fonda. I felt that New York was the center of things theatrical, and so I said that I would be happier in the New York company.

Logan answered for both of them. He adopted a fatherly attitude and suggested that at my stage of career, road experience would be more valuable than Broadway experience. He explained that we would have a few more months to go with the Chicago run; then we would have a long tour, mostly one-week stands. He said that would give me the experience of getting reviewed (there would, of course, be no more reviews of the New York company), the experience of first nights (every new town, each week, would be a first night), the experience of sampling different audiences (the folks in one city, he explained, will react in a totally different way from the folks in another city). It all made sense, but the real reasons I didn't argue, and accepted the road job, were that, first, I knew Josh

Logan was the reigning king of Broadway and I would rather please him than alienate him and, second, I knew my road costar, Forsythe, had a reputation as one of the brightest of the young Actors Studio actors. He had just finished a long run in *All My Sons*, with Ed Begley, directed by Elia Kazan, which had been a triumph for John.

I visited with Henry Fonda backstage one evening and discussed it all with him. We had worked together in a western before the war and had a semifriendship. He, too, said he thought that the experience of being on the road with the play and working with John Forsythe would be good for me.

At the time, of course, I had come around to the belief that I was a stage actor and that my future would be on the stage— preferably Broadway, but, failing that, at least on the stage somewhere. So when people like Logan and Fonda advised me to take the road job because it was a learning experience for me, I felt I should do it. In a sense it might be considered a comedown—after my being used to the center stage, so to speak, the road was certainly not Broadway—but I concluded that it was a comedown only for my ego. For my development as an actor, it was a necessary and positive step.

■ ■ ■

JOHN FORSYTHE: I had heard so many outrageous and possibly true stories about kids who grew up as motion picture actors—the Judy Garlands and the Mickey Rooneys—that I didn't know quite what to expect [from Jackie]. I knew that the child star, while talented, was usually on the kooky side. Well, Jackie proved to be everything but that. He was a pleasure to work with. It seemed to me that he was trying to find himself at that point. The relationship between Roberts and Pulver, as you may remember, is an interesting one anyway. It's an older brother/younger brother kind of thing. And he was like a puppy dog with me; he followed me around like you would expect a younger brother would with an older brother looking for the pat on the head, looking for approval—which I gave him, because I liked him tremendously. He was very generous, he was very kind, he was very warm, he was very outgoing—and he was very insecure. He wasn't insecure about his talent, however. I think he was always very secure about his acting. Marvelously secure as an actor.

■ ■ ■

A year earlier I had gotten to know Martin and Lewis, then the new comedy sensations, and I hung around the Copa a lot. One night Dean told me he was moving out of his apartment; did I want it? He knew I was still holed up in a little hotel room and that eventually I wanted to bring my wife and baby east. So I said sure. Dean's place was way up on the West Side, somewhere around 139th Street as I remember it. I went to my hotel, packed everything, got all my stuff from the hotel's storage area, piled it all in two cabs, and went to Dean's apartment—which was now my apartment.

I unpacked and put things away. The next night I went down to the Copa—a long taxi ride—and then went back home to my new apartment—another long taxi ride. The morning after, I decided I had to start living like all the rest of the Upper West Siders—I had to take the subway. So I went down all those stairs, put my dime—I think it was only a dime then—in the slot.

People recognized me, of course. There were the autograph hunters, and the pushers and the shovers, and everybody seemed to have bad breath.

"Hey, Jackie, whatcha doin'? Slummin'?"

"Boy, your career must really be slipping!"

"What's a big movie star like you doin' ridin' the subway?"

The whole experience really made me feel miserable. No matter how much I would like to be treated like a regular guy, I couldn't be. My new New York friends, such as Eli Wallach or Johnny Forsythe, rode the subways all the time, and nobody ever bothered them. When I told them what had happened, they laughed. They didn't really understand. I guess it's just that Hollywood people—and, I think, especially Hollywood people who were big names as kids—can't be allowed to be regular guys.

Anyway, I knew that if I stayed in that apartment, I'd be taking those long—and expensive—cab rides two or three times a day. And I was simply not making the money to afford

that kind of luxury. So that afternoon I left Dean's apartment—
forfeiting my rent in the process—and piled everything back
in two cabs and returned to my old room at the St. Moritz.
Then I found the apartment on Park Avenue, which was home
until I went to Chicago with *Mister Roberts*.

After June and John Anthony went away, I was upset and
nervous for a while. I would go to the Copa. I would go to the
jazz spots along Fifty-second Street. Sometimes I'd wake up
in the middle of the night—I had a lot of trouble sleeping—
and walk down to Fifty-second Street or go to Condon's and
listen and talk to the musicians and once in a while sit in and
play for a while. I was there, more nights than not, until they
closed up at four in the morning.

29.

Meeting Hildy Parks and gradually recognizing that I had fallen in love again accomplished two things, besides the obvious. It made the break with June final and irrevocable. And it woke me up financially.

When June and my son went back to California, I insisted on a financial reckoning from Norman Taurog and Myrt Blum, finally. I should have done that years before, of course, but I was led to believe that all that was beneath me, that agents and business managers and lawyers and accountants were created to free me from that sort of drivel.

It was New York and Hildy and the divorce and being on my own, totally and finally, that woke me up.

■ ■ ■

RODDY McDOWALL: There are reasons for the money thing with young actors. Number one, one's own sense of guilt coming from certain surroundings and making amounts of money that your parents never even made in their lifetime. And then the people who want you to be under [their] control. They're taking the money. Very few people...defend the money [they] make. A lot of people yell at you. You say, "Wait a second, you can't do this. Who do you think you are?" It takes people like Janet Gaynor, that sweet, adorable thing on the screen, who kept saying, "Wait a second, wait one fucking second." And she was right. You don't take all this away from me, you don't. It's not a pleasant profession. It's a brutal profession. It's the only profession I can think of where the accumulation of one's excellence and experience counts for nothing past the moment in which it is lived, absolutely nothing. And when anybody tells you that it does, they're lying, they want something. The majority of people really don't care. It sounds like a bitter remark, and it isn't; it's just a perfectly rational and true one. Sports figures, movie personalities, anybody larger than life—their professional death is received with as much interest as their professional life. If Judy Garland had fallen dead on the stage of Carnegie Hall, that audience would have screamed with as much joy of shock as if the opposite had happened. It's gladiatorial. It's an evil profession.

■ ■ ■

The "final accounting" they sent me was the first as well as the final. I found I had assets of something like $150,000.

I sat down and figured out roughly how much I had made. In the years between 1930 and 1942 I averaged about $1,500 a week. That was for twelve years, and then I added my vaudeville income and radio appearances and all the rest of it, and it was well over $1 million. And there was $150,000 left. I gave all but $5,000 to June and my son.

I converted everything into cash, like an idiot, and handed it over. No argument, no discussion. I just gave it all to June and figured I would start clean and fresh.

Later the physician I went to see—Dr. Arnold Hutschnecker wasn't a psychiatrist then, although he later became one—suggested that I wanted to get rid of that money because that was earned by somebody else. Perhaps. All I knew was that my instinct was that if I started over with nothing—without even that good old pot—then everything I earned from then on would be mine. Nobody else would have had a hand in the earning process—not Norman, not my mother, nobody.

The only thing I regret from the split with June is one hasty decision on my part. June asked me what I wanted to do with the scrapbooks—from the time I started, my mother had saved every clipping, and there were perhaps twenty volumes of thick scrapbooks. I was in my screw-the-past mood.

"I don't care what you do with them," I said.

Understandably she had no use for them (although, as others have suggested, you might think she would have saved them for John Anthony, who conceivably would have one day evinced a certain curiosity about his father). So she gave them away, to whoever wanted them. The gardener took a couple, the milkman, the mailman, whoever. They just went. Naturally I kicked myself about that decision many times down the years. A few of them have turned up. People occasionally write me and say that they have found or bought or somehow acquired one of my scrapbooks, and would I be interested in buying same? Damn right. I've gotten over a dozen back that way, but many are still missing.

When I went into *Mister Roberts*, I was paid $250 a week, and I sent June and John Anthony $100. That wasn't part of the settlement, and June never asked for it, but I just felt guilty, I suppose, and sent it to her.

The divorce had been no big legal battle. All very civilized. In fact, for a while after we separated, we didn't even think of divorce. Then Hildy got serious, and while I was on the road, touring with *Roberts*, she visited me. She came to Chicago several times and later to other cities—Milwaukee, St. Louis, Minneapolis. She was working in New York, mostly in television then, so she had to fit her visits around her work. We talked on the phone when she couldn't get to wherever I was. And there were lots of letters. But in the year I was on the road, I don't think we had more than thirty days together.

Finally, when we were going to play Boston and she would be able to get away for two weeks, we made the decision that we should get married. Then, of course, I had to contact June and arrange the details of a divorce.

I took a day off from the show and flew to Little Rock, Arkansas, where you could then get a one-day quickie divorce. I went into a building, saw a lawyer, signed a paper, and it was done.

That was 1948. I don't know what June did with her money, but I do know it was all gone by 1960.

I tried to get by on that $250 a week from *Mister Roberts*, less taxes, expenses, commissions, the $100 I sent June, the money I spent to bring my son to wherever I was once in a while. The poor kid logged a lot of air mileage in those days, flying alone both ways. He came to Boston when Hildy did, and they liked each other. That was nice, but hardly significant since they surely would not be together much.

Hildy and I went down to New York and got married—we did it on a Sunday, so I wouldn't miss any performances—and had the MCA suite in the Hampshire House for wedding and reception. On Monday we drove back to Boston, and I went on in the show that night.

I was still in Boston when Leland Hayward and Josh Logan came up to see me, and they offered me the part of Pulver in the London company of *Mister Roberts*. They were in the process of putting it together. Tyrone Power was going to play Roberts.

I was reluctant because I had a new bride, and the prospect of leaving her for a lengthy run in London was not appealing. But Hayward and Logan had anticipated that. They had earmarked the part of the nurse in the company for Hildy if she wanted it. We jumped at the chance. We considered it to be a kind of all-expenses-paid honeymoon, in a wonderful city, and a chance to act together on top of it. So when the Boston run was over, we went back to New York, and I moved in with Hildy in her place. I was really a New York actor type now—living in Greenwich Village, hanging around with my fellow actors, drinking red wine and talking about Proust and Stanislavski as if I knew what I was saying. I probably would have grown a beard, too, except it wouldn't have been right for Ensign Pulver.

We rehearsed together, the new cast, headed by Power and me. Naturally a different leading man changes the tenor of the entire production—the *Mister Roberts* of Hank Fonda differed from the *Roberts* of Johnny Forsythe, and Ty Power's *Roberts* was different again. A little stiffer, a little more naval officer.

■ ■ ■

HILDY PARKS: Ty, who was a very nice man, played Mister Roberts like an officer, and that was the one thing that Johnny Forsythe and Hank Fonda never had—they were civilians in uniform, and no matter how—it was never planned—but whenever Ty put the hat on his head, it was always at the right angle and the collar was always absolutely right. It was a dumb play to take to London. You took it to a country that was bombed and couldn't get away. And the leading character bitches for two solid acts about "please God, the war mustn't end until I get in it." Plus there was another one playing in London at the same time called *Seagulls over Sorrento* which was the British version of Navy people trooping around the world, and it was straight out of all the British music hall traditions with the off-color gags and all the rest of it, and it didn't have the selected moments of sentimentality and patriotism that

Roberts had, and the British thought: Oh, yes, of course, we all do that, but we don't talk about it.

■ ■ ■

Even though the British audiences were annoyed at the play, they loved my character, Ensign Pulver. He was a cad and a coward, cunning, an antihero. So they enjoyed Pulver and my performance in the role. I became the unofficial star because mine was a character they could understand. And over the months of our run most of the great figures of the English theater came backstage to visit—that's a London tradition, the backstage visit, even if you don't know the person you are visiting. Laurence Olivier came back to see me. Terence Rattigan. John Mills. And on and on.

Perhaps the only one of the major British actors who did not visit was Sir John Gielgud. It was understandable; he was in New York. And that was a fact I was delighted about because his being in New York made his Westminster house available, and that's where Hildy and I lived during our London stay. It was a narrow, 200-year-old place, four stories high but tiny, and we loved it. I adopt the protective coloration of my environment very quickly—in New York I became a New Yorker almost overnight, and in London I wore a tweed cap and bought an MG.

I seemed to fit into the English scene much better than Hildy did, I'm afraid. That fact was, I think, the beginning of our troubles. It is, of course, ordinarily very hard to pinpoint at what precise moment a marriage begins to turn sour. But with us, it was in London at some point.

Her problem—or perhaps the word should be situation, rather than problem—was that she was too strong for the English. She had been one of the earliest feminists, even before there was such a movement. She lived feminism. She had lived alone in New York since she was nineteen, always independent, always proud, always determined to say whatever it was that was on her mind. That was fine—in fact, it was sensational—in New York. But it didn't go over too well in postwar London.

I had had some problems adjusting to Hildy's strong will myself. I was then particularly old-fashioned about many things, especially some aspects of the man/woman relationship, but I believe I was tolerant and seldom tried to impose my feelings on her. We didn't understand each other—oil and water—but we never fought about that. I respected her, and I learned from her, and I think there was a little vice versa. Her friends, who had become my friends, had patiently explained to me the basis of her philosophy—I remember Anne Jackson telling me that I had to understand that a girl like Hildy doesn't grow up to be some guy's maid.

In London in 1950, when there was a serious conversation, men talked and women only listened. Hildy had her ideas, and it just never occurred to her to keep silent when she had something to contribute to a conversation.

So she would interrupt. The men would stop and listen and then carry on as though she hadn't even opened her mouth. It was very uncomfortable, actually.

Hildy didn't like that. By extension, she didn't like them and made no bones about saying so. The feeling was intensely mutual. Our budding circle of English friends was nipped in that bud. Pretty soon the only people we saw socially were fellow Americans. In particular, we exchanged visits with Allan Jones and Irene Hervey and, to a lesser extent, Ty Power.

Power was a strangely old-fashioned man, considering the fact that he was not particularly old. He was courtly of manner and unbending, although always pleasant and polite. I never saw even a hint of the supposed homosexuality he has been accused of practicing.

Together, we got along better with these Hollywood people than we did with the English people, but still far from ideally. Hildy was pretty anti-Hollywood then—I imagine she still is—and she rubbed them the wrong way with some of her derogatory comments about Hollywood and Hollywood people and Hollywood products. And again, vice versa. Besides, nobody got along very well with Ty's wife, Linda Christian. I got the impression, moreover, that Ty felt I was immature.

So pretty soon Hildy and I were left to our own devices socially. And the more we were together, and the more we discovered we had practically nothing in common, the more I began to think the marriage had been a mistake. But I didn't want to be one of those people with a string of broken marriages and a string of divorces, so I said nothing and determined to figure out some way to make this marriage work.

Since we had a lot of time on our hands and no friends, and since I felt if we had an interest to share, we might be happier, I searched for something we could do together. I had, of course, always loved auto sport. And I knew there was, in Europe, a new (to me) form of auto sport—the rally—which requires two people and is ideal for a couple.

I bought a Jaguar XK-120, gave Hildy the MG. For a while we both went our separate ways in our separate cars. I suppose we both wanted to be by ourselves, even though we never spoke about it. I would take long drives in the English countryside. In a few months, I drove my new Jag more than 7,000 miles, which is a lot in a small country like England. I drove to Wales, Scotland, York, Kent, Dover. That car was my toy— maybe even a surrogate wife—and I loved playing with it, tuning it, fiddling with it, even changing its tires.

I was branching out a bit professionally as well. When I was still touring with *Mister Roberts* in the United States, Josh Logan had visited the company on one of his occasional surprise drop-ins and had told me he sensed in me a potential as a director. I said the art of directing did fascinate and appeal to me. So he assigned me to direct the understudies in London, with periodic rehearsals so they would be ready if needed.

I was seated in the theater, watching my crew of understudies go through the play one afternoon, when I looked up, and there was Leland Hayward. He had flown over, he said, mainly to talk to me. There was a new play by Howard Lindsay and Russel Crouse called *Remains to Be Seen*, and I was the actor they wanted to play the lead. The character was an apartment house manager who was an amateur drummer, and they knew I was a drummer, so the part was perfect for me.

But *Roberts* is a play that has a strange fascination for people who appear in it. They somehow never want to leave it. I had been bitten by that exotic bug, and I told Hayward that I thought I'd rather stay with *Roberts*. I said I'd like to do it in New York or even on the road again. But Hayward was smart enough to talk me out of that notion and talk me into coming back to Broadway for *Remains*. I debated the offer awhile, then accepted.

Hildy and I had a month to ourselves in March of 1951 after *Mister Roberts* closed in London and before I was due in New York to start rehearsing for *Remains to Be Seen*. It was a marvelous opportunity to see something of Europe. And so we did, but what should have been our first real honeymoon turned into the prelude to the end.

The differences between us, which we had begun to notice, were magnified on that month-long vacation. Nobody's fault, just the kind of people we were and the kind of life we had been accustomed to leading.

I had always traveled, I suppose, first class. I had been taught that, I had grown up going only in the best way, and I must confess that I had become used to it, and I liked it. My costly traveling appalled Hildy. She was a very frugal lady, and the idea of spending money frivolously—and everything I spent money on she considered frivolous—was anathema to her. That was the way she was. And it wasn't the way I was. I liked nice things. Even in the days when I couldn't afford them, I bought nice things—I would spend $30 for a custom-made shirt, even if that was the only shirt I could afford.

So I am not totally blaming her. Nor am I shouldering all the blame myself. We didn't get along, that was all. Two different personalities, and neither one of us was about to give an inch.

As we drove through Europe in the Jag, I would want to stop; I would see something in a window and want to buy it. She would automatically say no. It didn't even matter if what it was was something for her; she would say no. If I bought something expensive for her when she wasn't around, she would rush off to take it back. And if she couldn't take it back, she would seldom, if ever, wear it or use it.

So the trip wasn't much fun. It should have been, but it wasn't.

The high point of the trip, for me, was the big Sestriere rally. It was at that time one of the biggest rallies in Europe, with hundreds of drivers. It was arranged so that you could start at any one of several points throughout Europe, and you then followed the prearranged route to Sestriere, a small ski resort town in the Italian Alps. We started from Paris, as did about sixty other cars.

In a rally it is not entirely speed that counts. You have to go from checkpoint to checkpoint, and you are supposed to make each leg in a certain time. The name of the game is consistency. Average times had been determined beforehand and were all given to each entrant, and the idea was to come as close to that average time as you could. I drove, and Hildy was navigator/timer.

Our route took us from Paris to Brussels, then down through eastern France to the Côte d'Azur, along the Mediterranean into Italy, and back up through the Italian Alps to Sestriere.

We had spent hours going over the maps and the instructions in our little Paris hotel room. We practically memorized the maps and the route—especially the last part, from Marseilles eastward across the Riviera and then up through Turin and on around a mountain and into Sestriere. They had given us alternate routes in case the main routes were weathered in—this was March, and winter has a way of lingering in the Italian Alps.

Before we left on the rally, I went back to England, to take the Jag into the factory and have the mechanics go over it. When I told them I was going into the Sestriere rally, they were pleased to work on the car. Mine was, they said, the only Jag XK–120 entered in the Paris group, so it would be a feather in their bowlers if I finished well.

The car was in good shape, and so were we, physically at least. We all left from the French automobile club building in Paris around nine one chilly March evening. They had issued us special license plates with the rally insignia, and all the police departments en route were supposed to recognize those plates, and we could, they said, go through some towns at speed as long as those plates were in full view. My car, of course, had a U.S.A. badge, but I took it off before we left. I'd heard that in rural France the people automatically threw things at cars with U.S.A. badges.

The game plan was to reach Sestriere in approximately forty-two hours. And everything went along beautifully. Hildy was an excellent navigator, and that's important in rallies. We arrived in Marseilles right on the button. Now we were first among the Paris group. They told us, when we checked in there, that there was some snow on the regular route ahead, but that there was a faster alternate route to Turin. It was steeper and curvier than the regular route, but a bit shorter. They said it had even more snow, but since it was shorter, I chose to take it. We knew that the tunnel through the Alps was our goal because beyond that it was downhill to Turin. It was only getting *to* the tunnel that might be treacherous.

It was.

We were halfway to the tunnel, with snow falling heavily, when, after driving for a couple of hours, I became snow-blind. Everywhere was white—white mountain on one side, a sheer white drop on the other, and white snow dead ahead—and I couldn't even see the instruments on the dashboard. So we stopped, but that was worse. The snow was falling in those thick, heavy flakes peculiar to the Alps, and the accumulation was wet and rapid. I knew that if I didn't get the car moving in a very few minutes, we would be snowed in for good. I saw that the road ahead was too steep for us to make it—no chains, no snow tires—and the only sensible course was to turn around.

But I was determined not to turn around. Hildy was yelling at me for taking that route. I was yelling back to the effect that there was no point in yelling about that now. Let's get out of here first, yell at me later.

I got out of the car to see if I could adjust my eyes; the interior of the car only looked black to me. I was angry and upset at everything—at the road, the car, Hildy, myself. I turned back and saw the car, with Hildy in it, was very slowly and steadily sliding toward the edge of the cliff in the turn behind us, and the drop could be a thousand rocky feet. I was so frustrated and so mad that for perhaps 1.7 seconds I actually considered letting the damn thing slip over the edge, carrying Hildy and all my problems with it. But of course, I jumped in the car, started the engine, and maneuvered it sideways so it would stay put. I never revealed that moment to Hildy.

I let half the air out of the tires, so they would have a broader surface. Then I asked Hildy to sit on the fender and direct me—I couldn't see far enough in front of me to steer, but she could see all right, and I could see her arm signals. I decided to go forward, not back—I realized it would be just as dangerous, maybe more, trying to turn around, and we were, I estimated, over halfway to the tunnel anyhow. Close enough to the point of no return that I figured we shouldn't return. So, at ten miles an hour, and worrying every inch of the way that the car would overheat, we crawled up the Alps to the tunnel. It took us somewhere around a half hour. By the time we got there Hildy's eyebrows and eyelashes were icicles. But we got there and sat inside the tunnel—the blessedly dry and snow-free tunnel—for ten minutes, gathering our strength. The other side of the tunnel, as forecast, was downhill, and we continued on to Turin. And at the Turin checkpoint we learned, to our utter amazement, that we were not only still on schedule but still first among the Paris group. Despite all that snowy delay and slow driving, we were okay because the road was shorter, and that had taken care of the delay.

Cheerfully we set out for the final leg, up another mountain, to Sestriere itself. We did fine until we got to a point where I estimated we had maybe another three or four curves to maneuver through and we'd be there. Then it began snowing heavily again. I stopped and again let air out of the tires because that trick had been helpful before. We set out down the road. There had been snow before, and the plows had carved out one lane that was open, with huge mounds of snow on both sides of the road. The plowed part was wide enough for one car to traverse, but no more. Ahead and above us I could see the lights of Sestriere. But smack-dab in the middle of that one-lane road there was a stalled Fiat. There was, obviously, no room to manuever around him. I tried to communicate with the driver in English and bits and pieces of French and Italian, and I understood enough so I knew he couldn't move his car. It had overheated. (Big gestures of smoke and steam spewing from his radiator, the same in any language.) I also figured out that he had been there quite a while and had already walked into Sestriere and arranged for a snowplow to come and get him.

I tried to convey my desire that he and I push his car into the snowbank so I could pass. It is difficult, without the proper words, to communicate vague philosophical concepts—such as what difference does it make to you, you cannot move anyhow, and the snowplow can get you out just as easily from there as from here—so he just automatically said no. When I gestured that I would push his car, he grew angry. I guess I would have, too. As we argued, I could hear the distressing sound of cars coming up behind us—certainly these would be our rally competitors. Well, at least, we were ahead of them. If I couldn't get around the Fiat, then neither could they.

Little did I know. The snowplow came. It mushed its way around the Fiat and, for some reason, pushed my Jag right into the snowbank. Then it turned its attention to the Fiat, pushed it aside also, enabling the other cars, which were by now not two hundred yards behind, to pass us both going on up to Sestriere and triumph.

I finally managed to shovel my car out of the snowbank

after a half hour and got up to the hotel where the final check-point was located. I lodged an official protest, but hearing my accent, all of a sudden nobody spoke any English. They just smiled and offered us a glass of wine.

We checked into the hotel, Hildy and I, and we were both exhausted. I went into the bathroom, drew myself a nice hot bath, and climbed in. And fell asleep. Hildy, lying on the bed in the bedroom, sensed I'd been in there too long, and she jumped up and pulled me out, just as I was sliding under the water. I wondered often if *she*—for 1.7 seconds—had considered letting me slip under the water.

We'd been up about fifty-some hours, so we slept somewhere around a day and a half. When we woke up, our bickering resumed. Nothing major, just a continuation of the incompatible trend. I wanted to go back to Cannes and relax. She wanted to go to Paris and visit the museums and art galleries. We went to Cannes, but I didn't have much fun, and I'm sure she didn't either.

That was the end of our glorious vacation. We shipped the Jag home to New York. When I reclaimed it, I worked with some top New York mechanics for a couple of days, getting it back into good condition, and then told Hildy I wanted to visit my son in California. So I took off and drove west and visited June and John Anthony, then went up north, to Pebble Beach, and raced the Jag there. I drove back to New York shortly afterward, and it was on that trip, in Kansas, that I damn near saw my father. It wasn't a great trip—there wasn't much I had left; there wasn't much I was going to; there wasn't anything in between.

■ ■ ■

HILDY PARKS: The rally. Ugh. Absolutely insane when you look back on it. We were in one of the first XK–120s and had not realized, being very naïve about weather conditions in the south of France, that we'd be apt at that time of year to hit snow when we got above a certain level. And as we started up the mountains over Nice, heading for Turin, suddenly there was a great deal of snow, and we didn't have chains, and we didn't have snow tires, and the French Police did not want to let us proceed, so there was a kind of insane race up the mountain, to elude the French police and get past the Italian border—the Italians didn't care—but by that time we were both sort of snow-blind because it was the middle of the day and the sun was shining and we did not have dark glasses and we couldn't see where the snowbank at the side of the road ended and the road was, and there was a lot of open air down there. It was a very hairy experience. But I think that was something he wanted to prove to himself.

■ ■ ■

30.

Remains to Be Seen was good for me. I opened on Broadway in a major play, by top New York playwrights, Broadway producers. I got a good salary—$1,500 a week plus a percentage—which at the time was extraordinary. I was thrilled to death at the whole prospect.

During the run of *Remains to Be Seen* I did more and more live television. It was all centered in New York then, and they were dying for Hollywood stars. But most Hollywood stars wanted no part of TV. Especially not live TV. To be honest about it, most of them couldn't handle it. They had, by and large, no stage experience, and the idea of acting without the protection film affords, the chance to do it again if you goof, was something they simply couldn't handle.

But there were a few of us who not only could do it but thoroughly enjoyed doing it. There were others who did it because they were just beginning their careers and took any job that came along. And so TV, in those days, was the elementary school for actors such as Paul Newman, Eva Marie Saint, Rod Steiger, Steve Hill, John Cassavetes. I acted with most of them on those great old shows, such as *Kraft Theater*, *U.S. Steel Hour*, *Philco Playhouse*.

I enjoyed it mostly because there was something about it that was like film, and something about it that was like the theater. It had the here today, gone tomorrow quality of film. You rehearsed, performed it once, and it was over. I hated the sameness of the stage—the same part over and over and over. And yet I liked the rehearsals, strictly a stage phenomenon. I liked the fact that, again as on the stage, live TV gave an actor a chance to build and sustain a performance, as opposed to the choppy work schedules of film. In a movie you can be doing a scene from the end of the film today and a scene from the beginning of the film tomorrow. That doesn't give an actor any chance at all to grow with his performance.

To me, therefore, live television was the best of both worlds. I enjoyed it. And I enjoyed the money—as the TV gimmick caught on, and it began sweeping across the country, productions were able to pay more. I began getting $750 for a half-hour show, $1,500 for a one-hour show.

When we began rehearsing *Remains*, I asked the producers to let Rosemary Clooney read for the leading female role. I had met her on some variety show or other, and I thought she had the quality the part called for. But I could see she really wasn't an actress, and Lindsay and Crouse, and the director, Bretaigne Windust, politely let Rosie read and just as politely told me she wouldn't do. I knew they were right. Then they brought in Janis Page, and I could tell the difference. Janis had a quality that was old show biz, and she looked sensational, and we all realized that the part was hers.

I realized something else about Janis pretty quickly, too. It was the same trap I had fallen into before—familiarity breeds romance. We were together all the time, Janis and I, together for rehearsals, for those quick lunches and dinners between rehearsals, for parties, for out-of-town tryouts and all that. Together for the excitement and the pain that goes with bringing a show to Broadway. Together for the good reviews and the bad reviews. Together for opening night and that wonderful old Sardi's tradition, waiting for the reviews.

And so, naturally, I fell in love again.

■ ■ ■

HILDY PARKS: He did *Remains to Be Seen* while we were still living together. And it was as *Remains to Be Seen* came into New York that the whole situation dissolved, the personal situation. You don't know what goes on in a marriage. Eli Wallach once said, and I don't know why he said it, but it may be true, "The same reasons that Jackie married you are why Jackie left you." And that's probably true—the wonderful part of living in Greenwich Village in an apartment that you had decorated with old oak pieces you had found at the Goodwill Industries and the Salvation Army and done brilliant things to with a can of red paint, and all those wonderful meals with mushroom soup and a can of tuna fish, everybody sitting around the floor, drinking plonk and talking about the theater, must have been very intriguing at one period. But [for someone] from his background, I think probably, as I say, I think the desire to get back there and to be reaccepted in a community that he really cared a lot about.... He was intrigued by this, and it began to pall. Or he saw that it wasn't going anywhere or something, I don't know. It was obviously the right career decision for him, and it certainly has worked out very well for me. Alex [producer Alexander Cohen] and I have been married for twenty-five years.

■ ■ ■

31.

On that trip back to the Coast, before rehearsals started for *Remains to Be Seen*, I had told myself it was just a visit. And on the surface it was. If anybody had asked me at that time what I did for a living, I would have said I was a Broadway actor. If anybody had asked me at that time where I lived, I would have said, "New York." Like all my fellow New Yorkers and fellow Broadway actors, I now sneered at Hollywood. Velvet trap. An orange grove in search of a meaning. A city with no point to it. All those clichés. And movies. That was all a good way to make a dollar, but it hardly could be considered A*R*T.

That was on the surface.

But inside me somewhere, when I went back and saw some old friends and some old sights, there was the beginning of a seed of a germ of a minuscule thought.

This was my home.

This was where I started, where I really and truly belonged.

I don't remember now if that beginning of a seed of a germ of a minuscule thought even made itself known to my conscious mind. I did what I had come to do—saw my son, primarily, and tried to get to know him a little—and then drove in a sports car race and then beat it the hell back to New York. And for a few more years I thought I was content there. But little by little, inch by inch, notion by notion, the thought that someday I would have to go back and reestablish myself in Hollywood grew in my mind.

I would not act on that thought for a while.

Meanwhile, there were some problems, mostly because of my romance with Janis Paige. Her early years, like mine, had not been out of the pages of a delightful children's book. Hardly. Once she told me the story of how when she had her first menstrual period, her mother physically shoved her into the bathroom, threw in a Kotex, and said, "Put it on," and slammed the door shut.

And other stories in the same gentle vein. So she grew up

and became neurotic as well as attractive.

We soon shared an apartment, and I found myself spending virtually every cent I made—and I was making a good living—on her. Jewelry. Dresses. All those good things. *Remains to Be Seen* had a respectable run, but it was not a huge smash, and after five or six months it closed. So neither of us was working, except for my occasional television roles. But that was enough—barely—for what I spent on her.

Janis's manager was a lady named Ruth Aarons, and Ruth knew Janis as well as anyone. She knew that Janis, basically a wonderful girl, simply had problems. So Ruth suggested she go to see a doctor named Arnold Hutschnecker. He was, as I've said, just an internist then, although he had written *The Will to Live*, a book that had made an impression on the three of us. Janis went to see Hutschnecker, and she was terribly taken with him and began seeing him regularly.

She said I should see him, too. At first, I resisted—I had no problems. But of course, I did, and eventually Janis helped me come to face that fact.

Twice, on the New York streets, my mental anxieties had led to physical attacks.

Terrible, sharp abdominal pains incapacitated me. I went to see Hutschnecker, and there was nothing physically wrong. It had to be as a result of anxiety, tension, call it what you will. And I realized, too, that many things were troubling me—career (should I go back to California?), and romance (I loved Janis, but could I continue with her?), and guilt (my son was in California, and what kind of father was I?).

So I began to see Hutschnecker regularly. I found I could talk to him the way I used to talk to my mother, and I had not talked to anyone like that since my mother died. Even when I was a teenage boy, full of secrets, my mother could get me talking. Hutschnecker had that same quality; he could listen.

I told him things I knew but had never really even told myself. I talked a lot about Janis, of course. I told him about my early love affairs, how none of them amounted to much or really meant much to me—except perhaps the one with Bonita Granville—until Janis. And I understood why this one meant so much. It was because of the ego thing. Janis was one of the reigning sexpots on Broadway at the moment, and any number of men would have gladly changed places with me. At the time we began going together, she was actively pursued by a platoon of rich and famous men. The thought that she had rejected them and had opted for me was naturally gratifying.

■ ■ ■

DR. ARNOLD HUTSCHNECKER: There was a period when he was very confused. Disturbed. Had problems in many directions. He was very lost and in very many ways not matured, not able to understand reality, struggling for an identity of his own, to get away from the childhood image people had and now be a man. He had no father and his mother—this is always a problem.... He got involved with a woman who was a patient of mine, and eventually that's how we met.... That was a bad period for him, and that lady didn't treat him too well. He helped her a lot in her career, but she helped him also. She is basically a very nice woman, a very bright girl, but confused. He needed a lot of reassurance, and he has not always picked the ladies who could give it to him.... There is a basic kindness in this man, and that made him survive. A child without a parent always feels deprived. He always has to prove more. But you could prove it by—my last book is called *The Drive for Power*—by resorting to power and then showing your position. That wasn't his way. He wanted to prove his worth in some creative way. And that probably saved him....

Jackie needed time, a year or more, to develop the ability to be assertive to a woman. A woman would understand his personality and would treat him with concern and affection, would have helped him to come out of his cautious, withdrawn state. But if you make demands, he will withdraw more. And so if he gets involved with a tough lady, then the situation is completely lost. And the woman, on the other hand, wants guidance but will fight it because she is convinced that he is a man who wants to take advantage.... If you have a strong woman, it's not in his makeup to be tough. Then you have problems. With that breed, you have to be tough. Because they regress, they start to whine. Toughness—not just to prove that you're tough, but you don't allow nonsense.

■ ■ ■

Janis was concerned that her career was slipping, and that only increased her neuroses. She had once appeared in the biggest movies and worked the top nightclubs—she was a very talented singer as well as an actress—but they didn't want her anymore. She still had offers for TV variety shows and night-clubs, only now these weren't the first string—these were the jayvees.

I understood. Of all people, I guess I could understand better than anybody, but I didn't sympathize. I had done something about it. I had left Hollywood behind and had carved out a new career and a new life for myself on Broadway. I thought that Janis should do the same; no point in riding the roller coaster down. Get down and find one going up.

After we closed on Broadway, they asked the entire New York cast to take the show on the road. (The cast included such stalwarts as Howard Lindsay and Ossie Davis.) We did a three-city tour, Cleveland, a city I have forgotten, and Chicago. It died in Chicago after two weeks. I was never lucky in Chicago.

We never talked marriage, although I tried a few times. For both of us, it was our first experience at what has become common practice—living together. I had the old-fashioned values, however, and I was sure one of these days we'd get married. That was how I stroked my guilty conscience, with the thought that marriage would happen when the proper time sailed in. When we separated, we both realized it was a lucky thing that we hadn't gotten married. We were just not that important to each other.

■ ■ ■

JAMES KOMACK: He told me Janis did him two of the greatest favors in his life. One was that she did not marry him, which he wanted to do. She said, "No, you don't want to marry me, you just marry people, that's your nuttiness. And on top of that, you ought to go to a psychiatrist." "A what?" She's the one who talked him into going to a psychiatrist. She liked Jack, and she said, "Don't marry me, Jack, don't try that. You don't really want to marry me. You think you do, and that's what you do with all the ladies, you suddenly get this mother thing going with yourself." Jack told me this much later, when we were forty years old. She said, "You get this mother thing going that you've got to marry them. You're not going to marry me. Go to a head doctor." She said, "I'll be your close friend. Go live your life." He's always been grateful to her for that.

head doctor." She said, "I'll be your close friend. Go live your life." He's always been grateful to her for that.

■ ■ ■

We were splitting costs of the apartment, everything but the rent—she had a thing about that—and she was working more steadily than I was for a time. She did those second-string nightclubs, second-string TV variety shows, and they paid well. I was mostly doing live TV dramas, and there wasn't much work. In '52 and on into '53, I did what I could—I'd do a *Robert Montgomery Show*, a *U.S. Steel* show, a *Kraft*, but those anthologies would use a name actor only once a year. Those years I made considerably under $25,000—for me, that wasn't so hot. I still had a lot of bills to pay and my share with Janis. I believe one of those years Janis made more than twice what I made. That bothered me, being old-fashioned.

I really didn't want the lady I was living with to work, but I knew better than to say that to her.

32.

When Janis and I split—it pretty much coincided with her going into *The Pajama Game*—I moved out of our apartment. I moved into a hotel. Even that was expensive, and throughout the rest of 1953 it was a struggle keeping my financial head above the swirling whirlpool of bills and more bills. Before long I found myself with debts—if I remember, the ones that troubled me most were around $400 at Sardi's and $300 or so to Saks Fifth Avenue. So, being old-fashioned, I began avoiding those places; I felt that until I could pay them in full, I'd better not go in and charge anything more. One day I met Vincent Sardi somewhere, and he asked me if there was something wrong because he hadn't seen me in his restaurant lately. I said it was very simple: I owed him too much money.

"Oh, no," Vincent said to me. "You have to be seen. You must spend at least fifty dollars a week in my place."

That came to about a couple of dinners or lunches a week, with a date, and I did what he said. Pretty soon the bill was up to around $700. When I got in my next play, Vincent Sardi was the first person I paid. Later he told me that he has carried a lot of people over the years that he's been in the restaurant business, and he's been stiffed only a few times.

■ ■ ■

VINCENT SARDI: Now Jackie, of course, had more ups and downs than the rest of the business. It was very funny when I met him. He really was not tuned into New York. He opened in a play, and the first thing he did was to suggest that if he had dinner here before or after the theater, what kind of discount? And it's a little hard for me to explain that we don't give discounts. I said if we gave discounts, half the dining room is theater people working in the neighborhood. But he was very naïve about New York.... And he was broke for a while because he had financial problems from his relationships with women. And

204

finally, he came to me one day and—I forget how much he owed me, but it was quite a lot—and he said, "There's no way I can pay you right away. Can you hold off?" Well, we've done that for other people. As a matter of fact, right now things are getting pretty tough, and I had to write eighty letters to people, most of whom I know well enough to call them by their first name, and they're all way overdue, and about half of them tell you, "Can you wait?" Well, Jackie paid every cent, every cent. I think Jackie's always been that type of person, always paid his debts.

■ ■ ■

My next play was *King of Hearts*, which, like *Remains to Be Seen*, was a mild hit. Another run of six months or so. I guess a few years earlier that would have been a smash, but on Broadway in the mid-fifties, it was only so-so.

It was another turning point for me. It was the beginning of the end of my long and costly (financially and emotionally) search for a woman to love, the beginning of the end of serious acting.

A few weeks before I signed to star in that play, I met Barbara Kraus. Janis was in the out-of-town tryout of *The Pajama Game*, and anyway, I knew that was over.

It was the same old story—I had to have someone to love. I wanted to be in love. I wanted to be loved. I flitted aimlessly, for a while, from one girl to another, not finding anybody who appealed to me deeply. Or even shallowly, for that matter. And then one day I met with Tom and Ann Farrell—Tom is Glenda Farrell's son, and he and Peter Marshall were then teamed up, doing a not-too-successful nightclub act together.

Tom and Ann said they had someone they wanted me to meet. Everybody had someone he wanted me to meet. Usually it was nobody. This time it was Barbara. Ann and Barbara had come from the same neighborhood in New York, and Ann said she was worried about her friend Barbara because Barbara was going around with a married man.

I didn't have many close friends during that period of my life. The Farrells were probably the closest. I saw them as much as I saw anyone. I was still very serious about my career in the T*H*E*A*T*E*R then. I had a lot of acquaintances—the stage actors I tried to curry favor with, a few doctors and lawyers I had met (mostly through auto racing)—but not even too many of them. My head was still pointed straight ahead, at a serious stage career, although I was beginning to get a few twinges of homesickness for California and motion pictures.

And so that night, when I saw Tom and Ann Farrell and met Ann's friend Barbara Kraus, I was very serious. At that point in my life I am afraid I had lost my sense of humor. Meeting Barbara Kraus was like letting a breath of fresh spring air float into the musty closet my head had become. Amazingly I found myself laughing for about the first time—really hard laughter—in some months. Barbara was always laughing at something or other, and our few months of dating were very happy times.

It happened quickly. I would be going with *King of Hearts* to Philadelphia and Pittsburgh for our out-of-town tryouts. I invited her along. She said no. She was still living home then, with her parents and her sister, and nice girls from the neighborhood didn't go away with men they had only recently met. But once we got back to New York and the show opened, we were together constantly. To adjust to my life-style—the typical Broadway actor's life-style, a postshow dinner around 1:00 A.M. and sleeping through most of the morning—she quit her job, so she could spend more time with me.

Her parents—great people, but understandably concerned about this development—gave her an ultimatum: Get married or get out of the house. They didn't want her sleeping all day in the house. She told me what they had said—as a joke, not as a threat—and I remember saying, "Well, then, what do we do?"

"Get married," she said.

That conversation, I recall vividly, took place in the dressing room of the Lyceum Theater before the curtain went up. In my nervousness I put on my second-act costume instead of my first-act costume.

We planned to get married on April 2, 1954, a Sunday when the theater was dark. But I hadn't divorced Hildy yet. That was no problem. Hildy was very willing and cooperative, and we worked it out with the lawyers and got a one-day divorce in Jacksonville, Florida. That held things up for a few weeks, and we finally got married on April 29. New York State wouldn't recognize the Florida divorce, so we went to Washington, D.C., for a brief civil ceremony.

We giggled all the way through it. We were the only ones

who knew the joke. We were the only ones who could see that the judge's fly was open.

■ ■ ■

JAMES KOMACK: Jackie's wife, Barbara, and my wife, Cluny, were close friends. Barbara and Cluny and I were close friends. I grew up with Barbara and Cluny, who was Marilyn in those days, and I met them in 1939, both of them together. I moved into that neighborhood, and there was Barbara Kraus, and there was Marilyn Cohen, and we became friendly.

All of her life, from ten years old up, Barbara was an attractive girl. Got up to seventeen, eighteen, nineteen, and then we all went off to the war, came back, Marilyn—my wife, Cluny—got married to her first husband; the other girls were moving around; her sister got married. But Barbara was not married. She always found some guy somewhere who was either not going to marry her or who was married, who was meeting her late at night. And one day—we were all a tight group out of the neighborhood, Bobby Goldworm, the dress manufacturer, and myself, and Greenie Horowitz, Larry Storch, Jay Lawrence, Don Adams (Don Yarmy then), and Dick Beenien, all from the same neighborhood—Kraus was twenty-six years old, and kids in the neighborhood were saying, "Hey, she'd better get married, she's getting older, and hanging around with this married guy is no good," so they designated me to take her to dinner to explain to her she should get married, she's twenty-six, it's about time.

I took her to Jimmy's Le Grange in New York, sat her down, she's a very cute girl, Barbara, very funny, and we're talking, and she says, "Why are you taking me out to dinner?" and I say, "All the guys in the neighborhood selected me—as a matter of fact, they're helping me with this check. Barbara, you're twenty-six years old. I got to tell you something, Barbara: You got to get married. Get married now, to anybody. In another year leave him. Then at least you'll be twenty-seven years old, and you've been married, and you'll be a divorcée or something. When you hit thirty and you've never been married, every guy's going to figure, what's wrong with her?" And I sold her this bill of goods. Had no idea what she was doing, just that she was going with a guy named Leonard something, he's married, he's Catholic. I said, "He's not going to leave his wife. Can't you find a guy, anybody, pick up a waiter, he can be terrible?" So she says, "Well, I'm going with a guy who says he loves me." I said, "Who is it?" She says he's an actor. Oh, Jesus, an actor, and I was one myself. I said, "What's his name?" She says, "Jackie Cooper." I said, "Oh, is he working?" She says, "Yeah, he's working in a show somewhere." I said, "Does he want to marry you?" "He keeps telling me he loves me." I said, "What do you think about him?" She says, "I like him, he's a cute-looking guy, but I'm not in love with him, he's nice enough." "If he wants to marry you, Barbara, marry him." "Why?" "I'm telling you, you'll be an old maid." I said, "Where's he working?" "He's working on Broadway, in a play." I said, "What's the name of it?" She said, *"King of Hearts*." I said, *"King of Hearts*? Are you talking about JACKIE COOPER?" "I told you his name." I said, "Barbara, I thought you meant some guy named Jackie Cooper—you mean THE Jackie Cooper?" "What do you mean, THE Jackie Cooper?" It never would have occurred to me that she didn't know who Jackie Cooper was. I said, "THE Jackie Cooper. I don't believe you, Barbara." She said, "Yeah, he dates me, calls me up. When I leave Leonard at two o'clock in the morning and he's got to go home to his wife, this strange man calls me up and says, 'Aha, with the married man, see, you're lying in bed alone at three o'clock in the morning. Wouldn't you rather be with a guy who stays with you all night?'" And he's laying numbers on her, trying to win her. I said to her, "Barbara, you're talking about THE Jackie Cooper." She said, "Why do you keep saying that?" I said, "For Chrissake, he's Skippy!" She said, "What does that mean? He keeps talking about Skippy." I said, "Jesus Christ, Barbara, I've known you since you were ten years old, you don't know Skippy?" She didn't know Skippy; she never heard of him; she never saw the picture; she never saw the funny little hat; she had no idea who Jackie Cooper was. At all.

■ ■ ■

I was never going to get married again. But you can't fool Mother Nature, or something. Anyhow, I met Barbara Kraus, and she was twenty-six years old, and she had never been married, and for a while I wondered what was wrong with her. Turned out there was nothing wrong with her—it was the rest of the world, people like me, who were wrong.

She was a sane person. A solid person. I hadn't had much truck with sanity or solidity before, not in the women I had dated or married.

We had a lot in common, too, as it gradually developed. Mostly we had our priorities in common. By that time in my life—and her life—I was tired of wild oats, and she was tired of that affair with a married man. We both wanted a sane, solid relationship, home, family, hearth, kids, garden, dogs, security. We wanted a station wagon kind of life.

■ ■ ■

RUTH COSGROVE BERLE: I knew Barbara before, yes—I knew Barbara after I knew Jackie but before they knew each other. I used to go out to Fire Island in the summer, and she and her family did, and so we knew each other for four or five years. Summers. And then after, I had lost touch with Jack—I think he married Hildy—and by that time I was going with Milton, and Milton knew Barbara's mother and father, you know, it was all kind of strange. And then when she started going with Jack, it was sort of like a full circle. It [Jackie and Barbara] would have been the least likely combination I would have thought of, and yet it's a very good marriage. I never would have thought of Barbara and Jackie together. If he had said, "Do you know anyone?" she would have been the last person I think I would have thought of.

■ ■ ■

Barbara was a "civilian"—not an actress, not tortured by actresses' neuroses, egos, demands, the frustrations of pursuing such a career. She was the first "civilian" woman I had become involved with. Barbara wasn't pursuing any career, although she worked. She was some kind of junior account executive with a small New York advertising agency.

After getting to know her and spending some time with her, I began to believe that for the first time in my life, I had fallen in love with someone who wanted to be my wife and a mother tc our children. I was old-fashioned in many ways, and perhaps 'nat is why I longed for just this kind of relationship—to share my life with someone who also wanted a home, a family, a garden, to build some sort of personal family tradition together. I saw in this bright, pretty, vivacious young woman someone who wanted much the same things out of life that I had always wanted and had missed out on. Barbara was a person who cared about what sort of human being she was going to become.

I was older now at thirty-one and, thank God, wise enough to appreciate Barbara. If we had met three or four years before, I wouldn't have been wise enough, and I probably would not have been the kind of person then that she would have been attracted to either.

Some people, when we began seeing a lot of each other, were surprised. They didn't think we were each other's type. But we knew we were.

33.

The live television era was beginning to grind to its tragic end in New York. Economy rules much of art, and economy certainly rules television if, indeed, TV can ever be considered an art. And economy dictated that television had to go on film, for the sake of ease of distribution, for the sake of rerun efficiency, for the sake of production values and costs. New York could not compete with Hollywood in film capability or the new filmed comedy series, so gradually the live TV shows in New York petered out. And when *King of Hearts* closed, live TV became my sole income.

I had been offered pilot films for potential series, off and on, for over a year, but I had been turned off by the quality of the material, the direction, the bit players, and everything else about those comedy series I had seen. Besides, I had left Hollywood to escape a series—even though it was a movie series—and I didn't want all that time I had invested in becoming a New York actor to have been wasted.

Even before I married Barbara, it had come to be a custom with me to stop in at Cheerio's, a friendly neighborhood bar, on Sundays. It was something of an actors' hangout, and I always knew several people there, and it was good to be seen, to see, to exchange chitchat with the actors.

Gradually, as the industry shifted west, there were fewer and fewer familiar faces in Cheerio's on Sunday afternoons.

One Sunday I was in the bar, and the only familiar face belonged to the veteran character actor Frank Maxwell.

"Frank," I said, looking around at the unfamiliar faces in the place, "I guess it's time we went out to Hollywood and did a series." I didn't really mean it; it was something to say.

"Hell, Jack," Maxwell said, "I'm not going to do that shit."

I went home and told Barbara about that little encounter. I said to her that even a character actor like Maxwell was probably right, it probably was shit, or whatever you want to call it, but that it was the coming thing.

We talked for a couple of hours about it. She knew our

211

financial situation. I couldn't save a quarter. She was willing to work, although not eager, and anyhow, I didn't want her to. We wanted home, family, etc., and I knew that would be much more attainable in California than New York.

Besides, I was getting homesick for the sunshine, the easy life, all those things I had grown up with. New York had been a magnificent interlude for me—a period of tremendous growth, a period of intellectual stimulation such as I had never had before, a period of reestablishing my self-esteem—but I was coming to the conclusion that it was only that, an interlude.

About the time we made the move back to California, my personal life was pretty well straightened out, but my professional life wasn't. I really was being pulled in several directions—I enjoyed Broadway and had established a solid reputation as a stage actor; I had begun directing, and that art intrigued me more and more; I knew that the big money was in the realm of those awful filmed TV series back in Hollywood.

I told my agents at William Morris that I would take the next film series deal offered.

And I did. In March 1955 the Morris people told me that Irving Brecher wanted to meet me in New York and give me the script of a TV situation comedy pilot. I knew Brecher's name and reputation—he was a movie comedy writer who had been the coauthor with Fred Finklehoff of *Meet Me in St. Louis*, and he had done the very successful TV filmed series *Life of Riley*—so I arranged to meet him.

He told me that George Burns's production company was behind this new show. He had the script with him and shoved it across the table. I said I didn't want to read it. I said that if I read it, I probably wouldn't want to do it, and I wanted to do it.

So I said yes to Irving Brecher and his series. He left me the script, but I still didn't read it. He had told me the plot idea in brief—a young man who worked for the city and was in love with the mayor's daughter and HAD A DOG WHO TALKED! That didn't really inspire me to read the damn thing.

I finally read it as Barbara and I were on the plane to Los Angeles. I felt like asking the pilot to turn back to New York. It was okay, cute, with this talking dog being the big gimmick, and I said, "Well, the dog is going to steal the show." It was strictly a gimmick show, and I was the star in name, but really I was supporting the gimmick. And I had worked very hard to get away from a gimmick—the gimmick of being an "erstwhile film moppet," as some reviewers liked to say.

When we got to California, it was a week until shooting was to begin. Brecher still hadn't cast the girl in the show. I had seen a girl in New York I thought was right, and I suggested her. Her name was Pat Breslin, and we flew her out, and Irving liked her. But Pat had broken her leg in a skiing accident, and the script called for a two-legged girl. Pat could hobble around on her cast and her crutches, and I said to Irving that we should use her anyway—"It's a small screen, Irving," I said, "and at least Pat isn't the typical Hollywood starlet"—and he agreed. So Pat Breslin became the leading lady. She is now Mrs. Art Modell, the wife of the owner of the Cleveland Browns pro football team.

Barbara and I disagreed about *The People's Choice* and its potential impact on my career. Over the years she was always—until just a few years ago—more enthusiastic about my acting than my directing. But I had long thought I had a better future behind the camera than in front of it.

That difference of opinion started when we went back to New York after we shot *The People's Choice* pilot. I was discouraged. I felt that the show would never sell—it was very lightweight. Moreover, I really didn't want it to sell. Yet, if it didn't sell, it would be a step back for me—an indication that my name and face meant little. Aha—but if it DID sell, I thought, it might be a step even farther backward because I would become associated in the public mind with a silly show.

Barbara thought it would reestablish me with the public. "And what's the matter with the money?" She had great confidence in me as an actor and felt that no matter how dumb the show was, the public would take to me as a personality in spite of the ridiculous talking dog.

We were both right, as it turned out. Maybe I was a little righter than she was in the long run.

The People's Choice sold. We made the pilot in April, the damned thing sold in June, and we began production in July. And I went right from that into another series, *Hennesey*, and each of them ran three years. So Barbara was right—the public forgave me the talking dog and bought me as a performer and watched both series by the millions.

But I was right about the fact that it really didn't advance my career. When *Hennesey* was over, nobody was beating on my door for me to star in a movie. Right about that time John Frankenheimer—an old friend; we had known each other when he directed many live TV shows in New York—was casting his film *Seven Days in May*, and there was a part I desperately wanted to play, an Air Force colonel. Frankenheimer told me he couldn't give it to me. It was because of my image, he said. The public thought of me as too young. I was almost forty then, and I told Frankenheimer that. I said that there were plenty of Air Force colonels who were only thirty-five, and I was some years older than that. He said I was absolutely right, and he couldn't argue with my logic. Nevertheless, my public image was still that of a younger man.

We started *The People's Choice* in 1955, and I had made eight of them, I think, when I had a terrible ulcer attack. I had never had ulcers before. In New York, as I wrote, I had something—nerves, I guess—but never ulcers. But filmed television in general and *The People's Choice* in particular gave me a pain in the duodenum.

I felt I was ruining my career. My years in New York had restored my self-esteem—I had become part of the New York stage establishment, which meant to me that I was an actor of some ability, some taste, some quality—and here I was prostituting it all for money. I was ashamed of what I had done, and at the same time I was angry at myself. I was doing what I had sneered at in others so often—selling my soul for a mess of money. Like so many actors before me (and after me, too), I hated what I was doing, but I endorsed every one of the checks. I had to go home every night and face the prospect of learning scenes which were written for your average, or below-average, twelve-year-old mentality.

Our situation with directors was virtually as bad as with writers. We did discover one good one—Peter Tewksbury—but *Father Knows Best* had a bigger budget and stole him away from us very quickly. George Burns, our boss, was very conservative in some areas. We had a twenty-six-week guarantee from NBC, but Burns would not, in turn, give a sizable guarantee to the writers or directors we had. So the good ones, like Tewksbury, we lost to companies that would and did give such guarantees. We wound up making directors out of cutters and writers, and that didn't work.

That's when the ulcers acted up. And that's when I said, mostly to Barbara, the poor girl who had to bear the brunt of my frustration, "I quit."

Brecher and I knew that writing and directing were our two biggest problems. Irving, always a facile writer, tried to write more himself, but he couldn't do every episode. We began to find some good younger writers. When it came to the direction problem, however, I volunteered. I said that perhaps we would lose something if I directed myself as an actor, but I believed we would gain more than we would lose. In the long run, we'd be better off—financially and artistically. And so, near the end of the first season, I began directing. And it worked.

There was no way, statistically, of measuring the qualitative change in the show, but I was told the episodes I directed were better than the earlier ones. And the fact that my directing was financially beneficial could be demonstrated in figures—the first year we lost around $75,000, but the next year, when I directed throughout the season, we made that $75,000 back plus an additional $100,000 in production profit. (As an aside, I must add that at that point, making TV films for George Burns's company was an honest, profit-sharing business.)

We lasted three years, a minor miracle. I think if we had grown, we could have gone on longer. What some people do not understand about TV shows is that they must grow. Broadway shows are necessarily frozen and never change. But a TV show has to change and grow as its audience changes and grows. We didn't change, with the result that our audience outgrew us and began seriously not watching. The audience grew up. We didn't. We still had the talking-dog jokes.

Still, three years was a lot longer than I had expected or than Barbara had expected. We had been so insecure in our faith in the show that we just kept renting. During the three years that *The People's Choice* was on the air, we rented a couple of apartments and a couple of houses. I always thought it would end and we would have to go back to New York, so why be entangled with any semblance of roots?

But it lasted those three years, and the people who were advising me on career matters—a manager and my William Morris agents—urged me, when it finally ended, to stay in California and give up my thoughts of going back to Broadway. I took their advice—and Barbara, the confirmed New Yorker, had become a confirmed Californian by this time and was urging me to stay, too.

I did some guest shots on TV. I wanted to get back into features, but had no luck. I knew I wasn't Robert Taylor in the looks department, but I felt that I was enough of an actor and enough of a name that I should have a place in the feature film hierarchy. Nothing doing. Evidently I had become a TV personality; since audiences were seeing me every week on TV for free (the two series did very well in syndication), they wouldn't pay to see me in a movie. That was the feeling then, and to some extent, it persists even today.

I tried to get some directing jobs in movies, too. I pointed to my TV directing work as a credit. Nothing doing. Success in one area meant absolutely nothing in the other area. At the time movie people still hated TV, were jealous of its phenomenal success, refused to recognize that a craftsman in TV could be equally artful in movies. There were some offers given me to direct cheapies in Australia and England, but I didn't want that.

So, gradually and reluctantly, I reached the conclusion that I was in the TV series business. Like it or not, there I was. It certainly wasn't what I wanted to do, but I was stuck with it. With a growing family to support, I accepted my fate.

The live television days in New York—with Barbara Bel Geddes in **The Hasty Heart**—a chance to work and a little money.

Top: Gracie Fields in the U.S. Steel Hour production of **The Old Lady Shows Her Medals**. Those were TV's greatest moments. *Bottom*: With John Forsythe in **Mister Roberts**. I learned more than just my part.

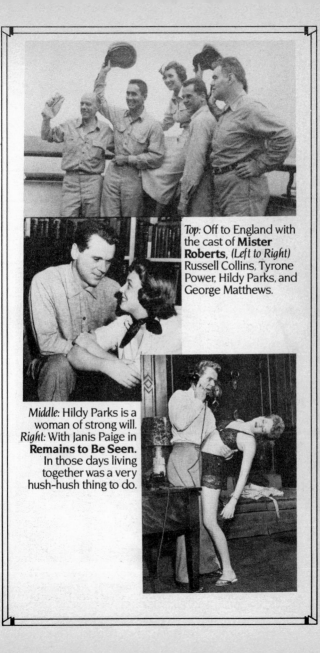

Top: Off to England with the cast of **Mister Roberts**, *(Left to Right)* Russell Collins, Tyrone Power, Hildy Parks, and George Matthews.

Middle: Hildy Parks is a woman of strong will. *Right:* With Janis Paige in **Remains to Be Seen**. In those days living together was a very hush-hush thing to do.

With Barbara, shortly after we were married.

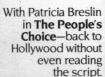

With Patricia Breslin in **The People's Choice**—back to Hollywood without even reading the script.

Cleo, the dog, and I were guest stars on Perry Como's show.

Top: The race car driver. It all started in England. *Bottom:* The auto racing team at Sebring, 1955, with *(Left to Right)* Lance Macklin, Roy Jackson-Moore, and Stirling Moss. When you start being too careful, it's time to quit.

With Barbara and our children—(*Left to Right*) Cris, Julie, and Russell. Three children, three different personalities.

Drumming with Lionel Hampton. The drums were always a release.

Sammy Davis, Jr., in **Hennesey.** Everybody wanted to appear in the show.

Left: As Hennesey in the series with a little class. *Right:* Clark Gable in 1958, doing a documentary on skeet and trap shooting.

Left: With our son, Russell, something to work for. *Right:* The Navy had a rule I followed.

The Steerman in Arizona. Planes can be expensive toys.

With Barbara Stanwyck on location for **Calhoun** in 1963.
We all did our best, but it was doomed.

Left: As the head of Screen Gems, I had to do a lot of executive things. *Right:* Elizabeth Montgomery had certain demands. *Bottom:* With Sally Field, in the Screen Gems days.

Top: In 1966 I congratulate John Anthony Cooper, after swearing him in. *Bottom:* With Roddy McDowall, two ex-child stars who made it as adults.

In the office of the *Daily Planet* in **Superman**.

Top: Directing an episode of **Quincy** with Jack Klugman, a man who likes a noisy discussion. *Bottom:* Directing Robert Alda and Lauren Bacall in a TV movie. Why was she bitter?

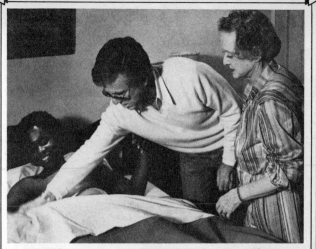

Top: With Bette Davis and Ernest Harden, Jr. in **White Mama** for TV. Bette loves to try new things. *Bottom:* Alan Alda's feelings, too, were masked.

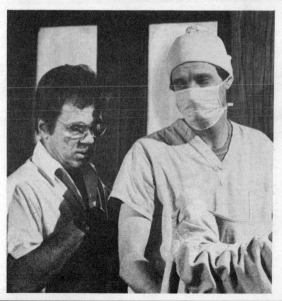

Barbara and Jackie today. There wasn't anything better than what we had.

34.

Barbara and I were married in 1954. Russell was born in 1956, Julie two years later, and Cristina—Crissy—a year after that. And of course, there was John Anthony, who, by the time he became a teenager, was able to call himself Jack.

Over the years since June and John Anthony had gone back to California, when our paths diverged, I had tried my best to be as good a father as possible under the circumstances. Obviously a cross-country separation isn't the best way to accomplish that, so I certainly wasn't the best father. But I saw him as often as I could. June cooperated because she knew that Jack needed a father. She did remarry for a short while—in 1953, when Jack was about seven—but as I understand the story, June thought her new husband was wealthy and he thought she was. Jack said his stepfather was nice to him and took them to Florida to live, but he was a gambler, and they had no money. June packed it in. She and Jack moved back to California.

June and I were not enemies. We had never been enemies. I think she pictured herself a woman scorned and tried very hard to stir up an inner anger. But she had no cause, although she worked desperately to create causes.

When I was on the road with *Mister Roberts*, I was awakened by a phone call one morning at three. I think I was in Pittsburgh. And June's voice screeched across the miles: "What do you mean, you're going to take my son away from me?"

I had never said that. I had never even intimated that. The thought had never even crossed my mind. I told her so, and she calmed down. I felt sorry for her.

I tried to have Jack with me as much as I could. Back in my touring days, if I knew I was going to be in a city for any length of time—two weeks or so—I would arrange for Jack to fly in and stay with me. June was always cooperative about that.

I went to Los Angeles as often as I could, in my New York years, to see him. The one time I drove out in my Jag was memorable. He loved my car. I always wore driving gloves behind the wheel (all of us keen sports-car types did then), and he'd put on his little mittens—ones he'd gotten to wear on trips to the snow—and sit behind the wheel and pretend he was me. He was a terrific kid.

I have always been delighted at how well Barbara and Jack have gotten along. He loves his mother, of course, and he takes care of her. Somehow, he and Barbara became best friends. He's a real brother to Russell, Julie and Crissy, too. There was a time when, for a lot of reasons, he and I didn't speak—it wasn't so much anger as neglect on both our parts that caused it—but Barbara was always there to bridge the gap, to be a link between us.

■ ■ ■

JOHN ANTHONY COOPER: There was a period of time that he and I didn't speak. We got to the point, late in the sixties, I went away to college, and that did not work out as well for me as it should have, and he was in that period when he was with Screen Gems; he really was the big mogul to me. I used to get letters on business letterheads, all typed up with his secretary's initials at the bottom, purporting to be from him. I don't blame him for that now or anything, but we got to the point where our communications became more and more difficult. And then I was making my own failings; I think I was trying to do a lot of things for him, whereas I really should have been doing them for me. It got to the point where I couldn't deal with the relationship. A lot of that was my fault, but some of it was his. So I just stopped calling him or seeing him, and with that came not being able to see anyone else—brother or sister. We didn't talk for five years. Not until about six years ago, 1974. By then I had moved back up here [San Francisco]. And he made the first move. He said, "I have to see you, and I'll be up." He made it like a throwaway thing; could we have lunch? I was rather apprehensive about it. I had wanted to call him, but I couldn't deal with him saying, "I don't want to talk to you," so I could not find a way to call him. But he was very understanding, and the first time I saw him, it was like it had never happened at all. I expected it to be awkward, but it was not at all. And we've been pretty close ever since.

Barbara has always been very nice to me. We have some differences about some things, and I sometimes have to remember when I talk to her that she's Dad's wife and she's going to have his point of view about a lot of things and so forth, but she always tried to make me feel comfortable there, including when I was a kid. She never tried to be my mother or anything like that; she never tried to usurp that away from June. She was always very nice to me, and I considered her even as a kid, as I do now, I considered her a close friend, like a big sister or something.

■ ■ ■

CRIS COOPER: There was a time when Jack wasn't with us, when he went off and did his thing. I found him, you know. I went and got him, and I said, "What is this?" I was thirteen years old, and I found out where he lived, and I had my friend take me over there—he was living there with his mother; this was before he moved up north—and I went and found him, and I don't know, after that he moved to San Francisco and Dad went up and talked to him. I liked him a lot, and being so young and he was so much older than I was, I didn't really know him very well, but I really liked him a lot, and it just seemed strange on the holidays and he wasn't around, you know, 'cause he was always there. So I looked in the phone book, and I went over there—and knocked on the door. His mom answered, and I said, "Hi, I'm Jack's sister," and she goes, "Oh, hi, I'm Jack's mother," and I said, "Well, is he here?" and she goes, "Well, yeah, as a matter of fact, he is." And he came to the door, and he was just like—he started to cry and everything. And I said, "Well, I just wanted to see if you were dead or alive, you know. What is this with you? I mean who do you think you are, just taking off and not saying anything to anybody?"

■ ■ ■

35.

The path of least resistance, that's what TV was for me then. I had hated doing *The People's Choice* despite its popularity, and I dreaded having to do something similar. So I decided that if I was saddled with television, at least I could try for something with a little more quality.

I got lucky. Don McGuire entered my life. I had known Don since he was an actor at Warner Brothers, before the war. So he was just a familiar face when I ran into him again. And Don said he had an idea for a TV series he'd like to talk to me about.

I was open to all ideas at the time, so we arranged a meeting. He had this idea dealing with an Army doctor because he had had a friend who was an Army doctor. And the friend had told him of some of the amusing things that happened. I said it sounded like it might be worth exploring, so he said he'd write something. And he did. It was good, but I was a little troubled about the Army doctor. I said that a man in an Army uniform just didn't look like a doctor, and besides, there had been a few other Army-oriented shows on TV (Phil Silvers's big hit, in particular), so how about making him a Navy doctor instead of Army? We'd be getting away from the Army backgrounds, and the Navy's blue suits looked more doctoral. Besides, I had Navy connections, and that might count for something when we wanted advice and the chance to shoot on Navy installations.

So McGuire rewrote it for a Navy doctor named Chick Hennesey. As usual with McGuire, he wrote only one draft. He was an absolutely brilliant writer, but he had an ego to match, and it was so enormous that it would not allow him to do a rewrite or a second draft. What he wrote first was what he wrote last. That ego, further, would not allow him to collaborate with anyone else. Had he been able to conquer it and go on to second drafts or accept advice or contributions from others, I am convinced he would have been as big a writer as this town has ever seen. But even as he was, he was great.

And that first (and final) draft of the *Hennesey* pilot script was very good and very funny.

We made the pilot. Lever Brothers—sponsors controlled TV then—liked it. But they told us they had no appropriate time period in which to air it. Back in those days, remember, the big sponsors owned blocks of network time, and they decided what programs went into which time periods. The Lever people thought we would have no trouble selling it somewhere else, and Don and I agreed; we were very bullish about our prospects. So we bought it back from them, and George Gruskin stuck it under his arm and began showing it around. He quickly peddled it to General Foods, who had a ten o'clock time period they wanted to fill and felt that *Hennesey* had just the degree of sophistication they wanted for that relatively late hour.

The whole process had gone rapidly, as it did in those simpler days. We had made the pilot in January 1959, and it was sold and we were into production by June. Don was grinding out the scripts, but our major problem was finding good directors. The going rate, then, for a director of a half-hour filmed show was only $750, not much of an inducement for top directors. But we lucked out—twice.

First, we found a young man who had been working around town as an assistant director in live TV, a bright fellow who wanted a chance to direct. The measly money was no deterrent to him; he just asked for a shot at a directorial assignment. We gave it to him, and Bob Butler came through for us.

Then there was the case of Gene Reynolds. I had known him, when I was younger, as a boy actor. A few years younger than I was, he was never a pal, but I knew him and liked him. So we hired him as an actor in the *Hennesey* pilot. He was, as usual, thoroughly professional. But he told me he had been getting disenchanted with acting and had been working part time at NBC in the casting department. That hadn't proved satisfying either, and he had been toying with the idea of getting out of show business entirely and going into real estate. Real estate seems like pie in the sky to actors in California; the real estate boom appears endless, and the talents they have as actors are the prime tools of real estate salesmen.

I asked Reynolds if he had thought about going into direction. The lack of good directors was looming so large on my personal horizon that I measured anyone I met then as a possible candidate for the job. Reynolds said no, he had never considered that. I said I thought he might make a good director—he certainly had been around enough movie sets; he was bright, inventive, creative—and I suggested a course of action that I felt would benefit both of us. I told him we would hire him for a nominal salary—enough so he could pay his rent and eat—and let him stand around and watch the next eight shows being made. I would direct them; Don would be on the stage (he always was), fixing the dialogue. And I said he would simply watch the way it was done, and then, if he felt he could handle it, he'd move in and direct.

I made Bob Butler the same deal. So we had two young men who turned out to be fine directors.

In 1973 I was the master of ceremonies at the annual awards dinner of the Directors Guild of America. And by the purest coincidence, when I gave the award for the director of the best half-hour show, it went to Gene Reynolds for the *M*A*S*H* pilot episode, and when I gave the award for the director of the best hour show, it went to Bob Butler for an episode of *The Blue Knight*.

Both Reynolds and Butler directed only four *Hennesey*s before they were both called to other things. But I felt proud at having given the two of them a start.

■ ■ ■

GENE REYNOLDS: Jackie gave me the opportunity to direct. I'd acted many, many years, then went into casting, cast *Peter Gunn* at Universal and a series called *Steve Canyon*. Jackie called me to do a part in the *Hennesey* pilot. Just a one-day part, and the *Peter Gunn* people let me go so I could do it, but at first the *Steve Canyon* people wouldn't. They finally let me go, and I did it, and the *Hennesey* pilot sold, and they decided to use new directors, so they hired Robert Butler and me. That's how I got started.

Jackie's enthusiasm is unique. He's been acting more than fifty years, but when he comes to work, he's read the script, and he's thought about it, and he comes on the set full of enthusiasm. It's almost a manic quality. He gets so fired up, and in these days that's memorable. He has technique, but he also still has enthusiasm.

He's always been a strong personality. Strong and aggressive. The problem of people who are aloof comes out of timidity. Jackie as a boy had normal interests—cars, music, that sort of thing. But like all child actors, he had hills to climb and a lot of maturing to do. I never talked to him about that, but I knew he went through some bad marriages and some periods of unemployment. We all had problems, and they manifested themselves in each of us differently. But he was resourceful. This town was murder after the war; everybody stole money during the war and got paranoid after the war, and there was very little production. So he went to London and New York. In London I saw him, and he was great company.

■ ■ ■

I directed all the rest of the *Hennesey* shows. It was cheaper, and McGuire and I were working with our own money, so that was important. And the show had gotten into a groove, and a very good groove it was.

It was THE comedy show for the business to watch in those years. It was to the 1959-1962 period what *M*A*S*H* became—a comedy show that worked on two levels. On one level, it had something that the mass audience enjoyed—nice people, people they cared about and took pleasure in watching, plus good jokes and a few wispy hints of sex. On the other level, it became a show the sophisticates could safely watch and talk about because it had a little class and wit as well as occasional drama. So it was, for those three seasons, a top show in many respects.

After the first season, McGuire—we're still good friends, but I believe he is very strange in some ways—decided he wanted to do a show that he would own totally. With *Hennesey*, he and I were splitting everything down the middle. So Don left the show and did another one, with Juliet Prowse, which, as it turned out, was canceled in the then-record time of six weeks. He never came back.

I carried on by myself, hiring other good writers and supervising everything very closely.

Jim Aubrey, the man who ran CBS with an iron talent, came to me in our third season and said that the government had taken control of TV time away from the sponsors and given it to the networks. He was, of course, pleased with that decision—he had fought for it—because he felt that was where the control belonged, in the hands of the networks. He said he wanted my show to continue on CBS. He offered me a deal—two more years as a half-hour show and then a third year as a full hour show. He talked money, and I would have made considerably more money than I had been getting from General Foods. But—and this was an enlarged but—CBS would retain all creative control. General Foods had had total confidence in me and my taste and rarely even offered a suggestion. I was afraid that Aubrey and his CBS committee would be breathing down my neck on every comma, every shot.

I understood Aubrey's position. Under the new FCC dictum, CBS was responsible for what went out under its auspices. It felt—and I would have felt the same had I been in Aubrey's shoes—that it had to have complete control; otherwise, how could it possibly assume that responsibility? But I wasn't in his shoes; I was in mine. And the view from my shoes was that I had to have control because I knew this show and its characters, and I certainly had the experience and the taste to do the right thing.

I also believed in the old saw "There's no room for democracy in show business." A play, a movie, a television show—whatever it was, it had to reflect the taste, views, and talent of one person. More productions have been ruined by committee decisions than by any other single cause. Anyway, I was having fun every day.

I couldn't have unqualified people looking over my shoulder and giving me advice, suggestions, or, worse still, commands. So, ultimately, I turned Aubrey's deal down. In effect, I turned down well over $1 million; had it gone to the hour format, two years down the road, it would have meant perhaps $3 million all told. It was one of the toughest decisions I've ever made, but I turned it down.

And so, in 1962, when General Foods lost control of its time period—it would have kept *Hennesey* on the air forever, if it could—we were off the air.

36.

I did three television series—*The People's Choice* and *Hennesey*, and in 1975 I made a serious mistake and got trapped in something called *Mobile One*. I made a lot of money, but I never enjoyed the work and was never happy doing it. And the cycle went on—I felt I should be happy because I was making so much money, but I wasn't happy, so again I began to feel guilty about not being happy, and that made me even unhappier. All this had its effect on Barbara, of course.

Often I would recall my New York days with galloping nostalgia. Professionally I had done good work, acting that I was proud of, acting that people whose opinions I respected, complimented me on. I enjoyed going to the New York restaurants and having people come over to me and congratulate me on a "fine performance." Nobody in Hollywood ever said anything about a "fine performance" in *The People's Choice*—how could they when I was playing straight man to a talking dog? I was doing unimportant things—even *Hennesey*, certainly a cut above the average TV show, was unimportant when measured against something like *Mister Roberts*.

The people out there—the millions of viewers—found the TV shows I did amusing. I suppose that is an accomplishment worth something. I have often heard the argument that if you can bring a measure of joy, pleasure, escape to the public, you have done a worthwhile deed and can take solace in that. I'm not sure I buy it totally. Certainly it is good to give the people a little pleasure and entertainment. But can't you do that AND do something that you yourself take more pride in? Are the two mutually exclusive and absolutely incompatible? Unfortunately the answer is yes, most of the time, on television.

My peers were not impressed with the work I was doing in Hollywood; they had been impressed with the work I had done in New York. I missed their respect. True, they respect success in Hollywood, they respect the big Beverly Hills house and all those status symbols, and so I was granted the respect of a man who was making good money. But my friendly neighborhood accountant and lawyer and shoe salesman and druggist and insurance agent and banker and theatrical agent got the same kind of respect if they were making big money. I didn't want that kind of respect; I wanted the respect of one artist toward another for his talent.

I thought I could get out of my trap by directing. If I could direct, then maybe I could go on to more creative work.

Actually I had long harbored the increasing suspicion that I had no real future as an actor. Acting had come so easily to me, and everybody said I was a natural, that at first I never questioned my career aspirations. I acted because I had always acted and assumed I always would act.

But being honest with myself, I knew that I didn't look like a conventional leading man. Yet I wasn't exactly a character actor either. I was in a limbo, and thus, I concluded that I could never be a motion picture star. For a while I listened to others who kept saying that I was wrong.

I kept hearing, over and over, from agents and critics and friends that I was destined to be the next Spencer Tracy. Even Barbara, who was often very objective about me and my career, jumped on that Spencer Tracy bandwagon. But I knew it wasn't going to happen—and it didn't happen.

Maybe I couldn't project sex appeal. It seemed to me that in real life I could project sex appeal, but there is a major difference between real life and what happens in a movie theater. And maybe what I could project in person simply was lost in the translation to film.

So, with a few minor exceptions, I made no movies after World War II. Certainly no starring parts. I had hoped originally that my part in the Broadway play *King of Hearts* might be my entrée back to the big screen. I was very disappointed when it was bought for films—with Bob Hope in the part I had created in New York. It was no doubt very selfish of me, but I was pleased when the movie flopped; it was one of the very few Bob Hope films that didn't make any money.

Okay, so I wouldn't be a movie star. Okay, I'd be a director instead. During the course of the runs of *The People's Choice* and *Hennesey*, I directed about two hundred of those shows. Then, afterward, my friend Dick Powell wanted to hire me for one of his shows at Four Star, and the network gave him trouble. They said (according to Powell) that I had done okay with my directing on my comedy series, but that wasn't "serious" directing.

It took a long time before anybody did take me seriously as a director—and as I write these words, I'm still waiting to be taken seriously as a director for theatrical motion pictures. I've won two Emmys as a director for television, and I'm in constant demand to direct TV movies, and I've directed some of the top-rated movies with some of the biggest stars in TV— but motion picture companies are reluctant to take me seriously as a director. Over the years I've had several chances to direct minor feature films, but schlocky things, films to be done on location, films budgeted at less than a McDonald's special lunch. I turned them all down.

In 1971 I was finally offered a $2 million picture at Columbia called *Stand Up and Be Counted*. It was one of the first films to deal with the women's lib theme. But the script emphasized bra-burning jokes and the like, not the sociological implications of what women's lib was all about, and so it was all pretty bland. We had a reasonably good cast—Jacqueline Bisset, Stella Stevens, Steve Lawrence, Loretta Swit, Madlyn Rhue—but it didn't do anything for my reputation as a director. I always knew the script was weak, and I should not have taken the job, but I couldn't turn down the chance to direct a major feature film.

When it came time to add a theme song, I started scouting around for a singer and a song. Somebody told me about a new singer from Australia who was heavy into the women's lib thing. So I went out and bought Helen Reddy's album—I think it was her first and, at the time, only—and played it. There was one song on the album called "I Am Woman," and it was perfect, in its message, for our women's lib-flavored film.

I took the album to the producer, Mike Frankovich, and played the "I Am Woman" cut. He couldn't understand one word she said, and I really didn't fault him for that. At the time Helen was doing the song very up tempo, and her Australian accent was so thick you could slice it with a boomerang. Besides, she was trying to affect a southern accent (why do all pop singers try to sound southern?), and that only compounded her unintelligibility. Later I found out that nobody had played the song, that the DJs hated it, and that even Jeff Wald, Helen's husband and manager, hated the song. But I knew we would never find a song so true to the spirit of our film, so I had my secretary type out the lyrics to it and showed them to Frankovich. Mike loved it.

I called Jeff to see if we could buy the song to use as the theme of the picture.

"Sure," he said. I could almost feel him shrugging at the other end of the wire.

When we got together, Jeff told me that both he and Helen were very discouraged.

"She's not happy here, Jackie," Wald said. "She wants to go back home to Australia."

The poor guy was upset about it because he was from New York and he had no desire at all to go to Australia. So we bought the song from them. We paid $6,000 for "I Am Woman"—and Helen was such a big women's libber that she insisted the deal be arranged so we paid the Walds $3,000 and the other $3,000 went directly to something called the Equal Rights Foundation, in Australia.

We used the theme as a part of the score of the picture and the entire song as the end title. Wald, on the strength of having a song in what was supposed to be a big movie (it turned out it wasn't a hit at all), went to Capitol Records, told them that the song was going to be part of a major film, and persuaded them to rerecord the song. And using our feelings about it, he had it rerecorded at a slower tempo, and Helen was much more careful with her diction. The result is musical history—that rerecorded version of "I Am Woman" was a monster hit, established Helen Reddy as a first-line pop singer, brought Helen and Jeff enormous success and huge sums of money.

But—human nature, again—in all the stories she has told since then about her life and career, she has never once mentioned the fact that "I Am Woman," the turning point in her career, had been in a movie or never once mentioned me.

It's curious how some people don't like to mention those who helped them along the way. It is, I suppose, insecurity in action; they don't want it noised about that they needed any help; they want the public to believe that they did it all on their own.

I had a lot of help, and I'm delighted to admit it. For a year, on the road with *Mister Roberts*, John Forsythe not only helped me as an actor but helped me find myself as a person.

■ ■ ■

JOHN FORSYTHE: Being so het up with the Actors Studio, having been an original charter member, and with all the zeal of the convert, I started some Actors Studio-type acting classes on the road. And he [Jackie] was enormously impressed with some of those things. I would just lead the classes—not a la Lee Strasberg—I was never in the position of criticizing—but I started and led the classes, and he was fascinated by that because that was a whole different approach to acting. He didn't need it because his talent was so instinctive that he knew right out. I mean, you don't jump into *Mister Roberts* the way he did with such incredible skill and authority, and you didn't, subsequently, go into stuff like that Lindsay and Crouse play or *King of Hearts*, in which he was just marvelous. He really didn't need it, but the Actors Studio was never a panacea for actors and acting; it was always a place where you could exercise, where you could stretch whatever acting muscles you had to stretch. And that was good for him.

■ ■ ■

Many people helped me, and in return, I've tried to help others. I started Gene Reynolds and Bob Butler directing. During my Screen Gems period Peter Deuel (he later changed the spelling to Duel) was a day player, had five or six lines in one of our shows, and made a few hundred dollars. I liked the way he came through on film and put him in a new series called *Love on a Rooftop*, which wasn't a big hit but did run a couple of years, and Universal picked him up and put him in *Alias Smith and Jones*, and he was on his way.

Somebody told me about a kid playing a guitar at some hole in the wall on Melrose Avenue who might be right for one of the new series in the works at Screen Gems. I went down to hear him perform, and I liked him—the performing was only so-so, but the look and attitude were great. So I hired him for *Here Come the Brides*. His name was David Soul, and he later became Hutch of *Starsky and Hutch* and a major TV star.

We were going to do a series called *Gidget* and had a terrible time finding a girl to play the lead. We didn't want a conventional fresh-faced Iowa farm girl kind of cutie pie in the lead but, rather, somebody with a little personality. So we had a series of what's known in the trade as cattle calls—open auditions and anybody can show up and be heard. Eighteen-year-old Sally Field came into one of those cattle calls, and in my opinion, she was Gidget, no question about it. And she's gone on to become one of our finest young actresses.

When it came to casting *I Dream of Jeannie*, we had our leading lady—Barbara Eden—but had problems finding her costar. I thought of Larry Hagman, but he had never done comedy. Until then Hagman had been a small-part dramatic actor, but I had a hunch he could handle the part and be funny, and we tested him, and it turned out I was right. Hagman was funny, and still is—perhaps one of the most dependable funny actors on TV, although as this is written, he's back to some kind of drama in the *Dallas* series.

And I've tried to help many behind-the-camera people, too. A bright woman named Renee Valente was working in New York as David Susskind's business affairs executive. I hired her to run the Screen Gems New York casting office in 1964 and, three years later, brought her to California to head up our total casting effort. She stayed for years after I left, then moved on and became a producer—she was the coproducer of *Blind Ambition*, the TV version of the John Dean book, and producer of the movie *Loving Couples*.

Rosalind Wyman was another. She had been a Los Angeles city councilwoman and wanted to get into television, but had no idea where to fit in. I brought her in and set up what we called a Public Affairs Department. That was really only a kinder word for an office designed to keep our stars out of trouble. Many of the young people we had—Judy Carne, Pete Deuel, The Monkees—had trouble handling fame and fortune and frequently got into jams. Roz was a magician at extricating them without the bad news' getting in the papers or on TV. Today she's executive director of the Producers Guild.

And there was Robert Altman, the brilliant, if erratic, director. When I hired him, he had only directed several episodes of the *Combat* series, which starred Vic Morrow. He did so well that he became one of my producers as well as director of many episodes, but he was so full of talent that I couldn't hang onto him for very long.

Paul Witt was a Harvard graduate who was in the Screen Gems mail room. He made a little film on his own and told somebody, who told me, and I saw it and thought he had a lot of promise and put him together with Bob Claver, and his career was off and running. He's now a highly successful independent TV producer.

Burt Metcalfe, now producing *M*A*S*H*, had been an actor and, in fact, had been a semiregular on *Hennesey*. When I was at Screen Gems, he came in one day and said he wasn't making it as an actor; could I find something for him at Screen Gems? I found a spot for him in casting, and he did well. Later, when I left Screen Gems, he moved to Universal and then joined another of my alumni, Gene Reynolds, on the *M*A*S*H* staff.

I brought a young man named Stan Kallis over from Four Star, where he had been an assistant producer, and made him a producer. Later he went on to produce the first four years (the best years, actually) of *Police Story*.

But then there was Jimmy Komack. I brought him out from New York nightclubs to act and write on *Hennesey*. Then came an incident which has always troubled me. The William Morris office, his agency, submitted his name to direct some shows for Dick Van Dyke. Jimmy asked me to say, if I was asked, that he had directed some *Henneseys*. I said no, I couldn't do that. He was upset with me.

I explained that you have to be truthful in this business. If I asked other people for information, I wanted the truth, and I expected the truth, so I'd damn well better tell the truth myself.

Then I got a call from Sammy Weisbord, who was handling Jimmy at William Morris, and he said, "How dare you hold up his career?"

I told Weisbord that far from holding up Komack's career, I had virtually made his career. Until we got together he'd never acted—except for his part on Broadway in *Damn Yankees*, all he had done was stand-up comedy. And he had never written a word until McGuire and I encouraged him to write for *Hennesey*.

He has done well, and I am very happy for him. He is a fine writer and producer and actor—anything he tries, he does well—but he never tells anybody else what anyone did for him. When we meet, he'll tell me how grateful he is, but he never mentions it to any third party.

■ ■ ■

JAMES KOMACK: I came to California in '57 and lived with Aaron Spelling. Aaron kept saying, "Your friend Jack has got this show, he ought to give you a job," ya-da-da-da-da, and he didn't. I came out here to screen-test for *Francis and the Mule*, to replace Donald O'Connor. I called Jack and Barbara, "Can I see you?" "Yeah." So I came by. I sat with Jack for a little bit, he was getting dressed to go out, and I said, "You know, Jack, I'm doing a screen test tomorrow, and I don't know how to do it, I've never done this before; between you and me I'm frightened to death, I don't know what to do." And Jack mumbled something, blah-blah-blah-blah, and I didn't understand him, and I went to Barbara and said, "I don't understand," and she said, "Jack, help him, Jack, help him, for Chrissake. The kid wants help." He came back and said, "Jimmy, it's all in the eyes." I went to work the next day. My eyes were wide all day. I saw Jack that night; he said, "How did you do?" I said, I did this [demonstrating the wide-eyed look]. He said, "That's not what I meant. That's not what I meant at all. It looks terrible." Barbara said, "You didn't tell him right. You should have told him better."

Then he got *Hennesey*. He hadn't been happy in *The People's Choice*; he felt the dog was upstaging him.

I'd go over to their house twice a month to dinner with Cluny. He used to sit and talk to me about this part, a Navy dentist, Dr. Blair, who had to be a good-looking guy, slick, rich, handsome. I suggested Larry Storch; I suggested Bob Dishy; I suggested everybody I could think of. One night I'm in La Scala Restaurant—I didn't know this, but I was sitting at the bar, and I had lost a lot of weight since I had come to California, had started to look like an actor, lost a lot of weight, slicked my hair back, sat in the sun (I had nothing else to do), got dark. The next morning Jackie is out having breakfast with a lady named Marilyn Reiss, a publicist, and he says, "Marilyn, I'm looking for a guy, can't find him, to play this dentist," and he describes him. She said, "I saw him last night at La Scala—Jimmy Komack." "Jimmy Komack? I have dinner with him twice a month." She says, "Well, he's the perfect guy." Jack says, "No, I need a skinny, good-looking guy." Marilyn says, "Don't you realize, Jimmy got skinny and good-looking?" Jack says no. Marilyn says, "I'm telling you, Jimmy is the guy—he's lost a lot of weight; he's slicked his hair back; he's got a nice suntan; he'd be terrific for you." Jack calls me on the phone, says, "I want to see you." I go over to General Service; he talks to me, tells me about this part. I said, "You're kidding." He said, "No, you're the guy." I still said, "You're kidding." He said, "Let's read the part." So he gives me the line readings, and we read the part—he fed me the right readings. So we go in and meet Don McGuire—McGuire had the bigger office. Sit down. "Jimmy, this is Don." Yeah, yeah. Dr. Blair. "Read for Don McGuire." So I read, and Don said, "Well, I must say, Komack, you got all the right readings, you really got it right." And Jack says, "I never told him a word, he's terrific." But something's wrong. I leave, and Jack says, "Don't worry." I went back three times, and every time I went back to read again for McGuire, Jack would take me off, give me the line readings, McGuire would say, "This is the way the part should be." Jack had told me what Don had told him, I'd go in, but each time something was bothering him. My hair was short—used to have the crew cut—and slicked back. My ears used to stick out. Jack is behind me, I'm reading for McGuire, and suddenly I feel him go like this, holding my ears in. You never fight with Jack—Jack's Jack—so I keep reading the part. McGuire says, "That's it! He's the guy!" I said, "What did you do?" "Your ears, your ears were funny, that was what was bothering me." Jack says, "I knew it, the ears." I said, "What's wrong with the ears?" He said, "If you were rich when you were a kid, you wouldn't have had funny ears like that; your mother would have fixed them right away."

Then they started to glue my ears, I got the part of Dr. Blair, and I became Jackie's inseparable buddy for about three years.

■ ■ ■

37.

The television business has been good to me. Certainly, when I compared the Jackie Cooper who ran away from Hollywood after World War II to the Jackie Cooper who had two hit TV shows, there is no comparison. I became somewhat of a force in the TV business, whatever that means. I prospered. Maybe I wasn't acting to the limit of my capabilities—I wasn't "stretching"—but I never starved once.

I think I could have done better, and maybe I should have done better. I would have liked to have done more directing—better things—and that's still my goal. I think I have the talent, but I am sorely lacking in the ability to play the game. I don't go to parties very well.

Maybe I should have gone to more parties. I had gone to hundreds—many in my honor—as a kid, and I grew to hate them. Maybe "hate" isn't the right word. I know they made me feel uncomfortable. I'm fine with a small group of friends, sitting around and listening to music, watching a football game, socially drinking, talking, laughing. But those big Hollywood and Beverly Hills affairs—no, they are not for me. And by now all the big Hollywood and Beverly Hills hostesses know that I won't go. So they don't even invite Barbara and me anymore. It doesn't take much, these days, to make me feel ill at ease and uncomfortable.

Parties, in a way, are like reading for parts. In New York I learned to hate readings and resisted them. Of course, as a kid I had never had to read, not since my very earliest days. So when I went to New York and discovered that reading for jobs was an accepted part of the hiring procedure, I was miserable. But I did it and got my share of roles that I read for.

Still, it was embarrassing and uncomfortable. When you read for a part, you quickly learn what a side of beef feels like when it is auctioned off at a wholesale butcher's. I think the worst moment I had in my professional life was in New York at a theater reading for a part for the playwright Arthur Miller.

When I came in, he didn't even shake hands, the polite thing to do. He didn't even get up; it may not be necessary but would have shown a certain breeding and respect. He didn't even take his feet down from the chair in front of him. I read; he listened; I left. I felt very uncomfortable.

In reflection and retrospect, I believe it is probable that had I been more adept at partygoing, especially in Hollywood, I might have advanced my career as an actor and director considerably. Parties, however, are always the most blatant form of display, and I've been on display all my life.

And yet people talk to me differently from the way they talk to the stars of the Redford-Newman-De Niro sort. Most people seem to find it easy to talk to me, and I suppose that's because they feel they knew me as a child and have watched me grow up. Some say I'm almost like family, and they have no hesitancy about starting a conversation. I've been with some of the other kinds of stars when this has happened, and they have noted the difference. Sinatra, for one. We were together somewhere, and he remarked on how the public approaches him with awe but approaches me with a very warm kind of familiarity. David Janssen, too—he said he was amazed at how easily people talk to me. He said they always seemed aloof with him.

Yet I don't really enjoy it, and maybe that's the big reason why I prefer being at home. To me, the public recognition is an integral facet of show business, and when I'm out, I am always polite and sign autographs and converse and smile and pose for pictures because all that stuff goes with the territory— but I don't really enjoy it.

Another part of the business I don't enjoy is the politics of it all. And that is something I don't tolerate and try not to have anything to do with. To me, that does not have to go with the territory.

There is so much politics in show business. I think political ability has become more important than talent in making a man successful. I haven't the time or inclination for all that; I have too much else to do, with my home, family, my Navy work, my flying. Most of the big entrepreneurs today have no real creative talent, but boy, are they great wheeler-dealers!

There was a time when I tried to play politics and tried to do the party bit. That was in 1946, when I was fresh out of the Navy and thinking only in terms of resuming my film career in Hollywood. I wanted to be seen then. I wanted to go to all the parties I could. I smiled at all the right people. I would never drive anywhere unless my car was freshly washed. I had to wear the biggest, brightest cuff links I could find. I bought only the most expensive neckties.

It didn't help. That was the period when I did those few clinkers of films, and everything soured for me in California.

New York changed me in many ways. It changed my attitudes on a lot of things. Hanging around with people like Eli Wallach and Anne Jackson and Hildy Parks and John Forsythe and Marty Ritt matured me. Going around during the day without any socks made me laugh, when I thought back to the days when I tried to impress people at Romanoff's by wearing out-sized cuff links. I wore jeans in Greenwich Village, and it was all very casual and warm and, somehow, innocent.

It was a period of marvelous growth for me. I found out there were other things in life besides movies. I found out there was a race problem. I found out there was religious discrimination. I found out there was political unrest. I found out there was a book called *Red Channels*—and that I was damn near in it. (A lot of people I hung out with, like Ritt, were in it.) I gravitated toward a liberal bunch of people and became one with them, in their attitudes and philosophies.

I am still angry sometimes about inequities. When the Hollywood Chamber of Commerce chose to deny Paul Robeson his star (that august body is in charge of the stars that are implanted in the so-called Walk of Stars along Hollywood Boulevard and Vine Street), I was angry. Many of us were sure that Robeson was being denied that honor, such as it is, because of (a) his color or (b) his politics or (c) a combination of both. Yet nobody was doing anything, so I got angry, and I started the whole movement that finally led to his having a star with his name on it. What galled me further was that a year or so later, when the Robeson star was finally unveiled, the people who showed up for the ceremony and basked in the reflected glory of the Robeson star included many black actors (Sidney Poitier, for one) who had never even written to the Chamber of Commerce and certainly had not spoken out publicly.

It's all politics, of course. The bigger the star, the bigger the director, the bigger the producer, the better he (or she) is at playing the political game.

I'm a rotten politician, maybe because I don't enjoy it. And that brings us to *Dick Daring*.

38.

When Dick Powell became ill, all his friends and associates banded together to help Tom McDermott keep things going at Four Star. Tom is still a friend of mine, but our business relationship at that time was not going too smoothly. I went to him with an idea to do a show about a county agricultural agent. After *Hennesey*, I kept thinking about other TV series ideas. I had achieved some degree of success in TV and had some clout, and people wanted me for other series because I had a "track record." But I felt that next time—if there was a next time—I wanted one thing that was missing from *The People's Choice* and *Hennesey*.

I wanted to do something that had some social significance. I didn't want to hit people over their heads with Message and Moral, but my years in New York—my indoctrination by all my socially aware Broadway friends—had rubbed off on me, and I felt it was important to make some kind of contribution. We all—actors, too—have an obligation to leave this earth a little better place than when we came in if we can.

So I had an idea about a county agricultural agent, a generally unsung small cog in the chain of command who, in reality, does some very good work. I believed that focusing on one such person and watching him work could be good dramatic entertainment and, at the same time, a vehicle for saying some things about our society and, maybe, how to improve it.

I wrote a few things down—very sketchy, very preliminary—and took it to Tom. I never heard a word back from him, either positive or negative. I think I never heard from him because of the old Hollywood politics. I know that Dick Powell had taken a fancy to me as a potential executive, and I think McDermott was concerned that I might be gunning for his job. Thus, if he okayed any project of mine, that would be ominous, but still, if he turned down any project of mine, that might turn out to be ominous, too. When in doubt, sit tight. So he just sat.

There was a lot of talk around Four Star at the time that everybody "should be nice to Jackie because he's going to be the next head of the company." If I'd heard that talk, Mc-Dermott had heard it, too, and naturally resented it—and therefore resented me. McDermott had come to TV from an advertising agency, and the politics in ad agencies is vast and all-consuming, so he knew how to play the game.

While I waited for the McDermott reaction that never came, I thought more and more about my idea and dug into it deeper and deeper. The more I discovered, the better the idea seemed. (And seventeen years or so later I think it's still a good idea, and it still hasn't made it to the TV screen.) Every county in the United States—even Los Angeles County or New York County—has an agent, an employee of the U.S. Department of Agriculture. He is required to help people with their agricultural problems; in Los Angeles County or New York County, that could be advice on how to grow geraniums in a window box. But in the big farming counties in the West and Midwest, the county agent is a very important figure. He's involved with big business in those counties.

In the Southwest there are many tenant farmers. (You must understand that all my information dates from around 1963, when I researched this and knew the situation; it may have changed since then, but probably not drastically.) In some of those huge counties in New Mexico and Arizona there are a lot of poor people and a few rich ones. Some of the rich owners are benevolent landlords; others are not. So the county agent often has to be a sociologist, a psychologist, and a judicial expert, as well as do his more ordinary duties in agriculture and veterinary science and medicine. With the poor farmers gone all day, leaving wives home alone and often lonely, the county agent frequently has to be versed in how to deal with the romantically inclined as well. And of course, the Southwest is a vast melting pot of peoples—whites, browns, blacks, reds, yellows.

It all combines to create, in my opinion, an incredibly rich lode of stories for a TV series. Focusing on the county agent in the Southwest—as I came to do in my mind—offered a vast spectrum of stories, everything from traditional westerns to comedies from social dramas to mystery, from science fact to love stories.

It all had come to me one evening watching a Marlboro commercial on TV. As my mind played with that figure—the rugged individualist in the countryside—one image led to another until suddenly the figure of the county agricultural agent popped into my mind.

After a decent interval of time, when I heard nothing from McDermott, I simply left a note for him: "I'm gone." And I left the studio.

I took my idea to my agents—William Morris—and they agreed with me that the concept certainly had merit. The William Morris people took me, in turn, to United Artists for financing a pilot script and, particularly, to Dick Dorso. Dorso, I am happy to say, is now in the clothing business and has recently written a novel. He is still an acquaintance, and I mean no disrespect, but when he was a TV mogul, we were in constant conflict.

United Artists liked the idea. More, they liked the idea of Jackie Cooper—a salable commodity to the public, on the strength of two hit TV series—as the star of the show. I told them that I wasn't interested in starring; I wanted to stay in the production area. I have subsequently learned that Dorso went to Jim Aubrey—we have met him before, the high muckamuck of CBS—and told him about my idea, and Aubrey agreed it was a good one, and Dorso told Aubrey, in effect, that we can get Cooper to star in the series, but the guy wants to produce, so they'd have to give me that if they wanted me to be the star.

So that was the way it came down to me. Yes, you can produce—provided you also star. Okay, it was a start and, once more, that Offer You Can't Refuse. So I went to New York and duly presented myself in Aubrey's office and told him my idea, and he loved it. First, though (there is always a proviso in TV dickering), he wanted to see a presentation, including a lot of documentation based on hard research. After that, a script for the pilot.

So I had to find a writer. United Artists had one of the best on staff as an editor. I'd known Robert Alan Aurthur from my old days of live TV in New York. He had written some memorable TV plays for such programs as *Philco* and *Playhouse 90* and the movie *Edge of the City*, a wonderful drama with John Cassavetes. I didn't need to look any further if I could get Bob Aurthur to write my county agent series.

I gave Aurthur a call, and we met, and I broached the idea of his writing the script. It was okay with him—he said he thought it was a very good concept—but Dorso nixed it. UA was paying Aurthur a big salary to supervise the writing of all its projects for TV, and if he was diverted to my project, that would take him away from his regular duties for too long. Bob said not to worry, he knew a writer/reporter who was pretty good. Let him do that presentation and all the research; let him do a first draft of the pilot script.

"Don't worry," Bob said. "I'll fix it up, whatever he writes."

So that's how a writer named Merle Miller got involved. At the time I hadn't read anything Miller had written. I had seen only one TV film he'd done, a show from Arizona about the tragic Indian figure Ira Hayes, and it had been very bad. The critics beat Miller's brains out on that one. I said to Aurthur that the only thing of Miller's I'd seen was atrocious, but Aurthur was a good salesman and said I needn't worry because he, Aurthur, would be on top of everything, overseeing it every step of the way.

Miller and I got together. I found him very effete, somewhat intellectual, a cold man who was difficult to know. Something about him bothered me, but I couldn't figure out just what it was. He was always gentlemanly, but always somewhat guarded and secretive. Four years later, on *The Dick Cavett Show*, Miller admitted to his homosexuality, which probably explains at least some of his odd behavior.

But at the time I knew nothing of that, not that it would have mattered had I known. We were going to work together, so we made the best of things. We mutually decided on New Mexico for our research and zeroed in on the poorest agricultural school in the Southwest, the one at Las Cruces, New Mexico.

Miller and I went to Las Cruces and spent two highly productive weeks there. The county agent was a fascinating man. We talked to farmers, farmers' wives, spray pilots, Indians, Mexicans. We were both stunned by the unrelenting poverty of the area. By the time we got back to New York—at the time all TV buying and decision making was in New York— we had a story line and a title. Merle had come up with *Calhoun*—"it has a good American sound," he said—and we had formulated the character of our leading man, the man I was going to play, Calhoun. Calhoun could fly, shoot, fix cars, knew almost everything about farming and animals, could get along with men and women and kids equally well. And we had established the character of his friendly antagonist, the female county agent, who was going to be played by Barbara Stanwyck.

Miller went up to Connecticut to write his script, and I went back home to Los Angeles. The script duly arrived, and I wasn't happy with it at all. I called Bob Aurthur in New York, telling him of my unhappiness, and he suggested that I have Miller come west and work with me on it. Miller agreed and came out and did what he called rewriting, but his idea of rewriting was simply to rearrange some words he had already written. It didn't help much. Miller sent a copy of the script to Aurthur. Bob told me he'd fix it, and he kept telling me that. Finally, he did do some work on the script, but that was bad, too. Aurthur had botched it if the truth be known. He had done things like taking out something from page 17 and later referring to that on page 50. When I said he was making no sense, he said that was how you pleased everybody at a network; everybody wants a particular something in a script, so you leave it in for him. He said you have to write for a committee.

There were rewrites and meetings and presentations and phone calls and flights east and flights west. As the days and weeks and months droned on, I saw my good idea being drowned in a welter of political moves and countermoves, and foundering in a sea of Miller's terrible pages, and just simply sinking—and there was nothing I could do to save it.

My agents at William Morris kept assuring me that I shouldn't worry, that I should go ahead and shoot the pilot, no matter how rotten the script was.

"So the script is lousy," they said. "So what? The important thing is that with you as the star, it'll test well, and CBS will buy it." But I didn't want to do it that way. I wanted to make a show I could be proud of. Besides, there was a major financial consideration—with that script, I knew damn well it wouldn't sell.

Dorso kept patting Miller and me on our egos and saying that we'd all get rich if we did things his way. Aurthur told me, "Jack, I want to get rich, so I'm going to do what Dorso says, no matter what you say."

I knew I had to get another script written. Down the hall from my office was the office of a top writer, Richard Alan Simmons, another Four Star producer-writer, and I told him the idea and showed him the script. He shook his head.

He said it was just too bad, a great idea, a terrible script. I begged him to rewrite it for me or just plain write it from scratch. I knew he could do it, and he riffled through the pages of the old script awhile, obviously thinking about it. He looked down at that script with disgust and shook his head again.

He said he'd love to do it, it was such a great concept, but he simply couldn't. I asked him why not, although I knew the answer already.

"I'm under contract to a competitor," he said, which was, of course, true. "It simply would not be ethical for a Four Star contract writer to write a script for a United Artists show."

Then he gave me a big wink and said, "But I'll hire you somebody." The wink meant that no matter who he hired, and whose name was down there on the script and on the payroll, it would be a Richard Alan Simmons script.

Simmons was as good as his promise. He sent me a writer.

As soon as I left Dick's office, I called Dorso. Now I was back on cloud nine—confident that the script problem would be licked. So it was time to get all the other pieces together. I asked Dorso if it was okay with him if I hired Stuart Rosenberg to direct. I told him I had Barbara Stanwyck all set as the costar, plus a great cast of TV actors in the main supporting roles—Robert Lansing, Barbara Luna, Howard Duff. They would all have been regulars on the show. I told Dorso everything was falling into place.

Then I laid it on the line about that elusive script. I told him bluntly that everybody had loved the idea, the presentation, everything—except the script. So I said I was giving him a choice: Let me get a good script now, or forget the whole damn thing. It was up to him. I sure as hell wasn't going to shoot that absurd Miller-Aurthur script, which made no sense. I told him that for a professional company, which I thought we were, we certainly had to have good dialogue, and Miller apparently was unable to write dialogue that sounded as if it came out of the mouths of real people.

Dorso hemmed and hawed and then said I could go ahead with preproduction; I could sign the director and cast, that sort of thing. Then he'd get back to me.

In the meantime (wheels within wheels), I later found out that my old pal Bob Aurthur told Merle Miller that I hated him and was his enemy. Obviously that wasn't so; I had lost a lot of respect for Miller's writing, but there was neither hatred nor enmity there. Aurthur added that I was trying to screw him, Miller. And he said that he, Aurthur, felt that Miller's work had been brilliant. Aurthur, of course, failed to mention that he had rewritten the script himself. So Miller concluded that

I was lying to him when, in fact, it was Aurthur who was lying to him.

The next time I talked to Miller I told him, very frankly, that I had to get another writer. I said that we would keep the Miller credit—"Created by Merle Miller"—on the finished product for all time. (Of course, I had been the creator, but I didn't need that kind of glory, and I felt he did.) Despite my attempts at fairness and honesty, Miller left in a huff, ran home to Connecticut with his script between his legs, and henceforth refused to answer the telephone when I called.

I reported all this to Dorso and repeated my ultimatum—no new writer, no new show.

"Okay, Jack, just exactly what do you want?" Dorso said. I went down my list of script changes I felt were mandatory before we could shoot a foot of film.

"Go ahead," Dorso said.

In a week the writer Simmons had recommended appeared at my office with a script that was everything I could have wanted.

Over the weeks that all this script hassling had been going on, I'd been working my tail off on other aspects of the production. I had hired a production manager and had scouted locations and found several places, between El Paso, Texas, and Las Cruces, New Mexico, for us to shoot. I had hired a plane to fly cast, crew, and equipment to the area and had contracted with a private airfield on which we would land.

It was all there, at last—script, cast, crew, details. All I waited on now was a corporate go-ahead from United Artists. I phoned Dorso, told him I had the new script and was sending it to him, and asked him to call me when he had read it. Then I called the local Los Angeles office of United Artists and told the minor functionary in charge that I expected a "go" any moment from UA in New York. I told him that since that "go" was almost a routine procedure now, I was going to set a date to commence shooting two weeks from that day.

The two weeks passed with no word from Dorso. So I called the local L.A. office of UA back and spoke to the same minor official.

"Have you heard from New York?" I asked him. He had not.

"Okay then," I said. "What do I do?"

"I guess you go ahead and start shooting," he said.

I had enough money to get started, money UA had laid out

as advances and first payments on various contracts. I had the fees and expenses I was being paid as executive producer. The only thing I didn't have—and this was my big mistake—was anything from Dorso in writing. I had no written okay to proceed or to use those funds for the purpose of proceeding with production.

But I proceeded, with my enthusiasm and innocence making me forget reality and corporate nastiness. I assembled my cast and crew, and off we flew to New Mexico.

The group was all very excited. They were unanimously very optimistic about the quality of what we were about to do. I kept hearing over and over, that this was going to be *"The Defenders of the West"*—at the time *The Defenders* was the class series on TV. We all warmed each other with the fires of our optimism.

We shot one day, and it was bliss. We were all so up, so enthusiastic, and so full of the rightness of our purpose that it was like floating. That day we could do no wrong.

But when we got to the set the next day, there stood two lawyer types—you could tell by their white-on-white shirts and narrow ties—and they immediately handed me a telegram.

It said, in effect, that UA had gotten word I was filming a blue script dated so-and-so when they had only approved shooting of a white script dated so-and-so. (In TV circles the white script is the original; the blue script is a rewrite. In our case, the white script was the Merle Miller/Bob Aurthur original, and the blue one which we were using was the new version by Simmons or whoever.) The telegram went on to order me to shoot the white script or reimburse the company $240,000.

Then it dawned on me that I had no witnesses to the phone call in which Dorso had told me to go ahead with the rewrite, or to the UA man in Los Angeles who had told me to go ahead. I had nothing.

■ ■ ■

RICHARD DORSO: His [Merle Miller's] script we just took and did a total rewrite on. We all got damned for certain things in his book *Only You, Dick Daring*. When the script came in, I read it, Bob [Aurthur] read it, we were very good friends, and we both sat down and said this script doesn't work. He has written the climax off camera. The climax wasn't on camera. So we said we have to have a meeting with Merle on this. So he came into the meeting and we presented all our objections, and finally, we got to the climax, and I said, "You haven't given me the lynching scene." It wasn't literally a lynching; it was just my way of defining the climax. "You've written the lynching off camera. You've got to put it on camera so the audience is there when the hero is beset and in desperate trouble." Well, he wrote the book *Only You, Dick Daring*, and he said that I demanded a lynching scene. Which was a total lie, you know, to make Bob and me look bad.

The plain fact of the matter is had that show gone on the air, it would have been a great success, because [of] the people—Barbara Stanwyck was wonderful, and Jackie—and it was a contemporary western-country story. It was *Dallas* before *Dallas*, told with some degree of integrity. But those are the vicissitudes of the business, Jackie's been through them; we've all been through them; you take your lumps. If it hadn't been for *Only You, Dick Daring*, the whole thing would have been forgotten, but that made it a *cause célèbre*. It was the most-talked-about thing that happened that year in show business, that whole book and everything. Then the Writers Guild did a whole sketch on it, and Jackie was there, and he got up like a little man, and he took his lumps, and the whole thing was wiped out forever.

There is only one funny bit, as far as I'm concerned. I had an appointment with David Susskind in his office in New York. We were going to do something together. As I came into David's office, Merle Miller was sitting there. And I only saw him out of the corner of my eye—he was sitting in David's outside office, and I went into David's office. When I came out, he was gone. Bob Aurthur told me later that when he saw me, he panicked, and he went and hid in the men's room until I left the building. I don't know what he thought I was going to do to him, call him names, what?

■ ■ ■

For a fleeting moment, I toyed with the idea of defying them and gambling that $240,000 on my judgment. Then I thought of my children and my wife and my house and all those things, and it was either acquiesce or hock everything.

Before I decided on anything, however, I called the William Morris office in Hollywood. They had power; they were my agents; surely they could do something. I knew from past experience and stories that have become Hollywood legend that William Morris people, when they want to exercise it, had power at the highest TV levels. Besides, they had a considerable financial stake in this.

But when I called, nobody at Morris would talk to me. I asked for all my friends. They were, the switchboard lady said, either all out or in conference—"Sorry, he cannot be disturbed"—and the number of people who were unavailable defied coincidence. After I had become belligerent and threatening, which I had to do with the poor defenseless switchboard lady, who was only following orders, she connected me with Sammy Weisbord. He was then second-in-command to Abe Lastfogel.

I told him what was happening down there in New Mexico and pleaded with him to do something, anything, to talk to Dorso or Aurthur or somebody and to fix it so I could shoot the good script.

Weisbord listened and then said I shouldn't have done what I did. "You should have told Dorso about that blue script," he said.

That conversation was like Nazi Germany. I was the innocent party, the wronged party, the victim of persecution. He was the Gestapo, twisting my innocence into guilt. It was the Great Lie all over again.

"Jack, Jack," he said, "what have you done?"

I hung up.

I realized the William Morris office was not going to side with an actor/producer when they represented "the package," no matter what they might privately feel about who was or was not telling the truth.

So we shot the white script. And the pilot is full of stilted dialogue and, what's perhaps worse, scenes that make no sense because they refer to action that was never shot because it had been cut from the script by Aurthur, to please the committee—UA and CBS.

The performances of the cast, script notwithstanding, were incredible. That morning, when it all hit the fan, I called them all together and told them that we had to shoot the original script. I passed it out, and the comments were unanimous—"This is garbage" was one of the kind ones. But they recognized my predicament and said they would do the best they could with what they had. And they did. And the director did, too. Barbara Stanwyck and Howard Duff both, I think, did the finest work of their careers in that botched-up pilot for *Calhoun*.

Through the entire filming those two lawyers in their narrow ties were on the set every minute of every day, script in hand, to make sure that we shot that script. To me, that's one of the saddest spectacles I've ever seen—two men whose mission in life for seven days was to see that we did the worst we could. One of them, incidentally, is now a movie producer for UA.

When it was over, I took the film back to Hollywood and, full of my usual enthusiasm and energy, got into the editing room determined to make something of the nothing we had shot. But the pieces weren't there; it was like trying to do a jigsaw puzzle with a few pieces from one puzzle and a few pieces from another puzzle. It was totally impossible to cut into a comprehensible whole. But Jerry Fielding, as a favor to me, agreed to write the score, and Mel Tormé wrote the two main themes, all of which helped give it some unity. So I cut it, added the music, and dubbed it.

I knew what I had was a botch, but I just hoped that CBS would recognize the intrinsic worth of the idea and the solid values of the characters. My contract was with UA, not CBS, so dutifully I screened it for the UA brass. Jim Aubrey of CBS later told me I was a jerk—he may have used a stronger word— for being so honorable. He said I should have gone directly to him when I was having trouble and said he would have set it all straight in nothing flat—and I believe he would have, too.

But I didn't. I went to UA and screened it, and the men watched it and filed out of the screening room without even looking at me. I was dead, and I knew it, and I wanted to cry.

■ ■ ■

HY AVERBACK: I was around during what has become the infamous *Dick Daring* thing. As a matter of fact, Jackie asked me to direct it first. Four Star would not loan me out. But I was very much involved in that production as a friend. I remember very carefully reading it because we were on the same lot, and aside from friendship, all that material coming in from Merle Miller, was marvelous re-portage coming out of New Mexico—it would have made two or three great *New Yorker* pieces—and I said, "My

God, this is going to be a very exciting project." And then that first draft came in, and it was a fucking mess. The descriptive things were marvelous. As he described the opening shot, it was almost poetry, as the glint of light came through the glass house and a prism of colors hit the lady's face, and then the dialogue started, and it was dumb. The bottom line was that it was just not a good script.

■ ■ ■

In due time, I got a call from Jim Aubrey. He was out in Los Angeles, staying at the Bel Air Hotel, and wanted to see me. I still had that faint flicker of hope burning inside me, and I told myself—I really knew better—that he had seen the pilot and recognized that buried under the crap was a helluva good idea.

We shook hands and Aubrey, never a bush-beater, said, "Well, Jack, what are you going to do with yourself the rest of the season?"

"It depends. If the show sells, then—"

"Forget *Calhoun*," he said, and in those two words was the epitaph of a great idea.

I asked him if he'd seen the pilot, and he never answered me. He just said to forget it, and think about other things.

Later, much later, I learned that the morning of our meeting at the Bel Air Hotel, Aubrey had, with a stroke of his pen, canceled his arrangement with United Artists. He had wiped out seven deals the network had with the studio, mine included.

That whole experience soured me on the entire TV series business. I had never been particularly sweet on it—it was money, not art or love, that had brought me back to Hollywood and money, not art or love, that had kept me here. But there had been a touch of art and a hint of love in the hoped-for series that came to be called *Calhoun*, so when that was yanked out from under me, I was doubly discouraged. I had thought I'd become tough, but I hadn't. It hurt because I had cared.

Then, about a year later, there came a book—*Only You, Dick Daring*, by Merle Miller and Evan Rhodes. It was, according to the subtitle, *How to Write One Television Script and Make $50,000,000*. The one script was, of course, *Calhoun*. I don't know where he got the $50 million figure, but then I don't know where he got most of the things in the book. I never read it—I read a lengthy excerpt that was published in *TV Guide*, but I just couldn't bring myself to read the book itself. What had happened to the show had been sad enough, but I didn't see why I had to read a jazzed-up, largely fictional account of Miller's participation in it.

It was, from all accounts, a very funny book. It attracted a lot of attention with its supposedly inside look at television and how TV shows happen—or don't happen. But it didn't make the best-seller list.

That year the *Only You, Dick Daring* thing was still so fresh in everybody's mind that they had a skit about it at the annual Writers Guild of America awards dinner. They asked me if I would play Jackie Cooper in that skit. Most of the writers doing the show were friends of mine, so I agreed to do it. And it was fun. I did all the dumb things Merle Miller said I did—kissing people, which I don't do, and saying, "God bless you," which I don't do—and the audience loved it. I got an ovation when I walked out onstage, and I got a standing ovation when the sketch was finished. In its review of that evening's proceedings, the *Hollywood Reporter* said "it was the measure of the man" that I had appeared in a skit about a book that had torn me to pieces, playing myself, too.

■ ■ ■

HY AVERBACK: I felt that he was very badly treated in the book, and I think that for all Merle had to say, he should have included his first draft of *Calhoun* in his book. I must say that I think [it was] to Jackie's credit, after all that nonsense, to appear at the Writers Guild in the sketch spoofing that made great sense. I think it was ballsy and marvelous.

■ ■ ■

39.

The combination of the sad death of the show and then the book about that death which maligned me made me completely fed up with the business. I never wanted to be in the position again where I was just a goddamn actor, where I had no power, where I presented a convenient target for anybody and everybody to kick around. No, the days when I was just Jackie Cooper, actor, were over. I would never again let myself get hurt that badly.

I remembered a conversation that had taken place during the preparation of the *Calhoun* work. When all that was swirling around my head, a friend had approached me from Screen Gems. They had said something about needing somebody to run the place, and would I be interested? It was in one ear and out the other—I was busy; I was riding a comet named *Calhoun*.

Afterward, however, when I was licking my wounds, that conversation came back to me. Who had said it? What had been said?

In the glaring, ugly light of *Calhoun* and *Dick Daring*, the idea of being the boss of a studio sounded tantalizing and very sensible.

There was one bit of unfinished business I had to attend to first, before I could commit myself. I wanted to get out of my William Morris representation commitment, after what they had done to me—or, more properly, what they hadn't done for me. I could never forget Sam Weisbord saying, "Jack, Jack, what have you done?" when I called him from New Mexico.

I called Abe Lastfogel, an old family friend, and told him that I wanted to see him. I said that I felt, after having been a client for all those years, I was entitled to talk to him, face to face, and I asked that he have his top six aides there, too. I said I was leaving and felt I had a right to tell them all why and to air my grievances.

"Abe," I said, "you owe me that much. Except for a few

years here and there, I have been a client of your agency since 1931."

So he agreed, and the meeting was held. All his top executives were there, except Weisbord. I said I didn't want to see him. The last time I had seen that man, it had taken two large lawyers to keep me from leaping over a desk and tearing him apart.

At the meeting with Lastfogel and his men I told Abe the whole story. He had not, until then, been told all the details. I told him that when I had called from New Mexico, desperate and needing immediate assistance, nobody would talk to me except Weisbord, who made like it was my fault.

I said that he was fortunate I wasn't suing. After all, his agency was representing two parties (me and United Artists), and it had obviously favored one client over another, and that seemed hardly ethical and possibly not even legal.

I reminded Abe that when he was asked to become president of William Morris, he had said at the time that he wouldn't have taken the job if it hadn't been for my mother's help. I traced our years of working together and then said I felt the agency had done me wrong.

Finally, he conceded.

"I think you've been badly handled," he said.

"I think I was mishandled," I said.

He said no, he wouldn't go that far—badly handled, yes; mishandled, no. I'm not sure I can see a major difference there, but I suppose to an agent that's a fine line that he can see without his glasses.

One last, revealing sidelight about *Calhoun* that I love to remember. Most of the rest of it I'd prefer forgetting.

When we were preparing the show, I went to see Barbara Stanwyck to persuade her to play the female agent on the show. We had a meeting at her house, and I went over everything— the early notes; Miller's presentation; the changes that would come in that; the first draft of the script.

As we talked, we were both drinking wine, and I think we both got a little high. She said she loved the idea and, just as important, loved the character she would be playing, as the work described her.

The character, Miller and I had decided, should be a woman who had had an unhappy love affair, the woman scorned. She had loved a man very much, but the man hadn't loved her back. He had been something of a rat, although all their mutual friends felt he was a prince of a fellow. As I talked and told her about those two and their relationship, she began to look a little sad. She said there were certain similarities between the story I had been outlining and her own life with Robert Taylor. Gradually the conversation switched (the wine working now). Instead of my telling her about the two fictional characters, she was now telling me the real story of Stanwyck and Taylor, and she told me incidents I doubt anyone else has ever heard.

I have something of a phonographic memory—I forget names ten minutes after I see them, but I remember dialogue for years—and when I got home, I wrote down most of Barbara Stanwyck's stories. When we came to work on the script, I added a few lines to the Stanwyck character's speeches, lines that were taken pretty much from what she had told me of her own life with Bob Taylor.

Later, when she read the revised script, she called me.

"You son of a bitch," she said. "You put in everything I told you."

I said I'd take out anything she didn't like.

"Don't change a goddamn word," she said. "I love it."

When we shot that part of the script, those lines were still in. Somehow they had survived all the butchery. I suggested to Stuart Rosenberg, the director, that he use two cameras when he shot that scene, just in case Barbara cracked under the weight of her memories.

Howard Duff was playing the man, and he was magnificent, and the combination of the words that were right out of her heart and Duff's beautiful portrayal were too much. Barbara did crack, and we had to send her home for the rest of that day. But we got the scene, and it was wonderful.

It's too bad nobody ever saw it.

40.

I thought, when they first approached me to become the head of Screen Gems, that they wanted me for my talent, my organizational ability, my knowledge of the industry, or any combination of the above. Maybe that had something to do with it—they wouldn't have hired just any klutz off the street—but there was something else on their minds.

My predecessor was Bill Dozier, a fine gentleman, a very knowledgeable man with thirty years in the industry, and, above all, an executive. He knows how to run things, and when he runs them, he runs them. He brooks no interference. He is the man in charge, period.

The Columbia brass apparently decided they didn't want that. They wanted somebody that they could control. They couldn't keep Dozier under their thumbs, so they bounced him.

They came to me because they felt I was young and, thus, controllable. They also knew I had a pretty good production record in TV. They had also heard, as had almost everyone in TV, about the pilot I had done, *Skippy*. It was a very classy pilot—it hadn't sold because the theory existed in network boardrooms then that series with kids as stars wouldn't make it; the theory lasted until *Dennis the Menace* came along, a few seasons later, and knocked it into a cocked duncecap.

Skippy, like my own two series, was talked about around town, and that talk and the knowledge of my production acumen reached the Columbia boardroom at about the time they had decided to dump Dozier. After the first feeler had been rejected—as I have said, it reached me when I was still involved with, and optimistic about, *Calhoun*—they waited patiently. Maybe they knew something. Anyhow, when *Calhoun* was interred, they came to me again. This time I was vulnerable. I liked the idea of being a boss, rather than being open to having my head handed to me—just a goddamn actor.

They offered me the same $75,000 a year that Dozier had been getting, plus stock options and a fat expense account. But I still hesitated. For once I felt I was in a good position, and

I waited. In the first place, I wasn't sure what I wanted to do. I knew I could still act—there were many offers—but was that what I wanted to do?

I recognized that I was very angry at that time—angry that somebody could write a book and say untrue things about me, angry that the higher-ups considered me just an actor, angry that my own agency had forsaken me at a time when I needed it. I think maybe that last thought—my anger at the William Morris people—really tipped the balance and made me decide to go with Screen Gems. I saw myself running a studio and issuing orders barring William Morris agents from the lot.

The genesis of the idea that eventually brought me to Screen Gems formed in the mind of Steve Blauner. In 1963 he was a talent executive for Screen Gems. For years before, he had been a friend of the company's treasurer, Bert Schneider, and Bert's father, Abe Schneider, the chairman of the board of Columbia Pictures, who owned most of the Screen Gems stock.

Blauner, then about thirty-five years old, had previously been the manager and partner of the late singer Bobby Darin for about ten years. They had matured in business together and had been very successful. At the height of Darin's career Steve decided he needed his own career, and the two parted amicably. That's when Steve, through his childhood friendship with Bert Schneider, was introduced to the New York management of Screen Gems. They recognized his unique ability to discover new talent. For one thing, it was Steve Blauner who established a publishing business, specializing in rock music, that is still one of the most successful phases of the Screen Gems—now Columbia TV—empire.

Blauner was ambitious, but Bill Dozier bracketed him with others as part of "the New York management team." So he had troubles fending for himself in California and communicated only with his friend Bert Schneider and the general manager of all Screen Gems divisions, Jerry Hyams.

Blauner and I had become friendly when, in my *Hennesey* days, I had wanted Bobby Darin to be a guest star on one episode and sing his huge hit "Mack the Knife." Blauner watched the way I ran that show—the business as well as the artistic ends—and after he joined Screen Gems, he started talking me up. He suggested to Schneider and Hyams that I might be the kind of creative executive the New York management could live with, better than Dozier, who was noted as being "network-oriented" and was also inclined to be much too autonomous to suit the New York "family."

There were conversations and more conversations, and finally, I became convinced that Screen Gems really wanted me. It was Steve Blauner who had convinced them to want me, but it was up to me to make the ultimate decision. It was my damaged ego that persuaded me I needed this attention, and I needed to be wanted and pursued, so I succumbed. I told my lawyers to go ahead and negotiate with Columbia, that I wanted the Screen Gems job.

They did a bang-up job of negotiating, too. By the time they were through I had a $150,000 salary, a healthy expense account, a projection room in my house, an annual trip to Europe, a three-year firm contract. That last made me feel secure for the first time in my life. Ever since I was a kid, I'd been living in a six-month-option world. Now I had three years ahead of me, knowing where I'd be, what I'd be doing, and how much I'd be earning for each one of those three years. It was a remarkable feeling.

After my first year they gave me a new three-year deal, with a raise in salary. At the end of the fourth year they added five more years—five years firm. But by then I wanted out.

At first it was the easiest thing I had ever done in my entire life. It was like a joke, it was so easy. You just have to make decisions. People come to you and say, "What do you think of so-and-so for this part?" and you think a minute and say yes or no. It doesn't really matter, in the final analysis, whether it is yes or no either. All that matters is that you make that decision. You quickly learn, as an executive, simply to go ahead and say one thing or the other.

I believe I did some things that were creative. Sometimes I had to fight for them, and when I felt strongly enough, I fought. I won as often as I lost.

I started the development of a daytime soap opera called *Days of Our Lives* in 1964. For a few days it created a big brouhaha with New York management. They felt it was going to be a big loser, and I stuck to my guns, even though a few of the older mossbacks said I should be fired. I am writing this sixteen years later, and *Days of Our Lives* is still going strong, and the studio is still collecting a fortune on it.

Some battles I lost. I could see, back then, that for a filmed half-hour situation comedy, the conventional filming techniques were too slow and, consequently, too expensive. I felt the answer was to do them the way Lucille Ball did her *I Love Lucy* show, only on videotape—three cameras, shot in front of a live audience, in one long take. I found a company that would install the equipment, run all the necessary cables, and I was all set to go with it on several of our new shows. But the mossbacks screamed no no no! They couldn't accept the concept that sometimes you have to spend a little money to make a lot of money. By 1969, just about the time I left the company, that was becoming the accepted way of shooting sitcoms.

By 1966 I wanted desperately to move the company into the longer forms of TV, which I felt was the coming thing. The big stumbling block to that was a man named John Mitchell, who was Screen Gems' sales manager. He had talked the Columbia brass into letting him do all the selling, and he was a crack salesman—but he had had success only in selling half-hour shows. You might think that wouldn't matter much—that's what I thought—but somehow it did. They kept telling me not to make longer shows; I knew that was because Mitchell couldn't sell longer shows.

We had creative people—I brought many of them in—and we developed some fine hour-long pilot scripts. No dice. We managed to get only two on the air—one was *Iron Horse*, which was sold on the strength of Dale Robertson's name, and the other was *Here Come the Brides*, and I still don't know how Mitchell managed to sell that.

In my first year at the studio we made ten pilots and sold six of them, a remarkable record I doubt anyone since has come close to. (The six were the long-running *I Dream of Jeannie* and three that were moderate successes, *The Wackiest Ship in the Army*, *Gidget*, and *Camp Runamuck*, plus two daytime soap operas, *Days of Our Lives* and *Morning Star*.) Four of our other shows were renewed—*The Donna Reed Show*, *Hazel*, *The Farmer's Daughter*, and *Bewitched*. So, for a time, Screen Gems was probably the hottest and busiest studio in town.

And as the man who had engineered it all I was on top of the town. I was suddenly the boy genius—I was hardly forty-one when I started with Screen Gems—and everyone was predicting that I would be the next big tycoon.

One of our biggest problems as a company—this goes for the combined Columbia and Screen Gems operation—was that at the time we didn't have a proper studio. No real plant. No back lot. Just a few battered, run-down sound stages. Along about 1966 I had a meeting with Elliot Hyman at Warner Brothers, a studio which then was doing very poorly. It had been dragged down primarily by a record division which was a total disaster and which, in turn, affected the entire WB picture.

The Warner Brothers studio in Burbank was beautiful—certainly compared to our Gower Street location in Hollywood. Visiting the Columbia/Screen Gems studio was like visiting a warehouse. If I had bigwigs to entertain—prospective advertisers or whoever—it was embarrassing. Even when Harry Cohn had run the studio, he had been embarrassed by how beat-up the place was, and it had gotten progressively worse.

Hyman told me he would sell us the Warner Brothers studio for $32 million. He leveled with me (I think) and told me that it cost $9 million a year just to open the gates every working day—that was because the payroll was loaded with old-timers, deadwood. Chuck Fries, one of my right arms, and I worked out the details and figured that if we took it over, we could cut that figure down so it would cost us only $5 million a year. To us, $5 million was only a couple of half-hour TV shows—and we had around eight of them going that year.

I wrote a long report to the Columbia brass in New York, telling them about this deal. I naturally advocated that we buy the WB lot for the $32 million asking price. I said it would be a bargain; we would realize millions in profits, both in increased efficiency on our own product, movies as well as television, and in renting out sound stages that we couldn't use. It was a sensational deal.

They fired an answer back—absolutely not! They said that Columbia was not in the real estate business. I thought to myself that maybe they should be; they had built a set out in the San Fernando Valley for the film *King Rat*, and they had merely leased the land, but the owner was currently selling it for three times what he had asked Columbia to pay for it. And Columbia had left a million-dollar set there.

Today, of course, Columbia is at Warner's in Burbank—but not as the owner of the studio, as a tenant at a cost of much more than $32 million.

I wanted to change the name of the company. Screen Gems was an old name and, I felt, a tired one. Actually Screen Gems had originated as a small company making commercials. The name didn't fit anymore, however. It smacked of cartoons and filmed commercials—Screen *Germs* is how we referred to ourselves. I said since we were part of Columbia, and since Columbia was an honored name in entertainment, we should simply call ourselves Columbia Pictures Television. Again, my idea was turned down abruptly. Jerry Hyams, the Screen Gems president at the time—my title was officially vice-president in charge of West Coast operations—had an ego, too. He felt that Screen Gems was his company, but that Columbia Pictures Television would not be his company. He wanted to keep a different name, so his title and position would seem separate and apart and more important. I tried to make that change every year for four or five years, without luck. Today, of course, it is Columbia Pictures Television.

By my fourth year I could see that my days were numbered. I knew that a clash was inevitable. They felt they could control me, and I knew they couldn't. I got a new contract—five years firm—and stayed another year. When I left, they owed me for three years and three months, something in excess of $450,000. I settled for less than that, of course, because I had to work in this town, and I knew that big studios don't look with favor on people who are difficult to deal with.

I settled for $150,000—and 5,000 more options of stock. By then the stock had stopped climbing, but had not yet begun to slide.

In my five and a half years at Screen Gems, Columbia's stock had gone from 19 to 44 and split many times besides. I am not saying that was entirely because of my genius, but I believe my administration had something to do with it. After all, for most of that time I was autonomous in running Columbia's TV arm, insofar as development of properties and production were concerned, and we were immensely profitable. During those years the tail was wagging the dog—Screen Gems was the heftiest part of Columbia's profit picture. I am the only one of the Screen Gems executives of those years still in the business—Hyams is now in the window washing business, and Mitchell is a consultant to advertising agencies.

I had to deal with their egos, however, and that was painful. At one point I optioned a little novel which had had an unsuccessful history. I was able to spend sums under $40,000 without getting New York's approval, and since this was considerably under that figure, I did it. It was called *The Flying Nun*.

Hyams and Mitchell asked me why I had optioned a dumb book like that. I said I planned to make a pilot out of it, using Sally Field. She was doing *Gidget* for us, but I knew that wasn't going to make it. I also had a feeling that Sally was going to be a big star and felt we should keep her under contract, and to do that, we had to have a property. One and one equals two—that's why I optioned *The Flying Nun*.

Hyams and Mitchell screamed. They disagreed with everything I had said. So I picked up the phone and called Tom Moore, a good friend and brilliant TV executive with ABC. I explained the situation to him.

"Say no more," Tom said.

He called Mitchell. And he apparently explained to him a few of the facts of TV life. Pretty soon Mitchell called me.

"Hey, Jack," he said. "I've been thinking over that *Flying Nun* thing we were discussing the other day. We should talk."

It was almost too late. We had no contract with Sally, so we had to renegotiate her whole deal. For *Gidget* we had been paying her $900 an episode. For *The Flying Nun*—because Hyams and Mitchell had dallied so long and forced us into a corner—we had to pay her $8,500 an episode. I had wanted to give her a contract for $1,500 a show, and she had been willing. But that was before.

More and more, that sort of thing was happening. They wouldn't listen to me—the name change, people I wanted to sign. So, after a series of business negotiations, I left.

I thought I was in great shape financially. I had all those shares of Columbia stock—thousands and thousands and thousands of shares, worth $44 a share. But soon after I left, the stock began to drop. The president of my bank warned me that if I sold, I'd get hit with a big capital gains tax. I said okay, pay the tax, but sell—I don't want to ride this thing down into the basement. He still said no, that wasn't smart business. I finally sold when it was $22. I estimate that at its peak, I had somewhere around $900,000 worth of stock.

I had blown another fortune.

■ ■ ■

GRANT TINKER: When Jack was at Screen Gems, I was at NBC, a customer of his. We had occasions to be together. He proved himself to be a good and organized executive. Some people have creative thrust which spills all over the floor. But maybe because of his Navy training, he was organized. I'm star-struck about good executives. Bill Dozier, Jack's predecessor, was also organized. But he is an executive. In the second year of Mary's [Mary Tyler Moore] half-hour show, I asked Jack to direct a couple. He said he'd love to. He did one, very well. Our policy always is to have writers come down to rehearsals regularly to comment on how the show is going. There's lots of talk back and forth. Other directors live with that. After he'd done the show, Jack came to me and said he couldn't be part of a group process; he has to be the guy in charge. He chafed under the democracy of a three-camera show, so he asked, and I agreed, to let him out of the rest of his commitment.

■ ■ ■

41.

Many people in show business, faced with a career decision such as mine at the time—direct or act?—rely on their agents to help them make up their mind. Many, in fact, let the agents do all the thinking for them.

I never had an agent who, I felt, was so totally in my corner that I could trust him (or her) that far. I always felt my agent had a personal ax to grind—the not-inconsiderable commission—and would therefore think about that first and my well-being and welfare second.

There are, I am told, agents who have the interests of their clients uppermost in their hearts and minds and thoughts. These paragons of virtue have been known, so the fables have it, to recommend a course of action to their clients that will result sometimes in a smaller commission to them, but a better future for the client.

I will have to see it to believe it. Maybe Abe Lastfogel forty years ago, I don't know.

My education regarding agents began when I was a small boy. I studied the four Rs—reading, 'riting, 'rithmetic, and rip-offs. I learned, at my mother's knee, what was what.

When, as a kid, I began doing vaudeville, my mother had to have somebody in the East handling our negotiations. Frank Orsatti, my agent at the time, arranged for us to meet Abe Lastfogel, and the William Morris people in New York. At the time William Morris was a traditional management firm, not just a booking agency. Lastfogel explained that he and his company were interested in career guidance, in supervising the growth of its clientele. To my mother, that sounded very good.

My mother became very friendly with Abe's wife, an ex-vaudevillian named Frances Arms. She had been a Sophie Tucker-like performer, shorter than Sophie, but built along the same general architectural principles. Frances and my mother found they had the same basic outlook on life: They were two very honest ladies; they had no time for nonsense or bridge parties or shopping. They were what Frances called *hamisch*—

show biz Yiddish, a word meaning something like "very comfortable and homey."

From then on, whenever we went to New York, we usually saw Abe and Frances Lastfogel. On one of those visits, Abe said that they wanted to make him president of the company and to move his headquarters to Los Angeles. The feeling was, he said, that the whole world of show biz would soon be centered in Los Angeles, and they felt the main William Morris office should be there, too. But Frances said she wouldn't go.

She told us that she had been to the Coast, as all New Yorkers then called California, and she didn't like it. She said she didn't drive a car and had no intention of learning how. Since she couldn't and wouldn't drive, she would be stuck in the house in Los Angeles every day, day in and day out, and what kind of idiot does Abe think she is, "to be stuck in the house, day in and day out, for the rest of my life?"

"Talk some sense to her, Mabel," Abe said.

My mother talked some sense to her. The biggest thing, she said, was that the move was important to Abe and his career. If he told William Morris he wouldn't go, they wouldn't fire him, of course, but he would probably never become the head of the company. That was number one. Number two was: "When you get out to the Coast, you won't be stuck in the house all the time. I'll drive you around," my mother said, "until you learn to drive yourself."

"Come out for a while," my mother said. "I'll make reservations for you. Just try it and see if you don't get to like it."

So my mother made reservations for them at the Beverly Wilshire Hotel—where Abe still lives, to this day. And she drove Frances Lastfogel around every day for six months until finally, one day, Frances said that she thought now she could survive, with an acquired chauffeur and car, by herself.

I learned from Abe, and a few others at William Morris, that there are some agents who are honestly and truly involved in career guidance. These are almost always men who are the higher echelons of the company—men like Lastfogel himself or Lew Wasserman. Lew guided Marlon Brando personally for years—slowly, methodically, carefully, successfully. Abe was always very careful with Judy Garland. His only problem was that he had led such a sheltered life himself that when people tried to tell him his little Judy was becoming a drug addict, he wouldn't believe them.

Abe Lastfogel, Lew Wasserman, Nat Kalsheim, George Wood—they were good men who cared deeply about their clients and gave them good, sound advice. But I'm afraid that the succeeding generation of agents was not so caring. Sammy Weisbord, the man who infuriated me during the *Calhoun* affair, had only a nodding acquaintance with the concept of career guidance.

The current generation of agents, the third I've been involved with, again has little of the sense of helpfulness of the Lastfogel-Wasserman-Kalsheim-Wood breed.

Today it seems to be unfortunate but true that when you sign with an agent, you also have to retain a lawyer—to read the agreement with the agent and make sure he isn't about to take your teeth, as well as your 10 percent. You have to have a personal manager, too—the agent today concerns himself solely with negotiating deals, so you need a manager for the career guidance bit, and a lawyer to watch out for *your* interests, and a business manager to make sure that some of your money stays at home. The personal touch is gone. To most agents-managers-lawyers-business managers, a performer is a piece of meat.

When I was a kid, Lastfogel and Kalsheim used to talk to me over and over about behavior. Good and professional conduct, they would tell me, is very important for a young man. They imbued me with sound ideas about being kind and courteous to young ladies, being polite to my elders, and how the show must go on. I doubt that the young actors today ever hear a word about anything like that. Maybe that's why the youthful actors I've had to work with have been, almost uniformly, difficult and unpleasant.

There was, for example, Andrea McArdle. She was the young singer who created the title role of *Annie* on Broadway. I directed her in the TV movie *Rainbow*, in which she played Judy Garland. She was fifteen—no baby—and should have learned something about respect by then. But she hadn't. We did the recordings of the songs first, and she was cold and unresponsive. She would take musical direction, but not emotional direction. When we broke, I asked her mother if something was wrong. She said Andrea was "disappointed" with the film's producers, who hadn't given her an extra week off she had wanted. I said that had nothing to do with me; I was the director, not the producer. The good lady said that in Andrea's mind, we were all one. Then she said something that horrified me.

"She's fifteen," Andrea's mother said. "We can't tell her what to do."

I was furious. I said that she should go tell her daughter to pay the director some respect. The woman shrugged and said it wouldn't help because she didn't listen to anybody anyhow. I had been around child actors a good part of my life, but I had never heard anything as pathetic as that.

Andrea wouldn't let her mother visit her on the set. Three times, when Mrs. McCardle appeared, Andrea sulked and asked me to have her mother removed from the stage.

The day before we were to start shooting, I had the whole cast over to my house to read the script, as a kind of minirehearsal. (There was no provision in the budget for a real rehearsal.) I asked her personally to come over, but she said she wasn't sure if she would or wouldn't. My assistant director phoned her and read her out, insisted that she come, and, in fact, picked her up and brought her over. We sat around and read the script—but at fifteen, she couldn't read well at all.

I wanted Don Murray, playing her father, to pick her up in one scene. She said no, she wouldn't do it because her underwear would show. I found out later that she had decided she didn't like Don, who is only the nicest man alive. I let her sulk for a half hour on that one, until she finally agreed.

All through it I remembered back to what I had been taught, and what I had practiced, about respect and good conduct from Lastfogel and the other William Morris old-timers. They would have chewed Andrea McCardle out until they saluted them.

Today bad conduct is rife on movie and TV sound stages. The younger stars, who have gone from nothing to something in one easy lesson, are the worst culprits, of course. The guys on *CHiPs* (Eric Estrada and Larry Wilcox), the guys on *Starsky and Hutch* (David Soul and Paul Michael Glaser), and even an older man like Peter Falk, who should know better, are most unprofessional in their conduct, in my opinion. The problem is that they begin to believe that they are indispensable; without them, the series will go down the drain, so they imagine themselves in the position of being untouchable.

I have an agent today, and I've been pleasantly surprised to find some genuine enthusiasm there. And there's some indication that we see eye to eye on the proposition that the big fat offer today may not be as good as what could come to-morrow.

I was recently offered a very tempting one-year deal to direct two half-hour pilots and one hour pilot—and for that I would have received a guaranteed $300,000 fee plus royalties (every time the shows aired I would get $1,000 per half hour and $1,500 per hour). My current agent, Bill Haber, of Creative Artists Associates, said he thought I should turn it down unless I needed that money. I had been inclined to turn it down myself—I want to direct features or at the least quality TV movies—and I was very encouraged when Bill said that. I turned the offer down.

Maybe the spirit of some of the old agents isn't dead yet.

42.

Besides my increased knowledgeability about agents, another by-product of my Screen Gems years was aviation.

Virtually all my life I suffered from that very common phobia, fear of flying. I can, however, pinpoint the cause of that frightening ailment. In 1938 my mother and I flew to New York for our annual vaudeville tour, and that was early in the history of commercial aviation. We flew on a DC-2, a plane which could fly no higher than ten thousand feet and had to land if it rained hard. And it rained very hard on our trip. For the better part of one day, we were grounded in Amarillo, Texas. The entire Los Angeles–New York flight took about two and a half days. And there wasn't a comfortable, peaceful moment en route. Both my mother and I were "shook up" by that experience. We had been scheduled to do almost a week of interviews in New York, before my first engagement, but my mother canceled the whole lot of them, and we spent that week just recovering from the ordeal of that coast-to-coast nightmare.

After that, no planes, ever. We took trains to all of our dates; I even think it went into a contract sometime that I was not to be made to fly for any purpose. I didn't fly again for years after that.

When the war came, one of the reasons I opted for the Navy was that the idea of small boats—as opposed to planes—appealed to me. But as luck would have it, when I was in the Pacific with Claude Thornhill, all we did was fly in unarmed aircraft, from island to island. I was scared every time we took off.

After the war I reverted back to my no-fly rule. I drove coast to coast a few times, as long as that took, so I could avoid the necessity of climbing into an airplane. And during my years on Broadway and my years starring on TV in Hollywood, I rarely flew—only if it was absolutely essential.

However, when I got to Screen Gems, flying between New York (our corporate headquarters) and Los Angeles (our studio and my base) became a way of life. In my first eleven months with the company I made twenty-one round trips. And I developed a system to cope with it. I'd drink before the flight, keep drinking during the flight, and then be hung over for a day or so after the flight. Between getting drunk and recovering, I figured out that I had wasted around fifty days, and it hadn't helped much. Flying still scared me to death.

On the last leg of the last of those twenty-one round trips, flying west on TWA, the captain introduced himself to me, and we were talking, and I mentioned my fright.

"Why don't you take flying lessons?" he said.

At first, the idea seemed ludicrous. A man afraid of flying should take flying lessons? That would be like a man afraid of mice volunteering to leap into a vat of rats.

"I'm serious," the captain said. "If you understand what flying is all about, you won't be so frightened."

I thought about it, and the following week I was in Palm Springs for a few days of sunshine. I remembered once passing the Palm Springs Airport, where there was a sign about flying lessons. So I screwed up my courage and drove over there, and before I could talk myself out of it, I took one lesson.

I caught the bug. That's all it took, that one lesson in a Cessna 150 at the Palm Springs Airport. The difference is being in control. Since then, I have flown more than three thousand hours—but I still can't climb to the top of a six-foot ladder. I do acrobatics in airplanes—but I cannot climb out on a roof.

After only six hours of instruction I soloed, one of the most thrilling moments of my life. At forty-three, I felt like a kid who had just taken the family car out alone for the first time.

After only thirty-three hours of flying experience, I went out and bought a plane. It had retractable landing gear. The recommendation is that you can't solo in a plane with retractable landing gear until you've flown at least one hundred hours; I did it after only thirty-five hours.

Pretty soon I was flying back and forth between Los Angeles and Palm Springs. At first, Barbara wouldn't fly with me; she still drove between our two homes. But after I had flown a few hundred hours, she relented.

In 1970, after I had logged nine hundred hours or so, the Navy made me a pilot. At the time I owned a twin-engined pressurized Aero Commander—one of several planes I've owned—and would land it at various naval bases where I was to perform reserve duties. One day, at Los Alamitos Naval Air Station, the commanding officer asked if I'd like to be able to wear Navy aviator's wings on my uniform. Of course, I said yes, and he put the request through the proper channels, and soon down came the recommendation, all the way from the Chief of Naval Operations. They would make me an honorary Navy pilot with the privilege of wearing the Navy pilot's wings of gold on my uniform. The Navy held a nice, low-key ceremony at Los Alamitos, and I had my wings. I was very honored.

I was even more honored when I learned that I was one of only three men in naval aviation history to have received Navy wings in that way. And one of the other two gave his back.

The first one was a Canadian who had saved the Navy millions of dollars on a wing design, and so they had rewarded him by making him an honorary naval aviator. Then they decided to honor Arthur Godfrey, an ex-Navy man, who had done a lot for the cause of private aviation. After he got his Navy wings, Godfrey, who had commercial and instrument ratings, asked if he could solo in a jet, but they told him the Navy rule was that nobody—absolutely nobody—soloes in a Navy airplane after he has reached his forty-fifth birthday. They feel that over that age it is too risky to allow anyone to fly such sophisticated aircraft. So they turned Godfrey down. The Air Force's General Curtis LeMay heard about what had happened and contacted Godfrey and said that if he came over to the Air Force, they would teach him to solo in a jet. So Godfrey gave the Navy back its wings and went with the Air Force.

The Navy doesn't like to talk about Arthur Godfrey and has been very careful about getting involved with show biz people since that incident, and I can't say I blame them. But I had been with the Naval Reserve a very long time, and they knew me and, I assumed, trusted me.

I felt that the Navy's rule of not flying alone after forty-five in a jet or anything else made good sense. So when I turned forty-five, in '67, it seemed sensible to me to hire a copilot on all my civilian flights. It was a precaution, so there would be somebody around in case anything happened to me. Barbara and our children flew with me often after I began doing that.

Then came an air taxi business, and on into the fringes of an airline business, with my Desert Commuter Airlines, flying back and forth between Los Angeles and Palm Springs. For a short while we prospered. But when Nixon's deregulation policies took effect, our operation became impossible. Western

Airlines was soon charging $1.50 less than we had to charge, and that was the end of that. Before long, I found myself with a bunch of useless and expensive airplanes on my hands. I'd signed notes for all of them, and I had to sell them quickly, and I took a beating on every deal.

I still fly when I can, although at the moment I do not own a plane of my own. I no longer am afraid of flying commercially, either, because I know what's going on in the cockpit. On most flights there are three men (occasionally these days one of the three is a woman) who know how to handle a plane.

But I worry—as do most informed people in the aviation field—about larger issues in flying. I am afraid that, one of these days, there is going to be a Watergate-like scandal dealing with aviation that will be a real shocker to the public. It will, I believe, reveal two parallel facts:

First, manufacturers of the big commercial airliners are trying to keep costs down so badly that too many corners are being cut.

Second, the discovery of what those economies are doing to planes (such as engines falling off, on more than just DC-10s, because of cost-conscious shortcuts and compromises) indicates the manufacturers are aware of what is going on, and so are the airlines and maybe even the federal regulatory bodies—but they are all getting together to look the other way. There is, most of the aviation insiders believe, hanky-panky, so the manufacturers turn out a product they know has some faults, the airlines accept them with full knowledge of those faults, and the federal agencies are looking the other way. And all in the name of economy and the health of big business.

I know that there is one popular aircraft flying today that the commercial pilots recognize as faulty. They have found that if they fly one of the engines on that plane at the engine rpm the manufacturer recommends, it vibrates alarmingly. So by tacit agreement, the airline pilots will not fly it at its recommended rpm. Maybe someday, to meet a schedule or to mollify some VIP, it will be flown at its specifications, and it will vibrate alarmingly—and it just might go to pieces. I will fly on that plane today because I know that the pilots in the Airline Pilots Association recognize its weakness and will take pains to keep that engine below the rpm the manufacturer recommends—and, incidentally, the speed the federal agencies have approved.

In my flying and my talking to pilots and others in the flying

business, I have learned that there are five basic causes of the
majority of air crashes:

1. Airlines, in their quest to save fuel for economy and for
basic fuel conservation, will make their pilots fly unsafe approaches. The big San Diego crash of a few years back was
thus caused—the approach the pilot took was the one his airline
said he had to take because it saved fuel, even though it was
hazardous.

2. People who live near airports, or own real estate near
airports, get on their noise abatement soapbox and cause all
kinds of fuss and furor. And so—as in New York—pilots must
make dangerous approaches and takeoffs rather than safer but
louder approaches and takeoffs over land to mollify them.

3. Airlines, again in a drive for economy, are cutting back
on their training programs. Thus, there are some people sitting
in cockpits whose education has been shortened and who may
have missed a few very important lessons, particularly engi-
neers—those in the cockpit in charge of the engine instruments.

4. Manufacturers, to keep costs down, are cutting corners
on the planes they are turning out and delivering to the airlines.

5. The rising costs of jet fuel, because of the twin pressures
of OPEC gouging and oil company profiteering, are putting the
screws to both airlines and manufacturers. And that, in turn,
leads to reasons 1, 3, and 4 above.

The whole area of politics and aviation is sickening. For
example, it was Nixon who first would not permit supersonic
planes to fly over the continental United States. He took bows
for that action, and even some environmentalists cheered, and
the papers applauded the fact that now there would be no noise
of a plane breaking through the sound barrier. It's all baloney—
military planes break through the sound barrier some fifty times
a day over the United States, and rarely is anyone inconve-
nienced. I myself, on training flights with the Navy, have
broken the sound barrier on an average two or three times a
year—and there are a lot of people like me flying.

I love flying now, now that I know what it is all about. And
I have recommended that anyone suffering from fear of flying
do what I did—take a flying lesson. Maybe it won't convert
you into a pilot, but I am almost positive it will cure you of
that fear. There is nothing like knowledge to chase away blind
panic.

43.

I think there was one other by-product of the Screen Gems experience I must mention. I learned quickly the art of dealing with people and, specifically, how to be an executive.

The background must be sketched in. My predecessor at Screen Gems, as I have mentioned, was Bill Dozier. One of his last pilot films, before he left in the fall of '63, was a show called *Bewitched*, which Dozier had made with Harry Ackerman producing. Elizabeth Montgomery was the star. The series, to be produced the following summer, had been sold to ABC.

I was convinced the show was a winner and looked forward to working with Liz. I had met her, years before, when I had done the show her father used to host, *Robert Montgomery Presents*. Bob Montgomery had invited Barbara and me up to his apartment after that show, which must have been in late 1954, and I had met his teenage daughter, already beautiful and already very strong and positive. I had met her since, socially, with her first husband, and then when she was Mrs. Gig Young, and then when she was Mrs. Bill Asher. I had known Asher, too, when he directed many of Lucille Ball's old *I Love Lucy* shows.

When I took over at Screen Gems in January 1964, Liz called and said she wanted to see me. Fine. But I didn't want it to be a business meeting, so I suggested we have lunch at the Beverly Hills Hotel. We had a pleasant lunch, chitchat and food, and then she got very businesslike.

She said she wanted to remind me of the promises Bill Dozier had made to her and make sure I kept those promises. What had Bill promised?

First, that her husband, Bill Asher, would be the producer. Harry Ackerman could be executive producer, but Bill would be the man running things. Second, she had ideas on what direction the show should take, and she wanted those ideas incorporated in future scripts. Three, Dozier had promised her casting approval and director approval. Four—most important—Billy would direct the first eight or nine shows in a row, in addition to producing.

I listened to these "promises" of Dozier's. They didn't sound like Dozier.

"Liz," I said, "Bobby Kennedy once told me that shortly after the President was shot, he went up to Lyndon Johnson and said that Jack had told him he wanted something or other done. And Lyndon looked down at him and said, 'I'm the President now.' Well, Liz, I'm in charge now."

She looked at me with her big blue eyes, which can become very steely when she wants them to, and she said, "It's too bad. It would have been a nice little show."

I explained to her that none of those "promises" were in her contract; I had made a point of getting out her contract and reading it before the luncheon meeting. She said she knew they weren't, but they were verbal promises Bill Dozier had made. I said that I was sorry, but I simply could not go along with any of those "promises." She smiled sweetly, thanked me for lunch, and said, as she left, that she wasn't going to do the show.

As soon as I got back to my office, I called her agent and told him about our conversation. He was very nervous. I told him I would, of course, have to report all this to the head of all Screen Gems divisions, Jerry Hyams, in New York. And he, in turn, would have to notify ABC. And ABC's first step would undoubtedly be to cancel the sale, unless (which was very unlikely) a mutually satisfactory replacement could be found. The agent said, "Please, hold the fort—don't do anything until I talk to her." In less than an hour he called back to say that she was firm; she was quitting. I hadn't expected her to have any other reaction.

This, I felt, was a good time for me to learn how I stood—and also how I could stand up to the pressure, real executive suite action. I hadn't been sure how I could handle that kind of thing. My psychiatrist in New York used to say I was too kindly, and I had to be more firm, especially with women.

If I was to be head of the studio, I was to be the head of the studio. But I wasn't merely being stubborn for stubbornness's sake; there were good reasons not to go along with Liz's demands. Ackerman was a tried-and-true TV producer; he should be in charge. No way was Billy going to direct the first eight or nine shows—nobody in his right mind did that. Casting and director approval? Not in my studio. And if she had ideas as to the direction in which the show was going, fine, but let her funnel them through the producer.

So I called Tom Moore, then the head of ABC, directly. Tom was a good, level-headed person, not given to hysterics. I explained what had happened. He said that maybe we could find a replacement, maybe not. At the least, it would mean a test film on the girl. They might even want an entire new pilot film. He said, "Let's wait and see who you can come up with."

I had our casting office begin looking for another girl, of the same general age and type as Liz Montgomery. I didn't tell the press (neither did Liz, I was happy to see), but there was a leak. In those days all the columnists in town had people in every studio on their payroll, at so much a tip, and there was no such thing as a secret. So the story leaked, merely saying that "Elizabeth Montgomery was unhappy at Screen Gems," and nobody denied it.

We found three girls we felt were good enough to test for the part of Samantha. We arranged for the tests to be filmed three days hence, and we hired a director, selected the scene, arranged for sets and costumes, brought in Dick York (already set for the costar) to work with the girls. All of this, of course, was money, and not an inconsiderable sum, out of Screen Gems' pocket.

The day before the tests a messenger appeared at my office, bearing a hand-delivered, handwritten note of apology from Liz. She said she had realized that her demands were outside her contract. She felt she should have respected and trusted me. She promised that she would not demand or insist that Bill either produce or direct. She would work well with Harry Ackerman, she was sure. She hoped that I would bear Bill in mind for the future.

I had won, but I wanted to nail the victory down. I showed the note to our legal department and asked if there was a way that note could be made a part of her contract. They said yes, if they prepared an instrument saying that and had her sign it. So they quickly drafted such an instrument, and we sent it over to her, and she duly signed it.

From that day on, for the first five years *Bewitched* was on, Liz Montgomery never spoke to me. On the other hand, she was never late, she always knew her lines, she never caused anybody any trouble, she was a perfect lady, and she made the show a huge success.

We did have Bill Asher direct a few shows during the first

two seasons, and in the third year Harry Ackerman became the executive producer and Bill became the producer.

In 1968, during the Christmas season, I was putting the lights up outside the house when Liz and Bill drove up. They were bringing a gift—a large and lavish Christmas wreath which I promptly nailed to the front door. There were hugs and kisses all around, and we became good friends again.

Soon after that gift it was time for negotiations with her for another contract. At the time of those negotiations I knew something she didn't know—and I hoped she would not find out. That was that ABC was making us an extremely profitable deal for the syndication rights to *Bewitched*. The deal was contingent on our signing her to another five-year contract. So it was to our interests to sign her before she got wind of that proviso; if she did find out, she could justifiably hold us up for a lot more money. So I became more generous with her than I might otherwise have been. I wanted her name on that contract very quickly, and very painlessly, so the syndication deal could go through.

And so I made her a most generous offer—involving cash, a big increase in her salary, a deferment arrangement. I believe she received maybe a half million more than she might have, had not circumstances dictated. And that wreath had contributed to my feeling of kindness. For years we kept that wreath, and whenever we put it on the door, every Christmas, Barbara and I joked about the "half-million-dollar wreath."

The show, as it was, ran on ABC for eight years. It became one of the big hits in TV series syndication and turned out to be a gold mine.

44.

When I left Screen Gems, I enjoyed my freedom for a few weeks. And I marveled at one of the phenomena of the Hollywood scene—the great hot potato act. As soon as somebody gets a big new executive job, there are hundreds of phone calls from old (often so old you can't remember) friends. And you get put on lists for party invitations and premieres and all kinds of inside extra-added perks. Ah, but the day after you quit or are bounced, all that stops. The letters and phone calls and telegrams stop coming. If you are sensitive, you can suffer from withdrawal symptoms of the most serious kind.

It didn't bother me, but I must admit that it was with a feeling of warmth, then, that I got a call from Bob Finkel a day or so after the announcement of my resignation was published.

He called to offer me the use of a desk in his office and a secretary if I needed them. I thought that was very nice of him. I didn't need those facilities, but the offer touched me.

Finkel was a very big producer in television. I'd first met him way back during the days of *The People's Choice*. When we first went on the air with that show, NBC felt that it was a bit shaky and suggested we use Finkel, an experienced director at the time. He came in and did a few of the shows, and we hit it off very well. But he didn't stay; he got tapped to do Perry Como's show in New York and produced that for some years. I once guested on Como's show—yes, with the dog from *The People's Choice*—and we had a good time. From then on, whenever Barbara and I went to New York, we visited with Jane and Bob Finkel. We often talked, hopefully, about someday going into business together, and we would thrash over ideas and projects and plans.

After his stint with Como was over, Finkel came back to California, and he was working steadily during my years with *Hennesey* and *Calhoun* and Screen Gems.

After my association with Screen Gems ended, Finkel and

I had a few lunches and a few dinners, without wives, and Bob said, "Jack, let's form a business."

He was under contract to NBC but felt that wouldn't be any problem. He thought NBC would be tickled to have me, too. We went to our lawyers and worked out a deal—he would still work exclusively for NBC, but our company and I wouldn't. Since NBC knew me—I had done so many things for it—we felt it would be receptive. In effect, it would be getting the benefit of my creativity, and our joint creativity, for the price of what it was paying Finkel alone.

We forgot one element in our planning. We forgot about human nature. Specifically we forgot that there were executives at NBC and that executives everywhere keep one eye on what's in front of them and another eye, warily, on their backs. They worry constantly about who might be approaching them from the rear, ready with a well-timed stab. Several of them—one in particular—worried about me. I was just off a successful run as head of a studio, and he evidently felt that I must be gunning for his job. I was, to him, a challenge and a threat.

If the truth be known, I would like to be head of network programming as much as I'd like to have a hemorrhoid. But Herb Schlosser, vice-president in charge of programming at the time, didn't know that. His worry caused NBC to act in a way that made it difficult for me, for Bob, and for the Cooper-Finkel Company.

At the time we began, of course, we didn't suspect this. So I moved into Bob's offices. We formed our company (tossing a coin to see whose name would go first) and invested $50,000 to develop TV and movie properties. The Cooper-Finkel Company was in business. NBC began objecting immediately to my presence, but its objection, at first, was minimal. The new logo of the Cooper-Finkel Company immediately went on Bob's shows. From then on, for several years, it became familiar to see the line "Executive Producers: The Cooper-Finkel Company" on many NBC programs.

We began developing properties. We were full of ideas and dreams. There would be half-hour sitcoms—that was an area I knew so well—and variety hours—the area that Finkel knew so well—and movies—the area we both wanted to explore.

But then we began running afoul of Herb Schlosser. Personally we had always gotten along fine. When I first met him, he was in the network's New York legal department—which somehow, in NBC's infinite corporate wisdom, seemed to it the perfect training ground for programming executives. He worked his way into a major programming position in New York, where our paths did not cross.

Schlosser was transferred to Los Angeles while I was still at Screen Gems. On one of his first visits to Screen Gems he got me aside and said, "Jackie, you have to help me. I know that in my new job I'm going to have to see dailies. And I've never been to dailies. What do I look for?"

I invited him to sit with me at Screen Gems while I watched dailies. It was impossible for me to see every inch of footage shot—that was physically too long a procedure—but I had worked out a system of spot-checking, seeing a little from each show. It is important that a studio head do so. One trick I found was to look at the faces of the cast and crew immediately after the director yells, "Cut." It always takes a few seconds for the cameraman to react and stop rolling, and in those few seconds you get a great insight into a company. Once they think the camera is off, they show their real feelings toward the director and toward each other. So you can tell if it's a happy company or one that's torn by hard feelings, and hard feelings mean problems for a studio head.

So I tipped Schlosser off to that and some other things I thought he should look for when watching dailies. He sat with me through dailies on several visits to the studio, before he actually took over his new job.

I used to kid him.

"Next year," I said, "if we sell you a show, and you watch the dailies of that show, I don't want to hear you say, 'Where's the close-up of the girl?'"

And a year later we did sell NBC a show—*Occasional Wife*, with Michael Callan and Patricia Harty—and Schlosser saw the dailies one day with me, and he leaned over and said, "Where's the close-up of the girl?" He wasn't trying to be funny when he said it either. I couldn't help it—I burst out laughing, and he was very offended.

Maybe that was the background of his reaction to my presence at NBC later, when Cooper-Finkel was formed. He obviously assumed that since I had been almost his mentor, I would surely be after his job. He proceeded to do everything he could to make life tough for Bob and me and our young company.

Our deal with NBC allowed it first look at anything and
everything we did. And with that look, it had the right to hold
those things for a certain period of time. Our friend Schlosser
held onto our things for every allotted second—so long that
it became too late to sell them to anyone else—and then turned
them all down flat.

I must admit that the things we did were not easy sells. We
are both, Finkel and I, creative and not ones to be satisfied
with merely copying other people's successes. We tried to be
inventive, and in television, that's two strikes against you.
What the public doesn't understand about television—and I'm
not sure that the network executives understand this either—
is that programming is largely based on a computer. The networks each year are offered literally hundreds of program ideas.
They don't trust their own taste and judgment. They rely,
instead, on their machines to rate the new ideas and tell them
if they are worth putting in the schedule.

But computers—and this is the hitch—can judge only on
what has gone before. They are programmed with data about
previous series and how they have done, and they subsequently
measure new ideas against old ones. That is all they can do.
They are electronically unable to consider that an idea could
be new and different and, therefore, appealing in its very
uniqueness. That's why most new shows are copies or switches
on old shows—because those are the ideas in which the machine can see merit. It is only rarely that a new idea is given
a chance, then, usually, only when a star the network wants
fights for it or a network has a financial stake in the program.

So the Cooper-Finkel ideas struck out—because they were
largely new and different, and the machine had nothing to
measure them against and so screamed out "Tilt" or whatever
it screams.

We managed to do two pilots—*Doctor Dan*, in which I
starred, and *Lily*, with Brenda Vaccaro. They were both good;
they were both inventive and ahead of their time; they both
died.

Incidentally, when we began working on *Doctor Dan*, I was
to be solely behind the scenes. But NBC—via Schlosser—
insisted that the only way they would consider it would be if
I starred in it. I think he reasoned that if I were stuck in a TV
show, I certainly would not be after his job, so they offered
me a rich deal to star in *Doctor Dan*. The machine rated me

highly, but not the show; it had never heard of a comedy series about a child psychologist, so it was another "Tilt."

Meanwhile, Bob Finkel was rolling along. He was doing a series of Bing Crosby specials, making good money, which kept our company afloat. I kept striking out in my end—the TV shows didn't sell; our movie ideas never got off the ground—and I began to feel that I wasn't pulling my share of the wagon. I tried to help Bob with the live variety shows, but I quickly got the idea that I wasn't welcome there. Bob would say things like "You do what you do, and I'll do what I do," which didn't sound very partnerlike to me. But he practiced what he preached—he stayed out of *Doctor Dan* and *Lily*, although when we had meetings about those and other projects, he was never shy about expressing himself and his opinions. I thought that was fine. In return, I felt I should be allowed to do the same in his meetings relative to the variety programs, yet when I did, I felt I was being tolerated at best.

Bob got an offer to produce Pearl Bailey's show at ABC so, to Schlosser's delight, the Cooper-Finkel Company moved out, to the Hollywood Palace. It was, officially, a Cooper-Finkel production, and even though I had nothing to do with the show, I moved in. I bought a desk and a couch for my office, but that was all—I never got the other things I needed, such as a coffee table or an end table—because I had nothing to do there.

So I began taking acting jobs again. I did guest shots, on shows like Raymond Burr's *Ironside*, and at least I was keeping busy. Gradually the partnership just sort of decayed, until Bob was doing his things and I was doing my things and we actually saw each other only very seldom. I started back directing then—I did many of the early episodes of *M*A*S*H*—and he continued to be doing well at what he does. I didn't feel good about it, because there was so much I wanted to say and couldn't. If I love somebody, I can't discuss my feelings very easily, and so things fester and get worse and you wind up with a full-blown incident.

Anyhow, we both realized that Cooper-Finkel was over, and so we got our lawyers to dissolve the corporation.

About a month later he invited me to lunch and said he hoped we would continue to be friends. I wanted to, of course, but I was still bothered by the way he had left me out of things. I never could talk about things like that. So I sat there at that lunch and smiled and said very little. We parted, and I didn't see him again for years, not until after Barbara and I separated.

He was the only person—the only person—who called me during the time Barbara and I were apart. He said he wasn't taking sides, because he and his wife, Jane, loved Barbara, too, but he wanted me to know he was thinking about me and he was there if I needed him.

During the time we had been partners, Bob and Jane Finkel had separated, after twenty-five years of marriage, just as Barbara and I did later. I remember yelling at him that he was a dummy to do something so stupid after being married to a wonderful woman for a quarter of a century. He could have returned the yell, but he didn't.

■ ■ ■

BOB FINKEL: As a consequence [of working together on *The People's Choice*], we became very good friends. Over the years Jackie and I have had differences, we had one major problem in our relationship, subsequently solved, but I said to him that I had only a couple of very dear friends, of which he was one, regardless of whether I saw him or not. Jackie is difficult, and so if you want to measure those kind of things on a scale, to be a good friend of Jackie's and a close friend is tough.

Jackie is many people, and I think that where he runs into problems in a relationship is when the actor in him comes out. Actors have certain foibles, and he does—impatience—that others may not have, and I think that in his relationships [that have gone bad] there was always an actor in that, or he was acting, or somebody else was an actor. When a difference arises, the sensitivity that Jack shows is that of an actor, not of a businessman, if I make myself clear.

When the Screen Gems period was over, we talked. And again the actor came out—it wasn't a businessman's bruise, it was an actor's bad performance, and he wasn't hurt like an executive, he was hurt like an actor, like his performance was bad, and there is a difference. And that bothered me because now I'm a friend and I'm emotionally attached, not business-wise. And I saw that performance, and I got worried.

He was a businessman, an executive of a company; I'm a working producer, a line producer, sometime director. That would make a good alliance, I thought. [So the partnership was established.]

It was not a healthy arrangement. It was not well received throughout NBC. Jackie had been a competitor, with Screen Gems, and all of a sudden he was in the building, a partner, and for reasons which still mystify me, it was not well received. I think Jackie, as an executive, had made a few business adversaries at NBC. We did a lot of good things. What I think went wrong was it was two producers in business together. Jackie didn't need another producer. I didn't. I needed a guy, a closer, a businessman, like I saw at Screen Gems, that would take an idea and get it on. But that other Jackie Cooper started to come out, and now you had two people doing it.

We started to run into those little irritations, like how do you split this, if we're moving, and you're moving your furniture, those little irritations, which I sorely regret in retrospect, and I think somewhere along the line in our dissolution I think I indicated to him that I was sorry those things happened, it was stupid. But its source was that two producers were talking.

My people came to me and said, "Bob, we said three years. You have done what you set out to do, you did *Doctor Dan*, and you did *Lily*. You said three years. But nothing is on the air, Bob. And you are spending and carrying this, and it is not a good business arrangement, and you should dissolve it and use the fact that you said at the outset it would be three years and you don't have to then go to Jackie on any other basis except that was the deal and that's it." Which we did. And I remember sitting there, and I looked at Jackie's face, and I knew that the minute it was mentioned that I was in trouble with him. He was hurt, acting-wise. He really was. I could see it as I looked at him. No, it's not actor-wise; it's something else. Anybody who is an actor, there's something about him that's different from somebody else. Sensitivity. Ego. And I prize that ego. And I saw it in his face, and we went on into dissolving the thing, and then it began to grow in him.

Jackie was very cold and distant, and I finally insisted that he meet with me to iron out anything that I didn't know about in our separation that was bothering him. And I think that it was all a matter of a couple of thousand dollars, charges that he was hurt that I would charge him for this and that, and I said, "Tell me what it is you want?" and I wrote out a check and sent it to him and thought that at least I had fulfilled the financial obligation.

But Jackie was through with me as a friend. I made many efforts to capture that again. He tolerated a couple of social evenings that we had. I had called, Barbara had answered, told Jack I called, he never responded. And I knew—that's Jack. I knew Jack, because when he's finished, he's finished. Jack had a little Italian in him, and it's one of those. He's tough to get back in good graces.

It was eating me up. I've had one or two of those things happen at other places, and I've made a *cause célèbre* out of getting myself back with those people. I can't bear this grudge—I had a problem with Yorkin and Lear, we had some legal problems about *The Andy Williams Show*. I finally went to Bud and Norman and said, "We can't—whatever it was, I'm sorry, I apologize, but let's not—life is too short, I like you. Let's not do this. I'm wrong. What do you want from me?" And we're back together—my daughter works for them. And this is the way I wanted to get to Jackie somehow, but to no avail.

■ ■ ■

45.

When we dissolved our partnership, I had no choice. I had to act to support my family. It had been so long since I had directed there was no chance of getting important jobs in that area. So I told my agent I was available, but please just good things, if possible only guest shots on the top twenty shows in the ratings.

Barbara said all along I was an actor and I should act, and she thought I would be happier and more successful acting. She had never been keen about my being a studio head or a producer or a director. I know her motives were purely unselfish; she honestly believed I would be better off, in the long run, if I simply concentrated on acting. I could keep acting for the rest of my life were I reasonably successful; that was her thinking. But as a director I would risk a shorter professional life and maybe be thought of, at sixty or sixty-five, as too old to direct. "It's a rough, physical life, Jack," she felt. And yet there are men who act, and successfully, well into their seventies and some into their eighties.

I played in one of the early TV movies—*Maybe I'll Come Home in the Spring*, with Sally Field. I did *Ironside*. I appeared in the first of the four *Police Story* episodes I eventually did.

So I worked. I knew at that point in my life the only part I'd play would be somebody's father, or the heavy, or the boss (of the bank or the hospital or the newspaper or the law firm). Okay. I knew I wasn't a leading man—maybe never had been—and I surely was well past the juvenile age. That was before the era of the character lead, which came later, enabling people like Gene Hackman and Dustin Hoffman and Carroll O'Connor and George Kennedy and Martin Balsam to have starring parts. At that time the leading man was still a cliché— young and good-looking, and I was past the young period, and it is debatable whether I had ever been conventionally good-looking.

But I did my father/heavy/boss roles. I did so many through 1971 and 1972 that I was doing them back to back. I was the guest star on a two-hour *Columbo* with Peter Falk and a ninety-minute *McCloud* with Dennis Weaver and another movie for TV called *The Astronaut* with Susan Clark.

More and more, though, I was doing heavies. I worried that I would grow into the modern counterpart of Charles Bickford. And so, when I got a chance to direct for the new show *M*A*S*H*, I leaped at it.

Gene Reynolds was co-executive producer of *M*A*S*H* with Larry Gelbart, another old friend. The associate producer was also a protégé, Burt Metcalfe, who is now the executive producer. When the pilot for the series sold, Reynolds called me and asked me to direct some of the shows. As soon as I could, I signed on. Hy Averback was also directing there.

Of the first thirty shows made, I directed fifteen. Occasionally, I would be asked to do two in a row, which was unheard of at the time. The pay for directors of half-hour shows even then was only up to $1,850, so I had to augment my income with acting. Reynolds was nice enough to let me take those lucrative acting jobs when they came up, so I'd direct a few, act somewhere, then go back to directing *M*A*S*H* again. It was a nice place to hang my hat, a good credit as a director, and as it turned out, I won my first Emmy with a *M*A*S*H* episode.

It was not, however, a totally comfortable situation. It led to one of the greatest disappointments of my life—a human disappointment.

Alan Alda is a contradictory personality. He projects warmth and wit and wisdom, intelligence and stability. Actually, in my opinion, he is concealing a lot of hostility beneath the surface. He speaks out in public on many topics, with his pet apparently equal rights for women and the Equal Rights Amendment. Yet he has, for almost nine years, played a character on *M*A*S*H* who looks on women almost entirely as sex objects. By playing a fanny-pinching, lecherous, boozing man, he perpetuates the very stereotypes he publicly claims to despise. The man must be torn inside. Maybe that produces the hostility I discovered.

My first contact with him was very positive. When I was preparing the only feature film I directed, *Stand Up and Be Counted*, I thought of him for the lead. After having sent him the script, I flew east for a meeting. He told me his problems with the script—it mocked feminism and equal rights. I told him that I agreed with him and that we were going to change it. On the basis of what I promised, he said he'd do the part, provided, of course, the terms could be worked out.

I came away from the meeting with a very good impression of the man. It was the same impression I had gotten from watching him on the screen. That seldom happens, so it is very nice when it does. It later developed, unfortunately, that producer Mike Frankovich would not let me turn the script around, and that left me with a dilemma. I knew the script was bad, but it was my first shot at a feature. If I walked out, I might be stuck with the label of quitter or someone who is hard to deal with. But if I stayed, I knew I had a guaranteed turkey. I decided I had to stay, for the sake of my reputation. I think now it was a mistake, but I did it. But Alda—and Sally Kellerman—walked, and I thought they were very sensible to do so. Gary Lockwood and Jackie Bisset took over their parts.

I didn't see Alda again until I began working with him on *M*A*S*H*. On the surface he was the man I had expected— very conscientious, very serious about his work, thoroughly professional about being on time, with his lines learned. However, beneath that serene surface, things were different.

On a television series the star's personality is very important to the company's morale. Everything flows downward from him or her. Alan Alda was determinedly uninvolved. He never ventured an opinion on things that did not directly concern him. If I had an argument with one of the other actors, Alan would deliberately turn and walk away. At first, I interpreted that as his way of telling me that he was behind me, that he was giving me free rein to run the set.

I ran the set on *M*A*S*H* as I've always done. I don't shout about it. I just do it. And I have generally become respected for that. I am open to any suggestion an actor cares to offer, and I have used hundreds of them. I have, however, found that in most cases actors like to be told what to do.

I have always tried to keep the atmosphere around my set light, happy, pleasant. That is generally done through the efforts of the star—as I have said, it all emanates from the star— although some of them can overdo it. Alda did nothing, so I did what I could. Mostly I kept the crew happy, which is important. I've always gotten along well with crews. On the *M*A*S*H* set I'd joke with them. I remember there was one grip who was a surfer and had the surfer's bleached yellow hair. Since my hair had been bleached yellow when I was a kid, that was an opening for me, and so I kidded him, and he kidded me, and everybody enjoyed it. It was a running gag, kept the set loose.

After I finished each of my shows, I'd order some booze and some cold cuts and bread and things, and we'd have a little wrap party. There was an assistant cameraman who had a Mexican mother-in-law, and he'd bring over some hot, hot Mexican food. Once in a while Gene Reynolds and Larry Gelbart would be the party. But Alan never did. On most sets the star, producer, director take turns footing the bill for the wrap party. On *M*A*S*H* the star's contribution was conspicuously absent.

Came our first Christmas. It is traditional, on a set at Christmastime, for a lot of presents to be exchanged. The star always—ALWAYS—gives a little something to everybody on the cast and crew. Usually there's a party, too.

Alan wished everybody a Merry Christmas.

Okay, there's no law that says he has to do it. It was just a little odd, and everybody noticed it. But still, everybody had a good spirit because the show was so intrinsically good, and it was beginning to catch on.

Gradually, however, the actors—several of them—began acting very strangely, for professionals. McLean Stevenson showed as unprofessional conduct as I have ever seen in more than fifty years in the business. After I'd worked with him on five shows or so, one day he announced that henceforth he was going to do only one take. Sinatra is famous for refusing to do more than one take. Stevenson said that, like Sinatra, he was good only the first time, and so he saw no point in doing any more. He suggested that I should favor him in all the master shots from now on, so he wouldn't have to do the scene again. He added that I should do less staging of the scenes—I was noted for giving my shows a lot of movement—because he wanted to sit down more and move around less.

He went to the producers, complaining about me, but Gene and Larry, of course, told him that he had to do what the director—whoever the director was—told him to do. After that, he behaved worse and worse.

I make a point, on my sets, of taking actors aside when I have suggestions or criticisms to make, so that the rest of the cast and crew don't hear what I have to say to them. Crews have a way of listening attentively when a director corrects an actor, blowing the whole thing out of proportion. That is often how certain things get in the Hollywood columns; a crew member sells a columnist an item about a fight between an actor and a director that is, in fact, only an artistic discussion. But Stevenson decided to let everybody in the studio in on his unhappiness and began criticizing me loudly.

So I said to Alda, "Alan, speak to Mac." It is really one of the unwritten duties of a series star to smooth things over on the set. But Alan just turned his back on the whole thing.

Again, I must say that a company takes its behavioral cues from the star. On *Columbo*, Peter Falk was continually late, and his set was constant pandemonium. And on *M*A*S*H* Alan Alda remained aloof, above it all, so cliques and wounds developed.

Gary Burghoff—Radar—became such a pseudo Actors Studio type, worrying about motivations and how he felt and all that, that he became a pain in the ass to everybody. Loretta Swit—I had given her her first break in *Stand Up and Be Counted*, which is where Gene Reynolds found her—became totally undirectable. She kept saying that her character—Hot Lips—wouldn't say this line or do that piece of business.

Through it all, Larry Linville's conduct—he played Frank Burns—was above reproach. And so was Wayne Rogers's, as Trapper John. Poor Wayne; some of the conduct of Mac, Gary, Loretta, and even Alan was beyond him, but he always tried, did his best, and smiled. He had poise, and he had class, and he kept his mouth shut.

But Stevenson, Burghoff, and Loretta Swit were terrors. So I again asked Alda to intervene with them, for the good of the morale of the entire ensemble. After all, he was there every week and I wasn't. He refused. If any problem arose, he'd stalk off to his dressing room and sit there until the clouds had blown over.

I was disappointed in that aspect of his behavior, but I was still in awe of him as an actor. He was also a joy to direct. He would take a direction and improve on it. He would embellish it and do things with it that I hadn't dreamed of.

Alan and I also shared political views. The Vietnam War, which we both thought was criminal, was on. He didn't particularly like the fact that I was active in the Naval Reserve, so we reached a tacit understanding not to talk about things military. But on issues like minority rights and social injustice, we saw eye to eye.

The show kept improving, but the morale on the set kept

deteriorating. For me, it was intolerable, except with Gene and Larry and Alan and Wayne and Larry Linville—and the crew. I still enjoyed kidding them, and vice versa.

Perhaps I should have realized—but I didn't—that my sense of humor was not Alan's cup of comedy. In fact, I didn't really believe he was aware of what went on between me and the crew. He was usually in his dressing room when we were kidding around because that happened mostly when they were setting up for shots.

During our second season Alan had gone off and made a TV movie, with Ruth Gordon, in which he played a sheriff. I remember Larry Gelbart and me discussing it, after we had seen it, and both of us had been struck by the same thing—Alda, famous for his hatred of guns of all kinds, not only carried a gun in the film but drew it out of his holster in one scene as he was about to enter a house.

The next morning all of us—cast and producers and I— were sitting around the table, reading the script for the following week's show. It was purest coincidence, but it was a script in which guns played a big part. It dealt with an enemy sniper, who fires at the hospital. They call for help, and a helicopter comes over, and a crewman aboard shoots the sniper. Then Hawkeye (Alda) goes out and treats the sniper.

Alda resented the script because of the shootings. It perpetuated violence, he said, and he would have nothing to do with that.

"What about you carrying that gun on that show last night?" I asked him.

"It was part of the costume," Alda said.

"But you drew your revolver. You didn't draw any other part of the costume," Gelbart said.

"But I knew that the character I played would never use the gun," he said.

"Maybe. But the people who saw it at home didn't know that you wouldn't use it. They just saw you draw it—"

Alda said he wouldn't discuss it anymore. This was the first real script problem we had had, as far as I knew. He simply refused to do that script as written. Gelbart and Reynolds huddled with us all, and a compromise was reached. Alan agreed to do the script, with some changes—the Army was made the heavy, and so the helicopter wasn't just any helicopter; it was an Army gunship, which is a very heavily armed helicopter.

I felt that the whole thing was now totally unrealistic. Those Army gunships had so much firepower that if they had fired at that sniper, there would have been nothing left of him for Hawkeye to go out and treat. But Larry and Gene convinced me that the majority of the audience wouldn't know that much about ordnance, and anyhow, the important thing was to get the show on the air. Alan was now pleased, even though the script had become ludicrous in my opinion.

From then on things got worse and worse. Swit kept trying to teach me how to treat women. Burghoff kept giving me acting lessons. Stevenson was giving me directing lessons. But the crew was happy, and Linville and Rogers were great. Then I began to notice that during the balance of the week Alan seemed to be very cold toward me. It was uncomfortable, but I had five shows left to do under the terms of my contract.

That afternoon when we had the blowup over the script, I had tried to patch things up later by telling them all how fortunate they were to be part of such a classy show which was a big hit. I told them of my own TV series, how much harder it had been then because the season was so much longer. I tried to talk to them like a Dutch uncle because I was older and had had so much more experience. I reminded them that they were actors, not comedians, even though they were involved in a funny show. I said, "If the producers had only wanted a funny person, they would have hired a Carl Reiner. But they wanted good actors, so they hired you."

I had hoped that would restore our rapport, but it didn't. I realized that as the week wore on and the atmosphere grew more and more tense. But we got the show done, despite it all.

On the last afternoon, as we finished our last scene, Alda said, "I want to see you." He led me around behind the cyclorama that surrounds the *M*A*S*H* camp built on Stage 9 at the 20th Century-Fox studio.

We were alone, behind the cyclorama, far away from the others.

"I want to tell you something," he began. "You have no idea what kind of people we are. How dare you say the producers should have gotten a funny man like Carl Reiner in the show?"

I tried to tell him he obviously hadn't been listening to what I said, but he just waved away my interruption and raced on.

"Nobody here appreciates your sense of humor."

"Then why does the crew laugh?"

"Because they're kissing your ass. And furthermore, I want you to understand one thing—you're not the star of this show."

And on and on he went. I can't remember the rest of the words. I just stood there, trying desperately not to cry. When he finally finished, he just walked away. Thinking about it, as I drove home that evening, I figured that there could be only two rational explanations for his outburst, both obviously triggered by jealousy. He was jealous (a) because the crew was mine, and not his, and (b) because the press, when writing of *M*A*S*H*, frequently publicized me. I still had a name the press felt the public might care to read about.

We hardly spoke after that. I wanted to quit the next day, when I told Reynolds and Gelbart what had happened. They talked me out of quitting. So I stuck it out and did the shows I was contracted to do—and it was a most uncomfortable four weeks. But one of those shows we did during that period earned me an Emmy. "Carry On Hawkeye" was a tour de force for Alan. We had to talk about the shows we did together, purely business, but didn't even say good morning or good night or anything in between.

■ ■ ■

LARRY GELBART: I remember that. I think I was more involved with what it meant to me in terms of my relationship with Alan than—I probably didn't appreciate what it meant to Jackie and Alan. I remember the script very well. It was called "The Sniper." There was somebody, one of the enemy, out harassing them. The original script called for the people at the 4077th to make an appeal to some fighter group to kill the guy, or knock him out, to take him, get him off their backs, because he was disrupting the life of the camp and, of course, threatening their lives physically. And in the original dialogue, they said, "Get this guy out of there, kill him, or wound him," or something—maybe not those words, but certainly, as happens in wartime, these people were not interested in being killed. It wasn't that Alan wouldn't do the script—I'm just making this a parenthetical observation—there was no such thing really as Alan or anyone else saying, "I won't do this script." There was in that time—and I can only speak for that time I was there, those four years—always the democratic system of people saying, "I object to this," or "I don't like this," or, "I find it hard to say this," or, "I can't say this." And Alan, who was very publicly a pacifist, was offended by the people in the unit, the *M*A*S*H* people, asking for that kind of help. I fought for the point because I felt strongly they should. I didn't and I don't take a back seat to anybody on that show in terms of being antiwar and antiviolence. Jackie and I shared the same point of view. I did change the script. I did change the passage. It was only a matter of a line or two, which didn't so specifically say, "Kill him or wound him." And in fact, what we did was we had the chopper come over and spray the area the sniper was in, and perhaps we went too far the other way then. Then suddenly the people were appalled that there was this sort of overkill; I mean, the 4077th people. Which I think was a piece of fiction really that doesn't sit so well on my own conscience now, as though we were supposed to sympathize with someone who only a minute ago was killing everybody else. And as a matter of fact, that was the point of the script—Hawkeye then went with his bag into the field and helped the man who was only moments ago trying to kill him. Jackie was on the side of the unit fighting for its life, in a sense.

Alan had, in fact, appeared in a movie on television just prior to this episode, in which he played a small-town sheriff, and I remember I was surprised to see him holding a gun. That always will, I think, remain a dichotomy to me—is it okay to draw a gun if you're a sheriff as opposed to a member of the armed forces? Guns are guns, and blood's blood, and life's life. But that's really something for him [Alan] to work out for himself.

■ ■ ■

At one point during that period my Navy superiors asked me to get some stars to do the usual Christmas season promos for Navy stations. They liked having stars saying Merry Christmas to the sailors on all the ships, things like that. Wayne Rogers did one, and even Mac Stevenson, but none of the others would.

I asked Alda to do one.

"I wouldn't encourage those kids to prolong the war," he

said, and walked away. But I wasn't about to let well enough alone.

"You mean some eighteen-year-old kid in a gun turret is encouraging the war?"

He kept on walking but over his shoulder he yelled back, "Yes, and I won't encourage it."

I replied with one last remark: "Well, okay, then, maybe you'd like to send a little message to the enemy."

He didn't respond.

■ ■ ■

CAPTAIN WILLIAM S. GRAVES (USN, Ret): He was directing *M*A*S*H* at Fox. I came over to the set because I wanted to make some Christmas tapes. It must have been in the fall of '73 or '74. And the Christmas tapes are nothing more than a greeting on a tape, and I would go in, go on a stage, I did quite a few of these, and people— I'd have a little script, and they could pick out the message they wanted. Some were thirty seconds, and some were twenty seconds and so forth. Or they'd read them all, or just two or three of them. And they'd say, "It's Christmas, and we miss all you guys, and you're doing a good job for your country, and we appreciate what you're doing, and come home safe and Merry Christmas." Just a very simple thing. They start out and say, "This is Joe Blow on the stage of *M*A*S*H*," or whatever.

Well, when I got there—I got there in midmorning, or something—they had had a big argument about this. No, by gosh, this was on a Friday because Alda takes off for the East Coast about four o'clock in the afternoon to go home on Fridays. They'd had a big argument that morning, so when I got there, Alan Alda had said he would make no Christmas greetings for the armed forces. So, of course, people sort of followed his lead, and Loretta Swit wouldn't do it, Gary whatever-his-name wouldn't do it. The only guys that would do it, and they were willing to do it even though it was against the policy apparently laid down by Alan Alda, were Wayne Rogers and McLean Stevenson. And this was my first encounter, and really my only encounter, with an antimilitary feeling against the individual serviceman in this community.

Jack had done his best to try to get these guys all to do it because he believed in it, and he was doing it, and every place I went I didn't have trouble—now, obviously, I didn't go to Jane Fonda and ask for it. I went places I knew I would be welcome, I supposed. So Jackie tried to help us, but it ended up he got into a real thing. I wasn't there, but that's what I heard. So the only people that did it were Wayne Rogers, who was a Navy lieutenant at one point in his life, and McLean Stevenson, who was a Navy pharmacist's mate during the Korean War. And they did a nice job. But nobody else on that show would do it.

■ ■ ■

At the Emmys the next year they seated Alan and me together. That year the show won everything that wasn't nailed down. There was a party afterward, and again, they seated the Aldas and the Coopers at the same table. It was a dull, terrible, sad evening. At one point Barbara couldn't take the silence any longer, and she said to Alda, "Isn't it a shame you boys can't enjoy this evening?"

Alan, with icy politeness, merely said, "Yes."

He was one of my greatest disappointments. If I was ever fooled by anyone, it was by Alan Alda. My son couldn't have hurt me any more than he did. Later, when I told Barbara that he wouldn't do those Navy promos, she cried. She felt so sorry for him.

I feel sorry for him, too. Something is eating him up, and he only occasionally—such as that last afternoon—shows how badly he has been affected. Ordinarily he is all charm—distant but charming. Mike Farrell, who is on the show with him now, says he's still that way, but he says he adores Alan. I guarantee him that one day he'll learn the truth.

46.

In my few retrospective moments, I look back at my history and realize that I got off on the wrong foot when it comes to friends. I have never completely recovered. I do not believe that wrong-footed start was entirely my fault. It is something that is part of the whole business of being a child star. Child stars cannot have friends; it is an impossibility.

With me, as I consider my catalog of friends, they were, when I was a small boy, either grown-ups or else kids of my own age with whom I had an awkward relationship. It was awkward for the reason that I was never an ordinary kid—I was a movie star, and they felt either that I was doing them a favor in playing with them or else that they were somehow not in my league (I had a bodyguard!), and therefore, we could never play as equals.

So there was never a really good, close, buddy-pal friendship. As I grew up, the girls I dated became my best friends. My wives were my best friends. And the guys I tried to become friends with either disappointed me or died.

Maybe I expected too much.

Maybe I had been hurt too often as a child and so refused—or never learned—to open up and accept their friendship.

The first person, aside from my mother, that I can remember feeling any friendly affection toward was Bill Smith. He was an adult, of course, but he was able to communicate with me on my level and he treated me with kindness. He gave me an electric train set—just a simple little one, a circle of tracks, an engine, two or three cars—before I was a kid star. He liked me. We could never have afforded a train set for me, but he bought it.

Bill, as long as I knew him, was a friend. But he was also an adult. He was probably closer to being a surrogate father, or an uncle figure, or a big brother figure, than he was to being a genuine friend. But at least, he never failed me. I had very few people I could trust, growing up. He was one. When my mother died, he was there.

When I was doing *Our Gang*, I wanted to become friendly with the other kids. But that turned out to be an impossibility. They all had mothers, ferocious women who guarded them and championed them and hated any interlopers who might in any way jeopardize their positions. I was such an interloper. I was the new kid in the group, and I got bigger scenes than the others. I got the crying scenes, which were more important. The mothers would have nothing to do with me, and their sons and daughters naturally obeyed them. I made friends with the man who trained the dog—and he was another adult.

My first friend, of my own age, was Jackie Searle. In both *Skippy* and *Sooky*, he was the mean kid. He became so expert at nastiness that it killed his career; he was typed as the mean kid and could do nothing else. But he was actually a very nice boy; at least I thought so, and we had a friendship. But it was of very short duration and a difficult one because we lived in different parts of the city. We talked on the telephone for a few weeks after *Sooky* wrapped, but then it just sort of ended.

Most of my pictures, after that, were with largely adult casts. I got along well with some of the actors—George Raft, Richard Dix—and not so well with others—such as Wallace Beery—but there were no friends. In the neighborhood where I lived, I knew some of the kids. But it was hard to become truly friends because of the total difference in our life-styles— I had a tutor and so could not share their school experiences. Because of my status in the business and because of the kidnapping scare during that era, I was watched very closely. So we had to play in my house and my backyard, where the bodyguard could watch. The studio carpenters built me a tree house in my backyard. Again, I was different because of that. I had more expensive toys—gifts and gold pieces from various people—and that was another mark of differentiation.

The bodyguard was always there. If I went to the movie show, he came along. He drove me. Generally I brought some of the neighborhood kids with me. Sometimes as many as six or eight of the kids came along. It was a big treat; Mom paid.

But usually my mother—out of misguided overprotectiveness—had called the theater ahead, to say Jackie Cooper and some friends were coming, and would the manager please save a group of good seats so the Cooper party could sit together? He would—but he would also, at intermission, turn up the houselights and introduce me and ask me to come up onstage and take a bow. Once in a while he would ask my friends to come with me and introduce "Jackie Cooper, the famous boy star, and these are his pals." They loved it. I didn't.

We moved to the beach again for a while, during the first days of my mother's marriage to Chuck Bigelow. That was a poorer area, a lower-middle-class area—now quite ritzy, of course, but that was more than forty-five years ago. I played with a couple of kids whose families were on welfare, which I guess was a good education for me. I learned a little bit about how poorer people lived.

I made a friend there. In fact, a few of them. One I remember clearly was Julius Bertrand, a year or so older, but short and solidly chunky. He was a good kid, pleasant and warm, and he soon began working with me as my stand-in. He even got to say a few lines in a few films. At the beach Julius taught me to surf and to ocean cast, which was a neat trick. My mother liked my being with Julius because he was a clean-cut kid; he wouldn't smoke or drink, and a lot of boys his age were already trying that. Since he was almost two years older, I listened to him and stayed out of trouble, too.

My other friends at the beach were Bob and Harv Dudley, who lived down the street. Bob was fifteen to my thirteen, and I looked up to him as I did to Julius because he was older and, therefore, automatically wiser. But where Julius had been a good influence, Bob was the opposite. He was sneaking smokes and drinks, and I had some adventurer in my soul, so I did, too.

When we moved back to Beverly Hills, I was ready for the practices of the older and more sophisticated gang I started to hang out with. They were mostly from the wrong side of Beverly Hills' tracks—there are poor people in Beverly Hills, you know—and many of them were football players at Beverly High. When I was fourteen, I was pretty good-sized for my age, and the six-footers on the football squad tolerated me. Because of my long exposure to adults, I was far ahead of the other kids my age in so many ways, and that automatically thrust me in with the older ones. So it was beer drinking and drag racing down Sepulveda Boulevard and chasing girls and all those good things.

They were friends, but merely superficial. We talked sex and cars and sports, but I never knew them, and they never knew me. As soon as we were finished with high school, we dropped each other. I never saw any of them again.

By then, anyhow, I had gotten in with the professional friend group—my first such—including people like Sidney Miller and Buddy Pepper and, peripherally, Mickey Rooney and his crowd, who were generally three to six years older. And yet, through my middle and late teens, I did not have one close, personal male friend; always my closest friend, the person I told my secrets to, would be the girl I was dating.

In all my films, or certainly many of them, I had played a guy who had a close pal, a bosom buddy, through thick and thin, and that had never happened to me.

I had plenty of acquaintances—Pepper, Miller, Rooney, Junior Coghlan. Then Forrest Tucker came into my life. Tucker was older, a smoothie, as we said then; he had money, he had his own house. But my mother feared that Tucker and his older friends were bad influences on me. She knew enough not to say I couldn't go there anymore; after all, I was eighteen by then, or close to it, and it would be difficult to tell me what not to do. She gave me alternatives, to break my behavioral pattern, had me go on trips, things like that.

After that, my Navy service was not very productive of friends. The guys at Notre Dame hated me—I stuck out like a sore thumb. In the band, touring the South Pacific, I buddied with Charley Graziano, half of the Graziano Brothers team of vaudevillians who were with us. When the band became riddled with cliques, Charley and I were outsiders, and we shared our loneliness and misery. With the war's end, that friendship ended, too.

At the end of the war, when I was in New Caledonia, I met Hy Averback. He's been a friend ever since, and that's now thirty-five years or so. During my eight years in New York Hy and I stayed in touch; he was the first one I called to say I was coming back to California. But Hy disappointed me, too. When Barbara and I separated, he never called me. I thought he should have just called to say he was my friend.

In my New York years there weren't too many male friends. I thought I had one for a while in Jerry Lewis. I had seen Dean and Jerry in Chicago, when they were new together, and touted them to everybody, and so, when they opened at the Copa in New York, I was at a ringside table, leading the cheering.

For a few days he was my friend, grateful to me for my support and friendship. But then the team became the toasts of New York, and suddenly all the big celebrities flocked around them. I never saw Jerry again until I was at Screen

Gems and had to talk to him about a possible deal with the studio. He never mentioned those early days in New York, and neither did I.

My best friends, as I have said, were the girls I dated—and the two that I had married. Hildy was my best friend, and her circle—Anne and Eli Wallach, Julie Harris, later John and Julie Forsythe—became my best friends through osmosis. During the year that I was on the road with *Mister Roberts*, Forsythe was more than a friend. He was the most influential person in my life at that time.

When Janis replaced Hildy, I saw no one. In those days, living together was a very hush-hush, secretive thing to do. So we rarely went to parties and certainly did not mingle. The only people we saw were her manager, Ruth Aarons, and Ruth's brother.

After Janis, for a while I palled around with Ann and Tom Farrell. It was the Farrells, of course, who introduced me to Barbara. With Barbara, friends are almost a religion. She came from a neighborhood where friends were sacred. She'd known most of the same crowd since she was a kid. I met them all, and they fascinated me—normal people. I had, I realized, met very few normal people in my life. These people were solidly married, most of them, and they had kids and dogs and jobs and apartments, and they talked about those things. We went to their apartments for dinner, and I found myself talking about those things, too, and it made me feel great. When Barbara and I got married, they came to our apartment for dinner.

It was a social life like that which people have all over the world—but I had never sampled it before.

And my best friend was Barbara.

She still is.

She has had a knack for making friends wherever she is and keeping them. When we were separated, dozens of people called her. Bob Finkel called me.

She is always on the phone, yakking with girl friends in New York from thirty-five years ago or to Mrs. Hank Greenberg, Mr. Larry Gelbart, or Mrs. Norman Glenn here in Los Angeles. I know their husbands, but she is thicker with the wives than I am with the husbands. She keeps after me to call some guy and go out to a football game—"Call David Janssen, he likes you"—but I didn't. And poor David died, too.

47.

Like most of the men and women who served in uniform in World War II, the day I got my discharge I wanted to forget all about wars and officers and other horrible things. We had served because we believed in the justice of what we were fighting for—compared to Korea and Vietnam, World War II was a very big hit war—but once it was over, we wanted to move on to something else.

The Navy hardly crossed my mind again for many years. It wasn't, in fact, until I got involved in the pilot for the *Hennesey* series that I thought Navy again. That had a Navy setting, so I went to the public affairs officer in Los Angeles to request assistance. Fortunately, the P.A.O. at the time was a man who was immediately sympathetic—he had been a child star himself and knew the film business. His name was Claude Jarman, Jr., and he had been the young star of that impressive 1940s film *The Yearling*. He was very cooperative, arranging for us to shoot on ships, on shore installations, to have whatever we needed.

Jarman and the Navy, in general, felt that *Hennesey* was a good image for the Navy. That was in marked contrast with some other shows of the period that they felt embarrassed them—*McHale's Navy*, the Ernest Borgnine show, for example, or its Army equivalent, Phil Silver's *Sergeant Bilko* series. Our show didn't hold the Navy up to ridicule. It was funny, but the humor came out of human realism, and our Navy characters did things pretty much by the book, and it was all shipshape, and the Navy loved it. So they spoke to me about being a kind of public image for them.

They had been so helpful to us that in the spirit of quid pro quo that the Navy understands as well as Hollywood, I wanted to return the favors. They asked me to make a few recruiting spots, and I gladly obliged. But they made me feel a little guilty—here I was, in a Navy doctor's uniform, acting as a Navy officer, asking young men to enlist in something which, in reality, I wasn't a part of. They said it was okay; that was an accepted procedure.

So the Navy and I became friends. The Secretary of the Navy invited Barbara and me to join them for the Army-Navy game in Philadelphia. Happily for us Navy won, so it was a joyful train ride back to Washington.

We were all very convivial—the Secretary of the Navy and a large number of top Navy brass—and they kept urging me to join the Naval Reserve. They were sure a commission could be arranged. I had heard that only college graduates could apply. The Secretary of the Navy can, however, make some appointments to other than college graduates: people who he feels have special talents the Navy can use. They felt that I qualified for one of those appointments.

I was asked to take some aptitude tests, and they ordered a full-scale FBI investigation into my past and my character. I wasn't surprised when the FBI gave me a clean bill of character, but I was pleasantly surprised at how well I did on those tests. Apparently all the reading I had been doing over the last few years—goaded by my New York friends mostly—plus what I had been subjected to at Notre Dame had sunk in deeper than I had believed.

So I was commissioned a lieutenant commander in the U.S. Naval Reserve, and it was a genuine thrill to be sworn in and receive my lieutenant commander's stripes. That was in 1961. Under naval regulations, a reserve officer comes up for promotion every five years, at which time a review board screens each applicant and studies the recommendations of his superior officers. All three times since my commission, I have passed those review boards and gotten my promotion.

I have done a lot of Navy business. I made many training films—they are called in-fleet films, meaning they are shown only to naval personnel. I've directed some, acted in some, narrated some—and various combinations of those three elements. Often the films have dealt with classified material of one sort or another, so I have been cleared to deal with highly classified information. I have also continued to make spots for both radio and television, promotional spots for various Navy activities, such as recruitment and public relations.

■ ■ ■

CAPTAIN WILLIAM S. GRAVES (USN, Ret.): What he does for the Navy and how he earns his reserve points is by...using his position, his professional position. For example, we get a lot of celebrity requests, people say, "I would like to have Jackie Cooper come and speak at this dinner," or this presentation or reenlist this kid, or this or that, and he tries to do those things. What's more important to us is when he goes to a big event, such as the Indianapolis 500, and rides in the parade with his uniform on, and is identified as a naval officer, as a reserve officer, and this is very valuable to us from a recruiting point of view. I think it's good for him, too, but it's very good for us, and he will make television spots, recruiting spots for us, make those Christmas greetings, or he will make speeches. He and I flew up to San Francisco for the decommissioning of the *Hancock*, an old aircraft carrier, oh, four years ago or so, and he presided at that, and cut the cake, and gave a little talk. It was just a draw, a celebrity.

■ ■ ■

I've often been asked how I reconcile my liberal political philosophy with my naval service. Aren't the two mutually exclusive? I don't think so. I find no problem in maintaining my left-leaning thoughts while I am wearing navy blue.

I have come to believe that we need a strong defense—actually, I have been privy to some high-level conversations, so I damn well know the reasons why a strong defense has become essential. I have watched, sorrowing, as the Navy's power has shrunk until, as I write these words, it is less prepared than it was on the eve of Pearl Harbor, in 1941.

I still am a liberal in matters of social welfare and human rights and such, but I favor a strong defense. I do not see any incompatibility in those two views. I still am a liberal in matters of justice and integration, but I believe in a strong police force. Again, I see no incompatibility there.

I have my own sets of values. During the Vietnam War the Navy asked me to go there to do a film. I didn't agree with the war, so I didn't go. At the time I thought that possibly might be a black mark against me in the Navy's eyes, but it has not turned out that way. Actually, there were many high-level Navy and Army officers who felt the same way about that regrettable war; they would have backed off if they could, but they couldn't. Fortunately I could and did.

I was making recruiting spots in the sixties, and some young people—even my own children—took me to task for that. They said that by doing that, I was backing the war. I said no, I wasn't—that I still believed a strong Navy was vital to our safety, Vietnam War or no Vietnam War.

■ ■ ■

CAPTAIN WILLIAM S. GRAVES (USN, Ret): The thing that always impressed me was that...when things were really tough in Hollywood, when things were antimilitary and being in the military or associated with it was not in vogue, Jackie was always, always willing to wear the uniform, do whatever he could and sometimes to his discredit, I suppose, by certain factors of our community, but he didn't seem to care too much about them, and he pressed on.

■ ■ ■

48.

I think if I had done nothing else but direct, after I got my foot in that door, I would have accomplished more, and today people would think of me as Jackie Cooper, the director, rather than Jackie Cooper, the actor who also directs.

But I didn't. I acted as much—maybe more—than I directed through most of the early and mid seventies. In effect, one career kept interrupting the other one.

In 1973 Grant Tinker offered me the chance to direct a pilot film. At the time I agreed to do it, there was no star signed, but the material—it was called *Second Start*—was, I thought, above average. The network—NBC—foisted Bob Crane off on us. Neither Tinker nor I was a big Crane fan, but NBC insisted.

With Crane in the show—they changed the title to *The Bob Crane Show* eventually—the concept was altered. Crane had somehow convinced NBC he was a comedian, even though on his only hit—*Hogan's Heroes*—he played straight man to the comic actors, such as Werner Klemperer, Richard Dawson, and John Banner, around him. Crane and I did not get along. It happened that we were doing the pilot when I won my *M*A*S*H* Emmy, and he put that down, saying, "You know, Jackie, those things you did on *M*A*S*H* were things we did years ago on *Hogan's Heroes*." To me, the very idea of putting *M*A*S*H* and *Hogan's Heroes* in the same sentence was a sign of a very immature mind.

But the show sold, and that was a plateau I had reached. Making pilots has become a very specialized area of television direction, requiring a lot of imagination and taste. A pilot is an on-the-air advertisement for a show, and it must, therefore, emphasize the show's intrinsic strong points, and if there are any intrinsic weak points in the show concept, the pilot director has to be able to spot them and somehow tone them down. For a director, too, pilots are generally more interesting to do because they have a larger budget than an ordinary show, and thus, you are allowed more time on the set.

One final advantage—if the pilot sells, the director usually receives a royalty for as long as the series runs. That can become a very lucrative feature.

Through 1972, 1973, and 1974 I kept going back and forth between acting and directing. I was battling with myself in effect. I was a little afraid to make a clean break and divorce myself from acting totally—who would get custody of my soul? I knew I was happier when I was directing than when I was acting. All I had to do was analyze how I felt when I got up in the morning—if I had an acting job to do, I faced the day without any great anticipation, but if I was to direct, I woke up before the alarm went off.

It was hard for me to get established as a director. To the movie/television business, versatility is a curse. They prefer it if they can stick people in pigeonholes or pin labels on them. If somebody has more than one talent, it screws up the system, and they hate it. I was showing versatility—acting and directing—and they didn't like it.

But I was muddling through anyhow. A little of this and a little of that.

I had directed a few pilots before the one with Bob Crane. I had done one under the Cooper-Finkel banner called *The Students Are Coming* in 1971; the writer was the same person who later was to be so successful with *Saturday Night Live*, Lorne Michaels. The problem was that ours was six or seven years ahead of its time. That same year I had acted in another one that was too soon—*What's up, America?* was from Ed Weinberger and Stan Daniels, hugely successful today, but they jumped the clock with that one. Consider the very similar 1980s hit *Real People*. In 1972 I directed a pilot for CBS called *Keep the Faith*, with Howard Da Silva, about an old rabbi and a young rabbi. It didn't sell. Neither had *Lily* sold in 1971.

The system, in those days, was that pilots were all finished by February and then submitted to the networks, which made their decisions by April. So I was startled when I was offered a role in a pilot to be shot in late February—too late for the normal buying season. Hy Averback was going to direct. The two of us talked about it and couldn't understand why Harry Ackerman, who was producing and who should certainly have known better, would make a pilot when it was probably too late to be bought. And to top it off, the script—a half-hour sitcom called *Keep an Eye on Denise*—was pretty dull. But at the time neither Hy nor I was setting the industry on fire, so we decided to do it. We figured it would never sell—and it didn't. Thank God.

I kept going back and forth. I acted in something called *Chosen Survivors*, which Metromedia made in Mexico. Science fiction and not very good. It paid well, so I did it.

In 1975 I directed a pilot I was very enthusiastic about. It was called *The Last Detail*, taken from the Darryl Ponicsan book and the very successful movie. It starred Robert Lyons, a young actor who has never lived up to his potential; he had a wonderful Cagney-like quality. It wasn't a silly sitcom, but a half hour of real substance and humor based on reality. But the network's computer had nothing to compare it with and so could never categorize it and rated it badly. That was a failure that almost broke my heart.

Then came *Mobile One*. Again the pain. I had done the acting job in it, a two-hour TV movie which served as the pilot, and it was another case of taking the money and scampering. The material was pretty bad. I first was inclined to turn down even the pilot. But I had enough friends in high places who tipped me off that ABC was interested only in me for the project. I'm not one to look a gift contract in the mouth. It isn't often that an actor has a company more or less over the barrel like that. If ABC wanted me that badly, then they would want me thousands of dollars badly, too. My agent drove a hard bargain.

So I did it. Of course, it wouldn't sell. How could it when it was so poorly executed? But as fast as it was made and delivered, the damn thing sold.

So now I was getting rich. I was paid $50,000 for the pilot, $30,000 for each episode, and a piece of the series. It turned out the series lasted thirteen episodes, which was enough to make Barbara and me finally financially secure, but it gave me headaches. And it also served as a most lengthy interruption in my directorial career.

When *Mobile One* ended, I decided to concentrate on directing again. In 1976 I did two pilots at Universal—one was good and didn't sell, the other wasn't very good and did sell, which is rather typical of network television.

The good one was called *SNAFU* and was designed as a *M*A*S*H*-like comedy. When we started, it had a lot of that flavor and classy humor, emanating from drama, and vice versa. MCA, however, saw fit to have its editors eliminate the drama, which took all the class out of the humor. They chopped it into a silly comedy.

The bad one was *Holmes and Yoyo*, a piece of froth about a cop and a robot. It sold, and I was happy for my accountant's sake, but it didn't run very long.

But even though *Holmes and Yoyo* was not a hit, I was beginning to get something of a track record as a director who makes pilots that get on the air.

Obviously, as you become desirable as a pilot director, you soon are offered more work than you can do. Therefore, I found myself in the position of having to turn down more projects all the time. This is ticklish because the people you turn down naturally hear of what you have accepted, and they often feel offended. There are only so many producers and studios to be employed by, so you find yourself having to explain, on the phone or at lunch, that "I love your property, but I just feel that I can make a better contribution to the other one." This is especially tricky when a network calls you directly and wants to know why you've turned down the pilot it is doing. You can't afford to make an enemy of any network because there are only three of them, and if all three are closed to you, where does a television director work? There may be a hundred production companies, but they all sell to those three networks, which approve everything in a pilot—star, script, cast, budget, and, most important to me and my work, director. So you have to learn to say no gently.

The pilots I directed that reached the air were, first, *Second Start* (alias *The Bob Crane Show*) and *Holmes and Yoyo*. Then came *Having Babies* (which became *Julie Farr, M.D.*), *The White Shadow* (I won my second Emmy for directing that pilot), *Paris*, and *Trapper John, M.D.*

But I didn't limit myself only to pilots. I finally began doing long-form television—*The Rockford Files*, a couple of episodes of *McMillan and Wife*, five of the first nine episodes of *Baa Baa Black Sheep*, and a few of the early *Quincy* shows.

In 1978 Gene Reynolds wanted me to come over and join him with his new one, *Lou Grant*, which starred Ed Asner. He offered me three of the first six. I wanted to direct them because theirs was a good concept and those were good scripts. So I said yes, and we were about two weeks away from starting in on them when I got a telephone call from London.

Keenan Wynn was suddenly taken sick, and would I rush over to London to replace him in *Superman*? I would play the editor of the *Daily Planet*, Perry White. Nice money was offered. I would, however, have to leave the next morning.

It was another inner struggle. I knew *Superman* was supposed to be a big picture, and it never hurts to be associated with a big picture. But it would mean giving up the three *Lou Grant*s and again interrupting my directing career.

Barbara felt that it was a feature film and it might lead—well, who knows? She thought I might learn something about directing big, expensive features. Or it might bring on a rebirth of a feature film acting career. She had never totally given up her feeling that I should be doing those Spencer Tracy parts.

So we packed up and flew off to London, and I did my first *Superman*. They wanted me to sign a contract giving them the option to use me in a total of six *Superman* pictures. I balked at that, but did have to agree to a four-*Superman* deal. We pretty much shot the second one, or at least my parts in the second one, at the time we did the first, although I subsequently had to fly back to London and do some added scenes.

This was, for me, a four-week shooting schedule (actually, the two *Superman* films took almost three years), and of course, I never did do any *Lou Grant* episodes. But when I got back, Paramount signed me to direct a two-hour television movie, *Perfect Gentlemen*, with Lauren Bacall. It was a comedy, and that scared me—two hours are long for a comedy. Some of the best Capra and McCarey movies—and I've seen them all, most of them several times—are short for features, running perhaps seventy minutes. Capra and McCarey knew, and I learned from their films, that you cannot stretch a joke too long. Most comedies have simple premises, and they just don't hold the audience more than an hour or so. Capra or McCarey or Stevens would usually make two hours' worth of movie, then preview it and slice it to seventy or seventy-five minutes, eliminating the parts where the audience was not held by the material.

So I was very careful to keep *Perfect Gentlemen* moving quickly, keeping the pace brisk. And it worked. I got good reviews and reached another plateau in directing—the television movie.

From then on, as much as I could, I specialized in television movies. I did several—*Having Babies*, with Susan Sullivan;

Rawbow, the story of the young Judy Garland, in which I had the unique experience of directing a young actor who was playing Jackie Cooper; *Sex and the Single Parent*, a comedy-drama I had to keep stepping along; *Marathon* with Bob Newhart; *White Mama*, which gave me the joy of directing one of the greatest of them all, Bette Davis; and *Rodeo Girl*, starring Katharine Ross.

49.

I thought I might have a problem with Bette Davis when I directed her on the TV movie *White Mama*. After all, she is a legend, and you might expect that a legend would know her own mind and insist on having things her own way.

I learned, however, that most of her motion picture life was spent working with star directors—Curtiz, Wyler, Mankiewicz, Cukor—and that she liked them because they took charge.

I knew that Bette Davis had acquired a reputation, along the way, for being something of a pain in the butt to some directors. But after working with her, I learned that reputation must be the result of exposure to weak directors. If she finds out she is smarter than they are, she'll have no respect for them. But the star directors, who wouldn't let her dominate them and who quickly demonstrated they knew exactly what they wanted, had no trouble with her.

She is a smart lady on the set. As an actress she wants to milk every moment she can out of every scene, squeeze as much time on the screen as is possible. So she has little tricks to help her do that. For example, if she has to walk from a table to a chair and has a line to say as she makes that move, she won't say the line until she arrives at the chair and sits down. That way the camera must stay on her through the move, as she sits and then as she says the line. If she had said the line as she walked, the scene could have cut to somebody else as soon as she said it. But her way gives her a few extra seconds on screen.

If you show her that you are aware of her tricks, and you show her why you need it your way, she will respect you, and she will acquiesce. Better yet, if you give her something new to try—it isn't easy, after all the films she's done—she will be as excited as a child and do it. She loves to try new things.

I had admired her for years. But I had come to feel that lately she had become an impression of herself. I wanted her to play a character, not to play Bette Davis playing a character. There is a difference.

It would be difficult, I realized, with an actress of her repute, to tell her how I wanted her to act. After all, to her, I was not a Willie Wyler or a Mike Curtiz or a Rouben Mamoulian. But I knew I didn't want to see Bette Davis up there; I wanted to see Mrs. Estelle Malone, the character she was playing.

The first morning we worked, I had made sure she had only a few light scenes to play, just some bits of exposition. It is always good, if you can, to start slowly on a production. That gives everyone a chance to get to know each other and work up to the heavy stuff; it's like giving a pitcher a chance to warm up before he faces a batter.

I watched her work. Good, but Mrs. Malone had not yet emerged. While they were lighting the last scene before the lunch break, I went to her trailer. I had to tell her what I felt and what I wanted, but I had to express it with the utmost tact. I knew that she is a woman of great pride—understandably so—and I knew that if I offended her on the first day of shooting, I could rock the boat so steeply we might all fall off and drown.

So I tried to explain. It was a very roundabout speech I was making, and she looked at me without any light dawning.

"Just what is your point?" she said.

All right. I would have to say it very plainly.

"I think you know that I have great respect for your work, Bette," I said. "But I believe that Bette Davis is not as naïve or as unsophisticated as this woman, Mrs. Malone. Nor has Bette Davis led such a sheltered life as Mrs. Malone has. I would like you to be Mrs. Malone as much as possible and Bette Davis as little as possible."

She thought for a moment. I could see she was considering whether or not she should be offended. She decided not to be.

"You're absolutely right," she said. "I'll do my best."

She did do her best, and her best is unequaled. A day later she was a naïve, sheltered lady, not the worldly actress. As she walked off, after doing a difficult scene, she passed me, close enough so I was the only one who heard her whisper, "You *are* watching carefully that there's not too much B. D. in Mrs. Malone, aren't you?" And she was dead serious.

That hastily whispered comment was, to me, one of the greatest compliments I have received as a director. It meant that one of America's finest actresses had recognized that I had shown her something, after she had been acting for almost fifty years. I knew that she was mine from then on, and the rest of the shooting went smoothly. The finished product brought her wonderful reviews, some saying it was her finest work in many years. She later told some mutual friends in the business that she couldn't wait to go to work every morning we were working together because she was having more fun than she had had for twenty years.

But she must be treated carefully. One has to realize her limitations. She works very hard—she was up at five or so in the morning—and she got tired by late afternoon. She would never admit it or ask for favors, but I could see she was weary, and I would arrange it so things slowed down for her late in the day. By Friday afternoons she was generally exhausted. I tried to let her go home early Fridays so she had a long weekend to recover her strength.

She is such a thorough professional that she learned the entire script—not just her own part—before the first day of shooting. On most sets, and ours was no exception, there are always script changes. Those are always difficult, for it means an actor has to memorize new lines. For Bette, it was doubly difficult because before she had to memorize her new lines, she had to unlearn the old ones.

Being a star of such stature, she has certain stipulations in her contract—she goes home at six; she has extra time for makeup and a full hour for lunch. She never abuses those privileges. In fact, if there is any kind of a bind she is in sympathy with, she will compromise and waive those privileges.

After we finished, the producers hosted a lovely party—not the usual wrap party, on the set, with everybody in grimy work clothes, but in a restaurant, the day after we finished, so we were all clean and pressed. Bette was there, of course, wearing a hat which has of late become a sort of trademark for her.

I made a goof when I spoke because I thanked her for her cooperation. I don't think she liked that—I believe she feels that cooperation is expected, and no one should be thanked for cooperating.

"COOPERATION?" she said, and she said that word with a reading only Bette Davis could give it. "What about love? What about performance? What about conduct?"

Cooperation was unquestionably the wrong word. But we still parted friends. She's not the easiest lady to please, but I guess she wouldn't be Bette Davis if she were. She is a dream. Even though she is almost fifteen years older than Lauren Bacall, in some ways she is a younger woman.

Bacall, at the time I directed her, was, I thought, an embittered woman. When you see her onstage, there are the footlights and the people between you and her. When you read her book, there are the pages between you. But when you know her and work with her, face to face, that bitterness is plain and obvious. She simply is not aging as gracefully as is Bette Davis.

I think it is age—the hard fact that we all grow old—that is the hardest thing for Betty Bacall to swallow. She seems to be living more and more in the past, reliving it in her mind, cherishing the old, resenting the new. She's bitter about the way movies and Hollywood have changed. She hates it when any of the films she and Bogart did, either together or separately, have been remade.

"Why would they do that?" she says.

It's foolish to ask such questions. They have always done that. In the last year or so people come up to me and ask me how I felt about the remake of *The Champ* and what I thought about Ricky Schroder, the young boy who played the part I played in the original. They expect me to say things that Betty Bacall says, such as "Why don't they leave things alone?," but I don't. For one thing, the old things often don't hold up. If we see the old things again today, we are disappointed; it is the tragic old story of not being able to go home again. I haven't seen the original version of *The Champ* for years, and I don't want to; I'm sure my memory of it is much better than it really is or than it would seem to be if I saw it after having seen the way current films look. You can't go home again.

I live in the present. Until I began working on this book, I hadn't talked about the past with anyone for years. But Betty Bacall is constantly talking about the past. She automatically brings it up in almost every conversation. The past is gone; that's why they call it the past.

She has younger people around her—her children and their friends—but she talks past to them, and I have a feeling it doesn't mean much. I'm sure her past bores their present.

She dresses beautifully, very today, up to the minute. But the rest of her hasn't kept pace. For one thing, she has no patience at all with equal rights—and this is a lady who once went with her husband as he tried to fight for the rights of men and women accused of Communist leanings, during the Hollywood witch-hunt days.

We had long discussions about that and about realism in movies. Like many, I feel the search for realism has taken some filmmakers too far, and they overdo it. I appreciate true realism, but Betty Bacall not only does not appreciate realism but doesn't understand what we directors are trying to do. She automatically equates realism with smut and pornography.

Bacall often said to me that nobody today can come close to the movies of the past. Consequently, I don't think she goes to see many movies now. If she did, she would find some good ones and some bad ones—just the way it was in her big era. Don't forget, for every *Casablanca* and *To Have and Have Not*, there were the *Four Jills and a Jeep* movies—dozens of B pictures, programmers, we used to call them—that Hollywood ground out.

Whenever Bacall caused a delay on the set, they would tell me that she was in her dressing room, getting her makeup redone. Or her hair fixed. Or whatever. We would wait an hour, and finally I'd make my way off to her trailer and find her.

"Come on, Betty," I'd say, trying to make light of it, "get your ass back on the set. We've waited long enough." On the other hand, Bette Davis always leaves her trailer door open, so she can hear when they call for the "first team"—the "second team" consists of stand-ins who are on the set as it is being lit. As soon as she hears that call, she is out of the door, even before the assistant director can get there to summon her.

I worked with Ruth Gordon, too, and she's even older than Bette Davis, but she doesn't live in the past either. She has humor and charm, but she's a tough lady. She tests you, as a director, right away. Once you establish your authority, she is a professional. She will always ask first if she can do something, then do it.

I could be becoming the George Cukor of my time—working with so many women. I've directed Bacall, Davis, Gordon, Susan Sullivan, Susan Saint James, and Katharine Ross. The man-woman thing has caused no problems. I appreciate the struggles any woman has had—on whichever side of the camera—to get where she is. I sympathize with the fact that it is, obviously, harder for her than for a man. But my sympathy doesn't turn to patronage. Women appreciate that. Maybe because I was raised in a houseful of women, I can feel for them. I used to hear my mother and my aunts talk about the plight of being female and trying to work. That was in the thirties. It is easier now, but it all really hasn't changed that much for the ladies.

I have, of course, worked with a number of men, too. One was Jack Klugman. We had met long ago, back in New York, because Klugman was in *Mister Roberts* with John Forsythe and me and Cliff Robertson. We rehearsed together in New York before we went on the road, and he told me he had been a fan of mine from my old kid days, and I told him I thought that he and Marty Balsam were the two finest young character actors I'd seen on Broadway.

I saw Jack a few times over the years. When he began doing *Quincy*, his show in which he plays a medical examiner who somehow always manages to become a detective, I had only done a few hour-long dramatic shows, such as episodes of *The Rockford Files*.

Late in 1976 they had an episode of *Quincy* which involved a good deal of comedy, so they thought they'd better get a director who was experienced in comedy. One of the producers then was David Shaw, an old friend from my New York live TV days, and he recommended me and got the network to okay it. So I directed that *Quincy*, and Jack, who is known to eat up directors, and I hit it off well.

He had become, I quickly learned, like a lot of stars. They make noises at the beginning, to test the director. If the director quivers and shakes, the star takes over and bosses the director. If the director is secure, then the actor subsides and lets the director run things. I was secure and can talk as loudly as Jack, too. He seemed to like that. Klugman is what they call in Yiddish a *tummeler*—he likes to discuss. Some say argue, but it really isn't an argument; it's a noisy discussion. I can *tummel* with the best of them, so Klugman and I got along fine.

They asked me back to direct some more. After I had done four of them, I happened to be in the office one day when Jack was having a big fight—that's worse than *tummeling*—about a script. He said he just wouldn't do that script. I think it had been written by one of the producers, who was just as adamant that he damn well would do the script. No, I won't. Yes, you will. I was there; I knew them both; I moderated.

I took Jack aside and explained a few things about the

realities of TV to him. I knew with him it wasn't just ego; he really thought the script stank and had valid reasons. He was fighting for the good of the show, not for the good of Klugman. But I said it could be fixed, and the producer/writer said he and I would change it, and Klugman said if we changed it, he'd do the show. So everybody was happy, temporarily.

"You know, Jackie," Klugman said to me, as we walked arm in arm away from the office, "there is no ego between us."

I think that may have been the highest compliment he could give anyone. He went on to say that he wanted me to do as many shows as I could do that season. He said I should just say a number, I had carte blanche, he wanted me there every week if I could do it. I said I would love it. He said he would have his producers call my agent to discuss terms.

That month I went off to do *Superman*, sure that when I got back, the deal would have been signed. I got back, and my agent said they never called. I never heard from Jack Klugman again regarding *Quincy* to this day.

50.

Psychologists tell us that the abused child grows up to be an abusive parent. I was a neglected child, I believe; the only one I feel who really cared about me was my mother, and she was magnificent, but she was away a lot and she was ill a lot. My father wasn't there at all. My grandmother really didn't give a damn about me.

But I don't believe I grew up to become a neglectful father. I love my four children—Jack, Russ, Julie, Crissy. When Jack's mother, June, and I separated, I think the mere fact that I was on the East Coast and he was on the West Coast forced me to neglect him much more than I would have liked. And even when I returned to California, he was in one home and I was in another, and the child of a broken home always is the poorer for it. But still, I tried my best to keep up a contact with Jack.

■ ■ ■

JOHN ANTHONY COOPER: Yeah, he tried to be a dad and so forth, and I have memories of the hunting and the fishing and all of that. Yeah, he tried very hard. But there were times when, you see, he was a stranger to me in a way. I don't know if I was awed by him or afraid of him, or maybe, deep back in my head, I resented him because he wasn't there. I don't know what the reasons were, but I was always kind of afraid to be around him.

And if something came up and he couldn't show up, I took it very personally. Or if I couldn't make it or something like that, I'd be afraid to call him. And then he'd get mad at me because I didn't call; it was that sort of thing. If he looked at me cross-eyed, I'd burst into tears because I was very afraid of him, not because he ever hurt me physically or anything, but he was a stranger to me. Maybe I didn't—I don't know if I'm any good at psychoanalyzing myself—but maybe I was afraid that he was going to go away again and I wouldn't see him again; if he got angry at me, then I wouldn't see him again for six months, I don't know. He tried to be a father. He was around. He was concerned about June and what was happening with June and with her mother, who we were living with, and it wasn't until I got older and started living with him or having an address with him, all of a sudden the concern for June wasn't there anymore, and I said to Barbara, whom I'd become close to by then, "Gee, Dad never calls Mom anymore," and she said, "You don't understand, he no longer has a reason to," and that never entered my mind. Then it started to dawn on me, as I got older, yeah, he was doing that for me, you know, he was concerned about me. I always thought it was so great that they were such good friends and so forth, but they were friends because of me; at least he was. Yeah, he tried to be a father.

■ ■ ■

I've tried to raise my daughters to have independence as human beings. I believe each sex is entitled to equality and to self-respect. Barbara and I have tried to give them both those values. It is curious, however, that one of the girls (Julie) has turned out to be very independent, not at all threatened by the males she meets. Her interest in men is very normal, and she evinces no feeling of being disadvantaged because she is a female. Yet the younger one, Crissy, has always used every feminine wile she can to win the favor of men, and she is certainly not above playing the helpless female to gain her goals. Maybe because of that attitude, she is the one who has continually had problems with boys and men.

That is only one of the endlessly fascinating, forever tricky, continually quirky aspects of parenthood. I have sat at cribside, cotside, bedside, and sleepingbagside, watching my four kids grow to maturity, and you never know what to expect.

When Barbara and I got married, we both wanted to have children. I had no brothers and sisters. Barbara has one sister. So we both wanted the joys and security of a family, of being the keystone of a brand-new family unit. And the children began coming, three of them in hardly four years.

Russell, the first baby Barbara and I had, was always a good boy—except that, in the troublesome four- to six-year-old period, he had the same temper that I had had. He outgrew it, though Barbara and I worried about him and his sudden, unreasonable fits of anger. Barbara was much better at handling him during those outbursts than I was.

Russell, as a boy, was always project-oriented: He saved things, and he collected things, and he put things in boxes and books and closets. But he wasn't much for sports. Julie, the middle of the three Barbara and I had, was the athlete. She was the one who would play catch with me. She was the one who willingly accepted my offer to learn horseback riding. Julie and I were very close until the tomboy phase ended abruptly at twelve, when her friends suddenly became more important to her than her father. Typically Julie picked friends who dressed down, not highbrow types. Also typically, she began smoking at thirteen.

And then along came Cris, the youngest, the Jewish princess. With Cris, it was always the makeup and the clothing and getting dressed up in her very best, and she never got dirty and never got messy. She wasn't interested in much of anything, certainly none of Russell's projects or Julie's sports.

■ ■ ■

BARBARA COOPER: It wasn't a family-oriented life, everybody eating dinner together. He got home too late. I regret that today. It was very rare when we all sat down together.

We'd go to Palm Springs, with help, and he seemed happier there and more the father there. He bought an old Model T. He'd take the kids to breakfast. He'd barbecue. He loved that place—he always felt if anything happened to us, we'd have that house in Palm Springs to fall back on. Russ and Julie had a swimming instructor there, but Jackie himself taught Crissy to swim. He'd go horseback riding with the girls there.

■ ■ ■

As they grew older, their individual characters and individual traits became stronger.

Russell's projects zeroed in on one area—music. He went

to college for a couple of years, but he was just going through the motions for Barbara and me. After his second year at Cal State, Northridge, he came to me and said, "Dad, you're just wasting your money." Okay, it was his life; we had done all we could. So he left college and went into music, and there he is today. And doing fairly well. He started out arranging windows in a record store, and he did it so artistically that MCA Records noticed and hired him for their promotion department. He wants to stay with music and preferably the recording business. He is not a musician himself, but he apparently knows music inside and out, and his ultimate goal is to produce records.

■ ■ ■

RUSSELL COOPER: My father has been more than a father to me; he's been my best friend, my confidant. There's no person that I can trust more than my father, and I told him after he had separated from my mother because I was more lenient on him than anybody in the family. Don't let anybody tell you anything differently. More lenient than my younger sisters, more than my brother, more than anybody. Not that I tried to understand, but I tried my best to love him during that whole situation. I remembered everything he'd done for me for the past twenty-four years, growing up, and getting me interested in things, in airplanes, all the material things and all the sensitive things, just everything. He made me what I am today. More than anybody, along with my mother, he helped me to be a better human being. And I think, because of that, I tried my best to love him, understand him, keep my fingers crossed, and eventually it did work out. I love him more than anything, and there's nothing I wouldn't do for him. He's the greatest, most marvelous person in the world.

They were both disciplinarians. She was the first one; if it got out of her hands, he got into it. The thing that set him off would be when I said something to my mother that he didn't like. That really set him off. He could be physical and I hated it, and my sister and he made a promise after one big incident that he would never do it again, and I really don't think he did. That big incident? Well, let's put it this way: It came down to a choice between a girl that I was seeing at the time or the respect of the family. It was a whole thing that I had to really learn the hard way. And something that will stick with me for the rest of my life. My father was absolutely, absolutely justified. I'm glad it happened to me at seventeen, when I was still in school, you know; I wasn't quite an adult.

■ ■ ■

Julie also balked at college. With her, as always, the big drive was for independence. As soon as she could afford it, she moved out of the house into her own apartment. The career wasn't important; the independence was. Earning her own living, paying her own way, being her own woman—those were the things that mattered to Julie. She is currently living in Indianapolis, with a guy she's been in love with for a few years now. He's in the real estate business, and she helps him.

■ ■ ■

JULIE COOPER: I think I was closer to my father than the others were. When we had our house in Palm Springs, when we had the chance, when Dad wasn't busy going back and forth from L.A. to Palm Springs on business, without my brother and sister or my mom we'd just get into the Jeep and run on down to—I don't remember the name of the stables—we'd go down to this huge outdoor arena and just ride and ride and ride. I was a tomboy, probably still am—I think I was born with my tennis shoes on. So Dad and I would probably do things with each other more than he did with Russ or Cris. Maybe because I was the firstborn girl; possibly. Also, like I said, just growing up a tomboy all the time. I don't think it was because he didn't want to be with Russell, but because I was always very, very eager to do it. To tell you the truth, I started to drive, Dad got me in the car, before I even had my driver's license. He let me get behind the wheel. Yeah, he helped me a lot, I got to do a lot of things, I'm a pretty lucky kid.

■ ■ ■

As for Princess Cris—no college for her either. Barbara and I have been very disappointed in that, the fact that none of our three really had a good college education. (Jack did well in college and is grateful for the education.) Cris wanted a job, so she could earn money, but not so she could move out and be independent, like Julie. With her, the money was for clothing primarily. She'd let Mommy and Daddy supply her with food and a roof over her head as long as possible. She even wanted to use one of our cars. Barbara and I suggested (she suggested; I yelled!) that our house was not a hotel. She went to business college and did very well. She is very fussy about where she works, and with that knack that some people are born with, especially royalty, she can quit a job and immediately get hired for a better one. Cris makes a better salary than Jack or Russell or Julie. She is now an executive assistant in a young law firm. So, although she plays the helpless female, she is tough as nails and always lands on her feet.

■ ■ ■

CRIS COOPER: No, I wasn't spoiled. Oh, for all intents and purposes I could say yes, I was spoiled, but I never had anything that anybody else didn't have, but then again, I was never said no to. But then again, I never asked unreasonable questions. I don't think I was spoiled. I don't think any of us were. I think they did a beautiful job with their children because we're all basically nice kids, you know. No serious problems. I mean, there's the usual, everybody goes through the dope thing and the money thing and the rebel-against-your-folks bit, but it's all over and done with in a matter of months, you know, so if you can pull through it and keep your head up, then more power to you, I think. But you know, we're all basically nice kids. And we love our folks, and we all love each other. That's nice.

■ ■ ■

I think Jack is the happiest of the four. He has made peace with himself and his life. He knows who he is. He has a good job, with a San Francisco clothing company, as manager of its mail-order division, and he raises his tropical fish, and he has good friends, and he appears to be content.

They've done whatever they've done by themselves. I've stayed out of their lives, at least from the standpoint of offering them employment. I have never approved of children working for their father, no matter what their father does. I think ultimately it is bad for the children, makes them feel inferior all their lives. Fortunately none of them wanted to act, so I never had that question to face.

During the fifties, sixties, seventies, when they were growing up, the big word in their life was "scene." Whatever the scene was, making it was the most important thing to them. They had to be a part of it, or they were left behind, lonely and lost. Unfortunately for many of the parents of that era, that scene often was an unparalleled world of sex and drugs and violence, plus some passive television watching. Barbara and I, like most Americans, totally unprepared for parenting, lucked out—there were no real drug problems, no arrests, no violence, no excessive drinking with any of the four. A good many of their friends came down with virulent cases of addiction or in jail or dead or suffering breakdowns. But even though ours grew up in wicked, wicked Beverly Hills, smack in the middle of the drug-protest-violence era, we had none of it.

Being the children of a Hollywood name, I think, could have been a handicap to them. That's why I perhaps bent over backwards to see that they thought of themselves as nothing particularly special. Once a notion like that gets into a kid's head, in his or her formative years, it is virtually impossible to dislodge. I thought public school would help keep those notions away. Maybe it did—but perhaps at the expense of not getting all that a good education has to offer.

■ ■ ■

BARBARA COOPER: He was never a father who put a diaper on a kid or gave a kid a bottle. Never did any of that.

He was the disciplinarian. They're nice kids—one's a little crazy. He'd take a lot out on them, and I didn't stop it, and that was wrong of me. He had nights of patience, nights of impatience.

After Cris, the doctors said to Jackie, that's enough

kids for her. I was thirty-three. Nobody consulted me. Vasectomies were not the in thing. We talked about it. I said, "It's up to you." Maybe I regretted it later. So he went and had a vasectomy. He even overanalyzed that because I went through change of life soon after that, very early. He attributed that to his having a vasectomy. Everything is psychosomatic with him.

■ ■ ■

51.

Many men, maybe most men, get the seven-year itch or the ten-year itch or the twelve-year itch. They find that life is going by too quickly, and they feel trapped, and they have to get out, taste a little of the excitement that life has to offer before surrendering to the blahs of middle age.

I had that. But I guess I always do things a little differently and a little late. The average man, if it happens to him, cuts out from home and hearth at around fifty. That seems to be the magic number, a signal to a man's psyche that old age is just over the horizon, and if he wants to avoid the rut of home life, now is the time to make the break.

It didn't happen to me at fifty.

■ ■ ■

BARBARA COOPER: When he was forty, he said, "I'm nearing fifty." At fifty, he said, "I made it." At fifty-seven, he said, "I'm nearing sixty."

■ ■ ■

It happened to me at fifty-seven. I had passed fifty-five, and I kept thinking: Every day I am nearer sixty than fifty. In 1972, when I was fifty, I had the worst year, financially, since my lean years in New York. But I was happy anyhow, juggling jobs, acting here and there, directing here and there. But at fifty-two things were going very well, and Barbara and I haven't had a financial care since then. It was so easy that I guess I had to look for trouble. I turned fifty-seven, and it's the cliché of all time—a man's middle-aged crisis.

■ ■ ■

BARBARA COOPER: Self-destructive, is what it is.

■ ■ ■

I made excuses for leaving home. I rationalized. I said to myself it was Barbara's fault. I said it was because she never had an interest in other things, and that now that all the children had left home, she just sat around, and I needed a woman with other interests. I said a lot of things to myself, and I came to believe some of them. I told myself that this had been coming on for some time, that I was drowning, and that I had to get some fresh air. It had been building up for six months, and I fought it, but in the end I had to leave.

■ ■ ■

CRIS COOPER: I gave him a terrible time about it and told him that was a selfish thing to do and he was rotten and crazy because, you know, the biggest go off and have their whatever, but they don't leave home. I just couldn't understand, because everything is always her. Since I can remember, I would just get my butt kicked if there was anything to upset her at all. Everything was Mother, Mother, Mother, Mother. He threatened us, for years, "If anything happens to your mother, I will hold you personally responsible." And I'll never forget him saying that to me, ever. And all of a sudden he was gone, and it was like "You jerk, you hypocrite."

■ ■ ■

BARBARA COOPER: I took it very badly. It was a complete surprise. The last two months he was, in my words, irritable and cranky. I thought that was because he was working too hard. He had always made me feel so secure, as a woman and as a wife. All that crap about actors falling in love with their leading ladies, I thought that could never be Jack. Oh, I knew he had had something fifteen years ago, when he was at Screen Gems, but that was fifteen years ago. I ignored it. You know, like the Jewish mother says, it never happened. I kidded around about this one or that one, but I never thought he was really involved.

■ ■ ■

I got involved with an actress. But that really wasn't the important thing. That gave me the excuse of leaving, gave me the strength to walk out or, really, somebody to walk out to.

■ ■ ■

JULIE COOPER: Dad called. At first, he didn't tell me what had happened. He just said, "Have you talked to anyone?" I told him no. Right away, I thought, My God, somebody got hurt. And before he even told me what had happened, he had me write down phone numbers of where he could be reached. And then he told me, "Daddy left home." He didn't say, "I left home," or "Mom and I had a fight." "Daddy had to leave home," that's what he said. "Daddy had to leave home."

■ ■ ■

BARBARA COOPER: Maybe I should have seen the signs. There were signs. When he went to New York to shoot *Marathon*, there were signs. He had always called me from the airport when he went somewhere. On this trip that was not the case. When he did call, it was the first time he didn't say, "I miss you," or, "I love you." Those are just words, but still—I felt he was tired or bugged. When he got back from New York—on a Friday—he was very sweet. Had dinner. Was tired. Went to sleep. I'd missed him a lot, but I felt something was wrong. Something was not right.

■ ■ ■

We had been married for twenty-five years, Barbara and I. Whenever I fantasized about old age, it was always with Barbara at my side. I loved her; that had never stopped. And yet it was a sickness; that's the only way to explain it. I didn't want to get old.

■ ■ ■

BARBARA COOPER: The next day, that Saturday, he went to the barbershop. He came home. He sat over there on the fireplace hearth. We watched the Gold Cup on television, and I looked at him and I said—my big mistake—"What's on your mind? You seem disturbed." Then he went into a number about drowning for two years. So I went into a crazy number about divorce. And I asked him who it was. I still don't know what he meant by drowning. It was very emotional. I only threw one thing, which was good for me. He left in an hour and said he'd call me the next day, which he did. When he called, he told me who the girl was.

■ ■ ■

I wasn't planning, when I left the house that day, on ever coming home. But I guess, deep down, I must have realized that I would. Actually, from the moment I left, I was thinking more about going back than about anything else. I suspect that it was just the mere act of getting up and leaving that was what I really needed, to show myself that I was still capable of some youthful and independent action.

But I knew, almost instantaneously with my departure, that it wasn't what I really wanted. I wanted to be back where I belonged, with my wife, in my house, in my own niche. And yet I was outside, and I had to go through with it.

■ ■ ■

BARBARA COOPER: That Saturday he left, he had told me that everything [a broad gesture, indicating the house and everything in it] was mine.

■ ■ ■

I didn't want anything. She should have it all. I had started from scratch a few times before, and I was still young (I told myself) and healthy (that I knew) and working steadily. Besides, I knew the pain I was causing her, and the house and everything else were little enough compensation for that pain.

■ ■ ■

BARBARA COOPER: I was catatonic. Oh, I got up and saw a lawyer. He gave me no big advice. He was surprised that Jackie had turned over the house to me. He told me to lay back. Everybody in the world called me. I called him once—you name a name, I called him that name. But then I got better. He acted well in having all his checks sent to the house, everything in the world I could have. My only real concern at the time was him—he'd lost his mind. In the past we had always been so close, and he had talked over all his problems, but this one he didn't.

■ ■ ■

I never talked to people—even my business partners—about things that troubled me. I'd try to work things out for myself.

■ ■ ■

BARBARA COOPER: You cut people off, that's what you mean.

■ ■ ■

I could never sit and talk about my feelings, about what is going on inside my head. I'd try to work things out, and then I'd explode when I had had it up to here.

■ ■ ■

BARBARA COOPER: I told him to go see a doctor. For the first time in my life, I was scared. First, you get to a certain age. And second, we've got a small family, just the kids, who really don't give a damn, they just want things to stay the same, and my mother and my sister, that's my family. I was terribly frightened.

■ ◼ ◻

But wasn't it clear to you that, even though I have work potential, that deep inside I never really could see myself going on like that?

■ ■ ◻

BARBARA COOPER: No, because the move was so— what does shock mean? You can die of shock.

◼ ◼ ■

She asked me if I was going to get married, if I wanted a divorce.

■ ◻ ◼

BARBARA COOPER: He said no divorce. He was emphatic. I didn't know what might happen later. You start to think about the things you've always taken for granted. I had to learn to live alone, and I'd never lived alone. I'd gone from my parents' house to Jackie. I came home one night, all alone, and said, "God damn it!" I wanted to go upstairs and draw the curtains.

◼ ◼ ■

I went through the motions of my new life. I was working, which was fortunate. I was working on the cutting of *Marathon*, and I was preparing to shoot the movie with Bette Davis. So I could keep my mind occupied. And there was this other girl, but I really knew that wasn't permanent. Every day, too, and every night I became more and more convinced that I had to go home. My separation from Barbara had to be only temporary.

■ ■ ■

BARBARA COOPER: I felt it was permanent. If he could leave me, then it was permanent. But then, he had never said, "I want a divorce," which would have been the thing to do if he wanted it to be forever. Even with that, I felt it was permanent.

He came over a few times. There were things that had to be signed. He was sweet and nice, but it was all negatives.

■ ■ ■

CRIS COOPER: Everybody kept saying, "He's never coming home, he's not coming home." And I really, for a while, started to believe that he wasn't going to come home. And then I said to myself, "Why doesn't somebody just tell him to either stop fooling around and get his ass home or, you know, for good, and don't call?"

I think he's bitter towards me now, and I put up with it. Yeah, he's bitter, he's angry at me, for a lot of reasons. I've stepped out of bounds too many times, as far as he's concerned, which is fine, you know, that's fine. I just kind of wheel in and wheel out the best way I can, you know, and try to make everything pleasant while I'm around. I just don't want, when I'm thirty, to turn around and go, "Where's my father?"

■ ■ ■

JULIE COOPER: I did probably a bad thing, but I'm kind of glad I did it. I called my dad after that article came out in the *Enquirer*. And I was very nasty to him, which I'm pretty sorry for now, but at the time I was glad I did it because I wanted him to know that just wasn't the right thing to do. He tried to talk real rational with me. He said, "I'm not going to scream and holler," because I was doing all the screaming and hollering, but while I talked to him, I said, "Is this going to last very long?" and he said, "I really don't think so," and when he said that, he said it in a way that I believed him.

■ ■ ■

I thought back, all the time, rather than enjoy the present. When I would go to the house, and she would be there, it was always pleasant—cold and reserved, which was understandable, but pleasant. After that first day and that first telephone call, no more recriminations. More and more, the thought occurred to me: What the hell stupid thing have I done?

And why couldn't she have seen the signs and stopped me?

■ ■ ■

BARBARA COOPER: I had not been aware of any of the clues. There weren't many to be aware of. He never stayed out overnight. If he was late, he was never very late, and there always was a good reason. And now that Crissy had left home, the two of us were alone, and because of Jack's working hours, it was boring sometimes for me, so probably boring sometimes for him. I had started to depend on Jack.

Some women are different. There are those who get massages and go to lunches. I was never one of those girls. My life was here. But then the kids were gone. Jack was absolutely right—all that was left was Jack and Barbara.

■ ■ ■

RUSSELL COOPER: I was really shocked. How did the Japanese feel when Hiroshima...? I mean, really, that's it. They had never fought, nothing. Total shock. I'd been living on my own for almost a year and a half at that point, and I hadn't been over to the house as much or seen them as much, but just before that, my sister had moved out of the house, my younger sister, Cris, and I said, "Gee, this is great, this is the time for them to be alone." You know. That's why it was such a shock, more than anything. I looked at him, and I said, "Geez, the best part of your life is starting, you know, you don't have any more kids and any more noise or any more crap to come home to. The worst noise you have is the dog barking."

The first time I saw him after I heard what happened, which was about four days after I heard, after my mother told me, I sat him down, and I, you know, I told him that I thought he was a hypocrite because of all the things he tried to teach me about telling the truth all the years, and all the things he tried to tell me—the one thing he didn't like, the worst thing that any of us, me or my two sisters, could do, would be to upset my mother. For any reason. He said there was nothing more important than that. And he always taught us to tell the truth, don't bullshit yourself. And that's why I thought—I really had to work hard to suppress the hatred that was building up.

I told him before the conversation started, I said, "You can say what you want, and I'll listen, but there's nothing you can say that will justify this. Nothing." His rationale was that he needed time; he needed to be by himself; he felt empty and depressed. I guess everybody is entitled to that to a certain point. But there was so much that he was giving up.

■ ■ ■

I worked very hard on the two films. I was really happy only when I was working. The rest of it was going through the motions. Working hard is something I do naturally. When I have an assignment, that is all I think about, all I have on my mind. At that particular time in my life, I was very glad to be working.

■ ■ ■

BARBARA COOPER: My girl friends got me to a psychiatrist because I was not coping with the problems—what does that word mean? I wasn't getting drunk or having hundreds of people over. I kept to myself, is what I did. I didn't leave my room all day long. I felt safe in this house. If he called, I felt better. Then we had dinner. It was pleasant—but saying good night to him at the door was a killer. We had dinner twice, and that was pleasant. He called me every day. Thanksgiving was terrible. I wouldn't get out of bed, and everyone was mad at me.

■ ■ ■

I had really become very home-oriented, very family-oriented, and being away hurt. I had a little apartment which was comfortable, but that's all. I had some friends or at least acquaintances. There was the girl I was seeing. But it wasn't home, and I came to realize that I was a fifty-seven-year-old man playing like he was thirty-five, and I didn't belong out there among 'em; I belonged at home. So more and more I would call home, and I would see Barbara, and I came to realize that I wanted to get back there—if she'd take me back.

■ ■ ■

BARBARA COOPER: Christmas. His son [Jack] came down. He was sweet. Christmas was always big in this house. I wasn't going to have a tree. But the kids put one up. Christmas night I really fell apart. I even asked the doctor to come over and give me a sedative. I never even heard the phone the next day. They thought I'd had a stroke. I had had a bad reaction. The doctor came over. I was okay. He told them to let me sleep it off. Jack came over, at Christmas, put all his gifts under the tree, then off to his little vacation in Big Bear.

■ ■ ■

CRIS COOPER: Julie was home for the holidays and had a miserable time because she was hurting so badly for her mother and she just wanted to get out of here, and I don't blame her. It wasn't a happy Christmas, but Julie tried so hard to make it real nice—she and Russell both did.

■ ■ ■

JULIE COOPER: When it first happened, I went back home [from Indianapolis] just for a weekend, just to be with Mom and to see my brother and sister because we are a family, and I thought: Well, even if they were in Alaska, I'm going home, because my mom, that's my lady, my number one lady. That was just for a weekend. And then in December I went home for ten days, which was the worst Christmas in my life. It was terrible. But I was satisfied because I was able to be with my mom and I was able to show my mom that wherever I am, however old I am, and whatever I'm doing, her little girl is here, whenever she needs me.

■ ■ ■

JUNE HORNE COOPER: Jack came down; he was really upset about it; he's very fond of Barbara and how sweet she is. He told me about it, and he said, "Ah, I don't know what's got into him—the thing that really bugs me is this girl is two years younger than I am. Jesus, Mom, what's the matter with him?" And I said, "Well, Jack, he's done it time after time." I said, "He did it to me, and he did it to Hildy. He did it to everybody."

■ ■ ■

I couldn't sleep very well. I wasn't eating much. The people I saw told me I looked terrible. That didn't surprise me because I felt terrible.

I went away to Big Bear Lake over the Christmas holiday with this lady. I couldn't face Barbara and the kids at Christmas.

■ ■ ■

BARBARA COOPER: I couldn't sleep at all most of the time. I even thought of putting the dogs away. The dogs were funny—when he came over, they wouldn't look at him. Honestly. They ignored him completely. Basil wouldn't even bark at him. After his little vacation in Big Bear, he came home, and the kids gave him his Christmas gifts. That was Saturday.

■ ■ ■

Saturday, December 29, I went back to the house, and I saw Barbara and the children, and I knew then, positively, that I was coming home—if I could. But I realized that that little step had to be handled very delicately, or it could blow up in my face.

■ ■ ■

BARBARA COOPER: And then New Year's Eve. Jackie called the day before. "Have you got anything to eat in the house?" I said to myself, "The son of a bitch isn't just coming over to eat." He came over, and he looked certifiable. He looked awful, crazy, ill. He scared me. I was going to put him in the hospital. He asked me what I was doing the next night, which was New Year's Eve. I asked him why. "Because I want to come home if you'll have me." I said to myself, "I'm not going to say good night to this man at the door again."

■ ■ ■

I just knew I was going to come home in the next day or two. I just didn't know how to do it. Looking back on it, I believe that subconsciously I always knew the separation would never be permanent. I think I consciously knew at Christmas. I knew I could never spend another Christmas without her. Christmas Day wasn't great for me, but Christmas night I was very sick—headaches. I tried to keep my mind off my troubles. I went for a long walk, Christmas Day, about two hours. And I knew, the day after Christmas, that I had to go home. But I wanted to do it the nicest way possible.

And there was this other person who was involved, and I had to end that. She and I had never talked about futures. Even so, it was difficult. To me, when the dawn came, it had not made any sense, none of it. It was insanity, after twenty-five good years, twenty-five happy, loving years.

■ ■ ■

BARBARA COOPER: Twenty-five years. You can say the number. It didn't seem so long. What's happened to me in twenty-five years? Three kids and change of life. But I didn't feel older. It was only when Jackie felt older that I did, too. He said he never could have left me if there was still a child in the house, which seemed so stupid to me.

But back to the night he came home. I said, "Jackie, don't do any numbers on me, no games, you can sleep in the kids' room, but I just cannot face saying good night at the door again." I think if I'd had to do that, there couldn't have been another night. You don't live with someone for twenty-five years and say good night at the door—it's uncivilized.

If it had gone on much longer, I would not have taken him back. By that time I'd have been a complete crazy woman, or I would have picked myself up and made another life.

■ ■ ■

JUNE HORNE COOPER: I guess he finally saw the light, and Barbara was smart enough to take him back, because it works both ways. And sometimes something like this makes things actually better. I know my son was very happy when Jack and Barbara got together again. He was really upset about that.

■ ■ ■

BARBARA COOPER: So he stayed that night, and the next day he went and got his clothes and came back. And then he proceeded to get very ill.

■ ■ ■

It was the release from the pressure that made me get sick. I've been under some kind of pressure, I realize, all my life. Very few young children know what it's like to have pressure, but I did. The pressure at home, with my grandmother forcing me to hide from whoever it was who rang the front doorbell—kids feel that pressure. And the pressure at the studio, to do exactly what everybody told me to do, to be a good boy and cry or be a good boy and laugh or be a good boy and say my lines. Kids feel that pressure, too. A lot of times a kid doesn't feel like working.

Life, for me as a boy, was a series of "You gottas." You gotta do what the director says. You gotta keep up your schoolwork. You gotta be nice to Louella Parsons when she comes to interview you. You gotta meet this person or that person.

Then, later, there was World War II and the Navy. Pressure, pressure, pressure all my life. The pressure was what could never let me sit still.

So I came home, and the pressure was off, and that had

been the worst pressure of them all. That had been pounding at me from all sides—my conscience was worst of all, and my own wants and needs, and my kids had been yelling at me, calling me stupid, and there was the pressure of what to do about this other person, and the pressure of Barbara just being there.

And how to handle her now. Do I try to pick up where I left off? Do I start all over from the beginning?

■ ■ ■

BOB FINKEL: We went out to St. Germain, sat down, and Jackie and I talked to each other differently than we did all the years I've known him. He touched my hand and told me that I was the only one, I think he said, who wanted to talk to him. During the time Jackie and I had been partners, I had had that problem, and Jack was very tolerant of me. It's funny, it seems to me that exactly the same thing happened to Jack. I was sick and didn't know it. When I say sick, it's a mental malaise, but not quite insanity; it's something in the juices of a man that goes awry, and he does things, comes out of a physical problem he has that he has to get over. And I feel that some men are fortunate, as I was and Jack was, that you recover, and your pride does not stop you from completing the recovery. So many of my friends went through the same thing, and they have so much pride that they cannot go back to their wives, can't pick up the phone, can't do it, are not capable. I said to him that you just don't walk back into the house, let's pick up, like that. You have to now court your wife; you're now starting from scratch, I don't care who the woman is, so that she believes you, falls in love again.

■ ■ ■

I could never relax. As the years went on, the only time I got in trouble was when things were easy. And that's what happened this time. Things were easy. I was in demand as a director. I had no financial worries. The children were grown and gone. There literally were no worries, no concerns, no troubles. And so I got this sickness.

But that started the pressures boiling again. And when I went home, the pressure was suddenly off. I was never so happy in my life as when I went home again—because I learned that I had recovered from a sickness that could have been fatal to my happiness and maybe to Barbara, but the mere fact that I recovered brought on such a violent reaction that I got physically sick.

■ ■ ■

BARBARA COOPER: When he got back, you really had to see him. All I could do—I knew in my heart and soul—was to send him to all the doctors, but it wasn't that kind of sickness. The man had to be in this house. I knew if he went out, he'd have an attack. But if he stayed home and stayed in bed, he'd be relaxed, and that's what he did. For days. He slept and slept and ate and ate. There was no strain between us.

The separation had nearly done me in. Everybody, including Jackie, told me to get away. So I went to Vegas. And I was catatonic. I sat there, staring. I fantasized: He's going to come and get me out of here. I realized my situation was real, but I fantasized.

One night the Averbacks and the Rickles made me go out. They were sweet. Five of us. There I was, the odd one. And I thought of silly things. Jackie had always been very attentive, but who would be now? If you need a drink, who do you ask? It's having that extra arm there. It was always one guy. It was being comfortable. Jackie always took care of me, even with his own ego—and he had to have an ego to survive.

■ ■ ■

I think, from the vantage point of today, that the episode was something that had to happen, for my psyche. If it had not happened, I might have always regretted that it didn't. It was painful for me, most painful for Barbara, peripherally painful for the children. But it had to happen.

So, from that standpoint, it was good. I got the whole goddamn stupid thing out of my system.

■ ■ ■

BARBARA COOPER: Now I feel maybe this whole thing was good, painful though it was. Don't take each other for granted. You listen a little more.

That day he left, he said, "I've done nothing to embarrass you or the children."

I asked him if he wasn't worried that I'd go crazy and blow all the money. He said no. I asked him if he ever considered the fact that I was in pain. He said no. Why not? "Well," he said, "I felt there was nothing you couldn't handle."

The whole thing made me a little more aware of myself. I'd lost weight before he'd left, and I'd been looking forward to good times together. Now maybe we can start having them.

He'll never know, I don't think, the pain he caused—I mean hurt, I mean real physical pain. And the no sleeping. And the waking up. The waking up was the worst, thinking about the Jackie I knew. This was a whole other person. All those years we had laughs, we had tears, we had good times, very few bad times.

■ ■ ■

There was never any dislike. Not for a moment.

■ ■ ■

BARBARA COOPER: I never hated him either. The people I knew would say, "When are you going to get mad?" The important thing now is it was an experience, a terrible, horrible experience. I'm going to be fifty-three; Jackie is fifty-eight. At this time in our lives what matters is comfort and devotion.

■ ■ ■

We both, in different ways, had an opportunity to look at ourselves and our choices. Do I want to be with her when we are in our seventies?

■ ■ ■

BARBARA COOPER: Who cares about our seventies?
Do I want to be with him when I am fifty-four and he is
fifty-nine?

■ ■ ■

Or is there something better? I don't think it took either of
us very long to realize there wasn't anything better than what
we had. That excitement—that other person—began waning
the minute I first left home.

We had choices. Everything else stunk.

■ ■ ■

BARBARA COOPER: The other choices certainly stunk.
As much as I thought I liked Jackie, I loved him more than
I thought I loved him.

He kept using the word "shame." He would say he was
so ashamed of what he had done. He said he was going
to see a doctor, but he hasn't said anything about that
lately. All he really needed was a vacation. Many people
need vacations.

I still believe him. I never believed in anybody like I
believed in him—and I still do.

It was awful, but you have to think positive. I remember
how he always used to say, when he got up in the morning,
"Well, we made it out of bed today." And we made it out
of bed this time today.

■ ■ ■

We both found something out. That's the difference between
the weak and the strong. If you learn from your adversity,
you're strong. You survive.

52.

For some weeks after I came home, I was troubled with attacks which I realized were psychosomatic, but that didn't mean they hurt less. They were centered in my head, seemingly an inch or so behind my right eye, and the pain was unbearable.

I saw all the doctors, who gave me all the tests, and the unanimous conclusion was that nothing was wrong with me— no tumor, no eye problems, nothing. So I had to suffer, and I suffered. Most of the time, for several long, agonizing weeks, I had to lie still. That was the only way I got any relief. And while lying still, I was forced to think, and the main topic of thought—naturally, since the separation had so recently ended—was that misadventure and its possible results for me and Barbara.

My self-analysis led me to several conclusions which, to me, were terribly important.

I concluded that I would no longer be concerned about the age thing. In the months that had led up to the separation, I was continually concerned with the question of how long I might have left to live. Now I realized that it didn't really matter. I was in good physical condition—I have an exhaustive physical examination annually from Navy doctors, and the conclusion always is that I have the health of a twenty-five-year-old, except for my eyes—so I may go on for many years yet. But if something happens and I have only a few years, well, then, good luck. At least I will relax and enjoy those few years and be with Barbara during them.

I also concluded that I didn't have to worry about money anymore. I am far from the wealthiest person in the world, but today we have our house—almost paid for—and the kids are set and I have things reasonably well organized so I can afford to wait for a good directorial assignment. I will never starve, and neither will Barbara.

Those two conclusions led me to perhaps the most important conclusion of all—I can now insist on doing only good things. I don't have to work as a means of beating the clock. I don't have to work just to make money. Therefore, the only point of working is to do exciting, challenging, exceptional things. And so I told my agent (and I trusted him enough to say this) that was what I wanted to do—that and only that—and from now on that would be my only criterion. If I will be doing TV films, then I will do only the cream of the crop, the ones the networks protect, the ones they push and promote, not like *Rodeo Girl*, which was good but which CBS threw away opposite one of the nights of NBC's *Shogun*. If I will be doing theatrical feature films, then I will accept only meaningful material.

So those weeks of lying on my bed, waiting for the attacks to go away, were beneficial. (The attacks ended when I had been home a month, after I had been treated by an acupuncturist. They might have gone away anyhow, of course.)

Today I know where I am going. I no longer have that nagging question "Should I act?" hanging over my head. I doubt if I will ever act again, although anything is possible. I look forward to directing—important properties only—for many years to come. Maybe someday the thought of having to get up at four-thirty in the morning to get to a set, the realization that I will be standing on my feet all day, the knowledge that I will not be getting home until eight or eight-thirty at night—maybe all that will seem insurmountable. That will be the day I quit. At least I'll quit directing. I might then do some producing or, perhaps, a little teaching. I cannot see myself totally idle.

The prospect of getting older no longer frightens me. I know now that it was fright that tore me away from my wife and my home. That fright caused Barbara real, physical pain—pain which I can never be sure has completely disappeared. But now, with that fright conquered and laid to rest, I am absolutely certain that I will never do those things again. There will be no more restless excursions, no more conjecture that perhaps I am missing something out of life, no more running away. I have flung my final fling.

I can look back at my life with some pride. Of all the kid stars, I think I came through with more of my buttons intact. Rooney is doing well now, but only after eight marriages and a lengthy professional dry spell. Judy Garland and her tortured soul are gone. All the kid stars had a tough row to hoe because the public smothered them with so much love they couldn't grow up, and after that, they never could find enough love to flourish.

I can look forward to the rest of my life—a year or thirty years—with quiet, peaceful expectation. In fact, I hope to do so much constructive living that fifteen or twenty years from now I will write another book about that coming period.

Glittering lives of famous people!
Bestsellers from Berkley

★ ★

__**BRANDO FOR BREAKFAST**   04698-2—$2.75
Anna Kashfi Brando and E.P. Stein
__**CONVERSATIONS WITH JOAN CRAWFORD**   05046-7—$2.50
Roy Newquist
__**HOLLYWOOD IN A SUITCASE**   05091-2—$2.95
Sammy Davis, Jr.
__**LADD: A HOLLYWOOD TRAGEDY**   05731-3—$2.95
Beverly Linet
__**SUSAN HAYWARD: PORTRAIT OF A SURVIVOR**   05030-0—$2.95
Beverly Linet
__**MISS TALLULAH BANKHEAD**   04574-9—$2.75
Lee Israel
__**MOMMIE DEAREST**   05242-7—$3.25
Christina Crawford
__**MOTHER GODDAM**   05394-6—$2.95
Whitney Stine with Bette Davis
__**MY WICKED, WICKED WAYS**   04686-9—$2.75
Errol Flynn
__**NO BED OF ROSES**   05028-9—$2.75
Joan Fontaine
__**SELF—PORTRAIT**   04485-8—$2.75
Gene Tierney with Mickey Herskowitz
__**SHOW PEOPLE**   04750-4—$2.95
Kenneth Tynan
__**FRANCES FARMER: SHADOWLAND**   05481-0—$2.75
William Arnold
__**TRUE BRITT**   05341-5—$2.95
Britt Ekland

 Berkley Book Mailing Service
P.O. Box 690
Rockville Centre, NY 11570

Please send me the above titles. I am enclosing $_____
(Please add 50¢ per copy to cover postage and handling). Send check or money
order—no cash or C.O.D.'s. Allow six weeks for delivery.

NAME_____

ADDRESS_____

CITY_____ STATE/ZIP_____   6Au